Sensational Internationalism

Edinburgh Critical Studies in Atlantic Literatures and Cultures
Edited by Andrew Taylor, Colleen Glenney Boggs and Laura Doyle

Available titles
Sensational Internationalism: The Paris Commune and the Remapping of American Memory in the Long Nineteenth Century
J. Michelle Coghlan

Forthcoming titles
Emily Dickinson and Her British Contemporaries: Victorian Poetry in Nineteenth-Century America
Páraic Finnerty

Following the Middle Passage: Currents in Literature Since 1945
Carl Plasa

Visit the series website at: edinburghuniversitypress.com/series-edinburgh-critical-studies-in-atlantic-literatures-and-cultures.html

Sensational Internationalism

The Paris Commune and the Remapping
of American Memory in the Long
Nineteenth Century

J. Michelle Coghlan

EDINBURGH
University Press

Edinburgh University Press is one of the leading university presses in the UK. We publish academic books and journals in our selected subject areas across the humanities and social sciences, combining cutting-edge scholarship with high editorial and production values to produce academic works of lasting importance. For more information visit our website: edinburghuniversitypress.com

© J. Michelle Coghlan, 2016

Edinburgh University Press Ltd
The Tun – Holyrood Road, 12(2f) Jackson's Entry, Edinburgh EH8 8PJ

Typeset in 11/13 Adobe Sabon by
IDSUK (DataConnection) Ltd, and

Contents

List of Illustrations

Acknowledgments

This book is about memory and the memories that most make us – most especially the ones that are not, strictly speaking, our own. One way to tell the story of its beginnings is to say it sprang from a single moment in a novel by Henry James, read for a class I was fortunate to take during my first year of graduate school. But another genealogy could be traced to a sight caught from the back seat of a car many years earlier. My father and I were driving back from Valparaíso – our first trip to Chile together and one of his first returns home since leaving it in the fall of 1973. In a sidelong glance I saw a name spray-painted across a shantytown wall: *Allende*. For years to come, that sight stayed with me. It forced me to grapple with what it meant, after nearly twenty years of military dictatorship under Pinochet, for someone to reach back to that name, and also what it meant for me – as a Chilean–American – that the first democratically elected Socialist in Latin America, Salvador Allende, would be toppled in a brutal military coup backed by the United States. (Nixon famously sought to "save Chile" from its own democratic process.) In the writing of that name I read a kind of hope, almost messianic, perhaps misplaced, in this figure then twenty-two years dead, and a dream of a world that the US frankly was not prepared to see happen.

No doubt much of my own preoccupation with the Commune lies, then, in its parallels with Allende's Chile, the mad optimism and aching loss of a moment that dared to be and, in doing so, was utterly crushed. No doubt my interest in the Paris Commune's American afterlife is bound up in the fact so many Americans were so very invested in seeing the Commune's suppression, even as they were so oddly preoccupied with returning again and again to the scene of it – because we were grappling, are still grappling, with what it means to be the great harbinger of democracy, but also, quite often, to be against democracy abroad in practice. It is, in other words, that great investment in democracy, and the move to crush it in when it suits our purposes, that most haunted me at sixteen, and certainly still haunts me now. There was, of course, another side to both these stories, a side signaled by the talismanic force of that spray-painted name: a way of finding not nostalgia and more than hope – indeed, something altogether more insurgent and more sustaining – in a past that could have been remembered simply as a defeat. As W. E. B. DuBois pointed out in his seminal rereading of Reconstruction, there can be something unexpectedly vital in moments otherwise regarded as failures.

There are many origin points, then, for this project and equally many intellectual debts to be enumerated; in no small way, this book is the product of the intellectual communities in which I have been fortunate to find myself over the many years of its making. My vision of why we do what we do was fundamentally shaped by Richard Halpern, Dorothy J. Hale, and Paul Stasi, and much of how I continue to read, think, and teach can be traced back to my time with them as an undergraduate at Berkeley. At Princeton, I was blessed with the ablest and kindest of graduate advisors: Bill Gleason saw this as a book before I could fully picture it as a dissertation and his continuing acuity and great generosity over the years helped to make it so; Maria DiBattista's graduate course on "High and Low Modernism," as well as her wonderful National Endowment for the Humanities (NEH) Seminar in Paris, shaped my vision of this project from the start and this book owes much to her wisdom and warmth; Michael Wood's ever-perceptive questions continue to guide my thinking from afar; and, finally, this book would have been *unthinkable* without the work and solidarity of Kristin Ross – though she may not, I see her mark on every page. Deep thanks are also due to Diana Fuss, Anne A. Cheng, Sarah Rivett, Meredith Martin, Zahid Chadhaury, Daphne Brooks, Eduardo Cadava, Jeremy Braddock, Ben Conisbee Baer, Nigel Smith, and Oliver Arnold for their encouragement and guidance as I was finding my feet with this project.

It has been both a delight and a vertiginous experience to teach American literature and culture in the UK; for their collegiality, advice in navigating a new system, and friendship, I thank my colleagues in English and American Studies at the University of Manchester, in particular Laura Doan, Dani Caselli, Monica Pearl, Eithne Quinn, Anastasia Valassoupolous, Iain Bailey, Rebecca Pohl, Noelle Dück-mann Gallagher, Andrew Fearnley, Doug Field, Natalie Zacek, David Alderson, Michael Sanders, Hal Gladfelder, Anke Bernau, David Matthews, and Ben Harker. Many thanks are also due to the friends and colleagues from outside my department whom I was fortunate to cross paths with early in my time here, most especially Joanne Jordan, Tom Allcock, Heather Inwood, Rory Horner, Jenny Gradwell, and Will Schroeder; to dear friends who relocated before I did and without whose humor and sagacity I could never have managed – namely, Charis Boutieri, Mimi Pillinger, Hilary Emmett, Hannah Charlick, Ellen Smith, Emily Coit, and David Russell; and to those colleagues from outside Manchester who made me feel at home right from the start: in particular, Scott McCracken, Angel-Luke O'Donnell, Lloyd Pratt, Bridget Bennett, Katie McGettigan, Christian O'Connell, Nick Grant, Mark Storey, Tom Wright, Peter Riley, Stephanie Palmer, Michael Collins, and Ed Sugden.

For their camaraderie, intellectual incandescence and unflagging ability to see more clearly than I could what I was trying to do in any given draft, all my thanks go to Adrienne Brown, Hilary Emmett, Cat Keyser, Lindsay Reckson, Britt Rusert, and Sonya Posmentier; J. K. Barret, John Bugg, Erica Fretwell, Nick Gaskill, Briallen Hopper, and Keri Walsh also pitched in at key moments along the way – I owe the finishing of this book, and much else, to your friendship. This book also benefitted enormously from the engagement and enthusiasm of my Occupy Everything seminar students over the past two years, as well as from the superb research assistance of Katie Welsh and Imogen Durant.

I presented work in progress from this book at Princeton University, Wayne State University, Manchester University, and Fairfield University, as well as at the Alt/American conference at Oxford, the 5th International conference of the Henry James Society, Dartmouth's Futures of American Studies Institute and meetings of C19: the Society of Nineteenth-Century Americanists, the British Association of American Studies, BrANCA (the British Association of Nineteenth-Century Americanists), and the Modernist Studies Association. Especial thanks to Barrett Watten, Jonathan Flatley, renée hoogland, Robert Aguirre, Elizabeth Petrino, Peter Bayers, Johanna Garvey, Cinthia Gannett, Colleen Boggs, Swati Rana, Ann Mattis, Emily Ogden, Shelly Jarenski, David McWhirter, Julie Rivkin, and Greg Zacharias, whose questions at these events enlivened my thinking and sharpened the questions I brought to this material.

Work on this book would not have been possible without travel grants and fellowships from the British Association of American Studies, the Program in American Studies at Princeton University, the Princeton Institute for International and Regional Studies, the Association of Princeton Graduate Alumni, the Dean's Fund for

Scholarly Travel, and the Princeton University Graduate School. Research assistance was funded by a Faculty Research Grant and Tuck Fund Summer Grant during my time as a postdoctoral fellow at the Princeton Writing Program, and later by a small but much-needed allocation of time from the Division of English, American Studies, and Creative Writing at Manchester. I am also deeply indebted to the staffs of several archives and libraries, many of whom stepped in to offer assistance when I had in mind only the faintest glimmer of what I hoped to find in their holdings or, as the book neared completion, provided invaluable help with its illustrations: Elsa Tilly, Laurence Goux, and Sylvie Gonzalez at the Musée d'Art et d'Histoire in St. Denis; Roberto D. Montoya and Mauricio Hermosillo at University of California at Los Angeles's Charles E. Young Research Library Department of Special Collections; Jim Green, Connie King, and Nicole Joniec at the Library Company of Philadelphia; Brianna Cregle and AnnaLee Pauls at Rare Books and Special Collections at Princeton University; the New York Public Library; the Tamiment Library at New York University; Rare Books and Special Collections at the Library of Congress; and the Harry Ransom Center at the University of Texas at Austin.

    At Edinburgh University Press I am indebted to series editors Colleen Glenney Boggs, Laura Doyle, and Andrew Taylor for their enthusiasm for the project and feedback in the final revision stages; editor Adela Rauchova for shepherding my book to completion, and project manager Rebecca Mackenzie for her help with the cover; and the two reviewers for the Press for their thoughtful engagement with the manuscript. Portions of this book have appeared elsewhere, and I thank the Arizona Board of Regents, Johns Hopkins University Press, Cambridge Scholars Publishing, and Nebraska University Press for their permission to reprint. A version of Chapter 2 was published as "Becoming an American in Paris: The Romance of the Commune in the 1890s," in *Arizona Quarterly* 67.3 (2011): 30–59. Earlier versions of Chapter 4 were published as "Aftertastes of Ruin: Uncanny Sites of Memory in Henry James' Paris," in *The Henry James Review* 33 (2012): 239–46 and "Aftertastes of Ruin: Uncanny Sites of Memory in Henry James's Paris," in *Transforming Henry James*. Ed. Donatella Izzo, Anna De Biasio, and Anna Despotopoulou (Newcastle upon Tyne: Cambridge Scholars Publishing, 2013): 77–93. Portions of Chapter 5 were published as "Tasting Horror: Radical Forms of Feeding in Guy Endore's *The Werewolf of Paris*," in *Resilience: A Journal of the Environmental Humanities* 2.1 (2014): 24–38.

My family and friends have lived with this project for nearly a decade and no thanks here could be enough. For this, and much else, great gratitude goes out to the Coghlan, Lyons, and Bunzel clans, as well as to Amy Converse, Tara Stearns, Rhea Sundquist, Jameel Alsalam, Emma Schwartz, Sean Labrador Manzano, Jamie Drysdale, Jennifer Luck, Nell Beekman, Wendy Lee, Nadia Ellis, Jacky Shin, Yaron Aronowicz, Yann Robert, Anne Hirsch Moffitt, Greg Londe, Rachel Galvin, and Leanne Wood. My grandparents, Cecil and Mayté Coghlan, first taught me the power of memory and the art of making a life in a country that is and is not your own, and although my grandfather did not live to see this in print, it would never have made it there without them. I am also very grateful to my sister, Meagan Coppage, for her faith in me, and to my Brussels Griffon, Gadget, for keeping me company and walking me on a regular basis. And, finally, to Nick, my lovely Welshman: thank you ever so much for arriving when you did.

Series Editors' Preface

Modern global culture makes it clear that literary study can no longer operate on nation-based or exceptionalist models. In practice, American literatures have always been understood and defined in relation to the literatures of Europe and Asia. The books in this series work within a broad comparative framework to question place-based identities and monocular visions, in historical contexts from the earliest European settlements to contemporary affairs, and across all literary genres. They explore the multiple ways in which ideas, texts, objects, and bodies travel across spatial and temporal borders, generating powerful forms of contrast and affinity. The Edinburgh Critical Studies in Atlantic Literatures and Cultures series fosters new paradigms of exchange, circulation, and transformation for Atlantic literary studies, expanding the critical and theoretical work of this rapidly developing field.

Revolutionary Preoccupations: Or, Transatlantic Feeling in a Radical Sense

In light of recent events – in particular, scenes from Zuccotti Park in the fall of 2011 – the Paris Commune of 1871 no longer *feels* quite as distant from our own historical moment. On the morning of March 18 of that year, in a protest at once social, political, economic, and spatial, a mass of men, women, and children "occupied" a major urban center. Their move to seize it as their own and to question the social order of their day immediately puzzled and inflamed the press on both sides of the Atlantic and prompted swift action by displaced city officials and government forces. A mere seventy-two days later, the uprising that Engels would famously dub "the dictatorship of the proletariat" was brutally put down by the French army, even as the events in Paris and the name that came to stand in for them – "the Commune" – went viral, provoking at once transatlantic anxiety, international leftist solidarity, and ongoing coverage across a variety of mass-cultural media.[1]

That the Commune seems curiously new, when viewed from the rearview mirror of Occupy Wall Street, and that its legacy has come to feel tangibly vital can be evidenced not only by a spate of US and international newspaper articles that turned to the Commune's defeat to make sense of Occupy Wall Street, but also by David Harvey's recent account of Occupy in light of earlier urban uprisings, the Commune foremost among them, and by Occupy blogs from across the US that made readings of the Commune and its history more or less de rigueur for those who claimed they wanted to "occupy everything."[2] Put a little differently, in the fall of 2011, and in the immediate aftermath of the razing of the Zuccotti Park encampment, the Paris Commune seemed to arise out of nowhere as the new objet trouvé of choice for the US leftist imaginary wrestling with the pangs of defeat, the politics of occupation, and both the promises and the perils of collective action. As Kristin Ross aptly puts it in *Communal Luxury*, her powerful recent book on the political imaginary of the Commune and its lasting influence on the development of both Marxist and anarchist European thought, "There are moments when a particular event or struggle enters vividly into the figurability of the present, and this seems to me to be the case with the Commune today."[3]

In March 2012, for example, a guerrilla theater troupe, led by artist Zoe Beloff and wielding period costumes and cardboard cut-out props, resurrected Bertolt Brecht's 1949 play, *The Days of the Commune*, in Zuccotti Park, explicitly linking its staging to the politics and aspirations of Occupy, and suggesting the Commune's ideas "are just as alive and urgent today as they were then."[4] The following year, the investigative theater company, The Civilians, launched a bigger-budget return to the Commune in the form of a ninety-minute musical staged at the Brooklyn Academy of Music and the ArtsEmerson theater in Boston. Both productions claimed not just to channel the Commune at a moment when it was most needed but rather to remind audiences of a past that, unlike 1789 or 1830, did not already have a Dickens novel like *A Tale of Two Cities* (or the recent blockbuster musical film, *Les Misérables*) to keep it in circulation. "The relatively low profile, at least in current cultural memory, of what happened in March of 1871 is part of what attracted Steven Cosson and Michael Friedman, the creators of 'Paris Commune,'" suggested *New York Times* theater critic Ben Brantley in his glowing review of The Civilians' show.[5] Their aim was, then, to re-occupy a foreign past that seemed altogether long lost, and perhaps most crucially, to revivify a moment they figured to have had no previous currency in the US. While these productions echo wider claims often made about American historical memory – namely, that as a nation we have been most often prone to historical amnesia – they nevertheless bring into relief just how much we have forgotten about how radically transatlantic the experience of the Commune was, how much of a sensation it made in its own moment, and – most of all – how often, and to what cross-purposes, the Commune was fashioned anew over and again in US memory long before Occupy came onto the scene.[6]

When the largest national strike in US history broke out a mere six years after the Communards' failed revolt in France, headlines shrieked in 1877 that "the French Commune had suddenly been vomited over us."[7] American suffragists were instantly linked to the so-called "man-women" of the Commune in an array of Gilded Age sermons, editorials, and visual and literary texts, while in a variety of bestselling fin-de-siècle page-turners American boys become men by returning to the scene of – and, more to the point, witnessing the destruction of – that short-lived but not at all forgotten Parisian revolution. Postbellum pilgrimages were made time and again to the Commune's spatial remainders, visits that generated magazine remembrances that, more often than not, mourned lost landmarks and damaged buildings as if they were bodies and condemned the insurgents whose "savage fingers" had torn them from the city's landscape. Southern whites consistently mobilized anti-Communard rhetoric against African Americans in the postbellum period, while W. E. B. DuBois turned the tables by christening the South Carolina Reconstruction government the Black Commune. Turn-of-the-century American radicals looked to the Commune as an affective and material blueprint for revolution; mainstream audiences went to Coney Island, in 1891, to see its fiery demise at the hands of government troops restaged as a pyrotechnic spectacle, and two decades later, more than 7,000 "Reds" assembled to watch a two-hundred-member production of *The Paris Commune* on stage at Madison Square Garden. The Commune was, in other words, never far from reach in Gilded Age America, and, despite or perhaps because of its sensational afterlives in US literary, visual, and performance culture, it remained a vital touchstone of leftist internationalism well into the modernist period. While McCarthyism did much to efface the tangible traces of its presence and role in US memory – bringing an end to, among other things, the pamphlets and yearly commemorative pageants that had kept it in circulation for some five decades in the US leftist imaginary – the Commune nevertheless emerged once again in the 1960s, offering both a nomenclature and a model for student radicals such as Mario Savio and Mark Rudd, who, in re-occupying revolution and occupying public spaces, were reliving the future via that once again not so distant past.

Sensational Internationalism recovers this now largely forgotten story of the Paris Commune's spectacular afterlife as specter and spectacle in late nineteenth- and early twentieth-century American culture. In so doing, it aims to remap the borders of transatlantic feeling and resituate the role of international memory in US culture in the long nineteenth century and beyond. In putting 1871 – and, more particularly, the Paris Commune's "audacious internationalism" – on the map of American literary and cultural studies, this book contributes to the conversation begun by the seminal work of Michael Rogin and Larry J. Reynolds to recover the influence of the European uprisings of 1848 on the literary imagination of writers like Emerson and Melville and the literary history of the American Renaissance, as well as more recent work to trace what Anna Brickhouse has termed the lingering "Franco-Africanist shadow" on American literary and cultural history in the wake of the Haitian Revolution.[8] But this book offers another angle on that story of distant uprisings resounding at home: namely, how a foreign revolution came back to life as a domestic commodity, and why for decades another nation's memory came to feel so much our own. Chronicling the Commune's returns across a surprisingly vast and visually striking archive of periodical poems and illustrations, panoramic spectacles, children's adventure fiction, popular and canonical novels, political pamphlets, avant-garde theater productions, and radical pulp, my book argues that the Commune became, for writers and readers across virtually all classes and political persuasions, a critical locus for re-occupying both radical and mainstream memory of revolution and empire, a key site for negotiating postbellum gender trouble and regional reconciliation, and a vital terrain for rethinking Paris – and what it meant to be an American there – in US fiction and culture. For Americans felt Paris to be curiously their own long before the Moderns made it their hometown.

Whereas scholars of memory in US literature and history have primarily focused on the domestic contours of events, centering their attention on, for example, the Alamo, the Civil War, Vietnam, and 9/11, *Sensational Internationalism* reveals the necessity of approaching cultural memory as a phenomenon within and beyond the nation and, in turn, rethinking various media – in particular, the newspaper, the panorama, and the novel – as crucial sites for the construction not simply of national but also of international – I am tempted to say extra-national – memory.[9] For as I argue, the tenacity of the Commune's second life does not simply attest to its continuing usefulness in American culture for making sense of revolutions past and future: it also crucially reverses the assumption that transnational circuits of memory – that memory without borders, as it were – are uniquely or definitively a product of our *own* hyper-mediated historical moment.[10]

What little attention that has been paid to the Commune's unexpected second life in America by historians has so far focused almost exclusively on the relationship between the events in Paris and anxieties about labor unrest at home, and these accounts suggest the

Commune's presence begins to fade in the aftermath of the failure of the Great Strike of 1877.[11] As Philip M. Katz elaborates in his compelling study of Americans and the Paris Commune, while "a lurid image of the Commune continued to haunt [the mainstream US] vision of domestic social unrest . . . even this image dimmed shortly after the Great Strike, as the image of the Commune ceased to be an active force in American culture," and after 1877 only "foreign-born workers – and not even all of them" kept the Commune's memory alive in the US.[12] My book crucially revises this narrative by revealing the ways the Commune as spectacle and specter continued to garner a variety of literary and affective responses well into the 1930s, and always meant more than labor in US memory. It also contributes to recent work in American Studies on the global dimensions of late nineteenth- and early twentieth-century US radicalisms by taking seriously the way the Commune's sensational presence in print, visual, and performance culture offered pre-Popular Front radicals a foundational blueprint for action and touchstone for internationalist feeling.[13] In so doing, this book addresses a critical ongoing blind spot in American Studies by extending the borders of transatlantic affiliation beyond the confines of Anglo-American attachments.

In refocusing attention on the Paris Commune as a key event in American literary and cultural consciousness and a vital site of late nineteenth- and early twentieth-century transatlantic feeling, *Sensational Internationalism* intersects and complicates previous studies of Americans in Paris and the role of Paris in US literature. Modernist Paris has long been considered the prime time to be an American in Paris, and studies of that moment in US literature most often focus on the ways that American writers engage with the mythic rather than historical dimensions of the city.[14] By contrast, I analyze the ways that the specter of the Commune took up residence in the US, haunting and electrifying even those writers and readers who never left home. My book thus draws attention to the way that, in the Gilded Age and beyond, Francophilia was as much a structure of feeling that shaped Americanness as was the Anglophilia to which Elisa Tamarkin's work has directed our attention and that Americanist scholars have come to more commonly associate with this period. Like Tamarkin, I am interested in the "productive vertigo" of extranational feelings, or more precisely, in how and why Americans "feel the deepest reality of attachment without the reality behind it."[15] I draw on her reading of the ways in which we might be "the most national while lost in fantasies of belonging elsewhere" in order to understand the ways in which transatlantic feeling might equally work to complicate and counter our national attachments (and fantasies).[16] I term this extra-national structure of feeling "sensational internationalism" rather than simply Francophilia to highlight both that flux in national feeling and the role of a variety of print and visual media in shaping the memory culture around Paris and the Commune that sustained it for over five decades.

Sensation and Solidarity

The keywords at the heart of this book require further elaboration, not least because the meanings of "internationalism" have shifted dramatically in the past century. The *Oxford English Dictionary* informs us that the radical, extra-national valence of the term – implying "a movement or doctrine advocating international proletarian revolution" – is now largely defunct, or as it puts it, "chiefly historical."[17] Yet for nineteenth-century Americans the term provoked profound anxiety and affiliation in equal measure, for in the aftermath of the *Communist Manifesto*'s exhortation to cross-national working-class solidarity ("Workers of the World Unite!"), the formation of the International Workingmen's Association in 1864, the rise and fall of the Commune, the emerging international movement for an eight-hour work day, and the Haymarket bombing and execution of the Haymarket anarchists, *internationalism* was both the bête noire of American culture in the long nineteenth century and a radically embodied form of extra-national political identity and lived counter-cultural memory.

Yet post 1989 and 9/11, the term has largely come to be defined, on the one hand, by the erosion of national culture in the homogenizing, and seemingly ever-triumphant, face of global capitalism, and, on the other, by sensational media accounts of "radicalized" Muslims leaving their home countries to embrace a fight in faraway places to which religion rather than the nation-state connects them, a phenomenon often portrayed as a terrifying new form of transnational solidarity. This era (or iteration) of radicalism *as* jihad and internationalism *as* globalization has its roots in the Cold War "US internationalism" that sought to counter (not to mention vilify) the USSR's Comintern global revolutionary solidarity with Marshall Plan-sponsored mass consumption efforts in Europe and an ever-expanding project of exporting both Fordist production and American consumerism abroad.[18] At once occupying and co-opting the foundational term of leftist transnational solidarity – internationalism – this vision of internationalism "American-style" was deeply nationalistic and hegemonic in bent, directly identifying, as Bruce Robbins has pointed out, US national interests with those of global capitalism and vice versa.[19] Such nationalist internationalism was, in turn, predicated on a new form of global imperialism, or what Paul Giles has aptly described as "a putative triumph over the coordinates of physical space, the replacement of an imperial design based on territorial possession by one driven instead by liberal internationalism, through which American economic and cultural ideas would penetrate overseas markets."[20]

Recent scholarship on the culture of diaspora and Black radicalism has, however, recovered the ways that twentieth-century African American radicalism and artistic production were vitally animated by an altogether other vision of international belonging.[21] As Brent Hayes Edwards, Robin D. G. Kelley, Cedric J. Robinson, Kate Baldwin, and Minkah Makalani have powerfully elaborated, this "Black Internationalism" was marked by its commitment to anti-colonial struggle, participation in transnational artistic and political movements, and, most of all, by its vision of Black identity and solidarity that superseded national affiliations. While these studies focus on the Bolshevik Revolution as the key catalyst of radical internationalism and most often locate the watershed moment of Black internationalist feeling and cultural production in the 1920s and 1930s, they nevertheless shed light on earlier cultural formations and affective modalities of leftist internationalism in the US. Building on this body of scholarship, as well as on recent work by Shelly Streeby to recover pre-Popular Front radical world movements and US internationalisms, *Sensational Internationalism* uncovers the Commune as a vital, if now largely forgotten, site for living and remembering within, as well as beyond, the nation-state in a radically anti-capitalist sense throughout the postbellum period and well beyond it.

Perhaps the most singular and least remembered aspect of the Commune uprising is, as Ross has recently pointed out, its "non-national" orientation:

> an insurrection in the capital fought under the flag of the Universal Republic, the Commune as event and as political culture has always proved resistant to any seamless integration into [a French] national narrative. As one of its former members recalled years later, it was, above all else, "an audacious act of internationalism."[22]

Yet postbellum radicals like Victoria Woodhull and Wendell Phillips, who supported the Commune in the 1870s, celebrated its legacy precisely as a "universal republic" rather than simply a

Parisian event by way of marches and yearly gatherings that united spiritualists, socialists, and free-thinkers with Communard refugees, German immigrants, and Cuban revolutionaries. Turn-of-the-century supporters, such as the Los Angeles-based socialist organizer N. L. Griest, heralded the Commune's memory – and annual celebration – as the cornerstone of radical internationalism as counter-cultural remembrance: "Other men may have their days, but to the American workingman the anniversary of the Paris Commune will be the greatest celebration in the calendar."[23] But while remembering the Commune helped to consolidate leftist internationalism as an affective, material practice and counterpublic in the US in ways that have so far received scant critical attention, the injunction to remember the Commune was *not* simply a leftist pastime or structure of radical international feeling. Indeed, the desire to witness it, and the lingering sense of possession of its memory and the Paris it scarred, was also viscerally underwritten by an extra-national attachment to Paris and a form of internationalism that allows Americans to feel we possess places that are not ours and support state-backed violence when "civilization" is under threat.[24] (*The New York Times* insisted in 1871 that the Commune waged war "against civilization itself" and that claim was resoundingly echoed across the US press in the 1870s.[25]) Both these versions of late nineteenth and early twentieth-century internationalism – the radical and the reactive – were in turn facilitated by the Commune's *virality* as a sensation circulating across US culture by way of ongoing newspaper coverage and literary representations, as well as spectacles and pageants.

If I invoke the term sensationalism in my title to signal the layering of memories of the Commune made possible by postbellum media technologies and the forms of international feeling enacted through them, I do so also to highlight the way the Commune *itself* marked the advent of revolution as instant media sensation. That the Commune entered the American news scene and public sphere as, in Russ Castronovo's formulation, a "mass spectacle" had much to do with the rise of the illustrated weeklies and the recent laying of the first transatlantic telegraph cable, as well as Paris's role as the "capital of modernity" in the nineteenth century.[26] And as historian Samuel Bernstein points out,

> No political or economic issue in the United States, save governmental corruption, received more headlines in the American press of the 1870s than did the Paris Commune . . . Anarchy, assassination, slaughter, incendiarism, streets covered in human gore – such blood curdling scenes were monotonously reported in the news.[27]

But if I am interested here in the sensational as at once a spectacular genre and a narrative and visual–cultural media modality, so too am I concerned with reconnecting us with the sensory valence and somatic immediacy of that register: the way that ruins could be experienced as aftertastes or amputated limbs, and panoramas allowed viewers impossibly immediate sensations of the Commune years after its end.[28] The term thus points to a larger argument I make across this book about the sensational and the sensory modes working at once to mediate and produce cultural memory and international feeling.

My approach to the affective and material *afterlife* of the Paris Commune in US literature and to the study of cultural memory combines detailed reading of specific literary texts and performances with a wide-ranging engagement with transatlantic print and visual culture. By excavating the ways that representations of the Commune echoed and resurfaced across an array of periodicals – beginning life, for instance, as a periodical poem in a highbrow periodical like *The Atlantic*, immediately finding a second life alongside Marx's *Civil War in France* in a radical publication like *Woodhull and Claflin's Weekly*, and ultimately enjoying a final incarnation in the first "poems for workers" anthology in the late 1920s – *Sensational Internationalism* uncovers how circuits of remediation and reprinting reshaped the borders of international feeling within both radical and mainstream US culture and chronicles how America's unexpectedly lasting fascination with the events in Paris crisscrossed rather than crystallized nineteenth-century social and mass cultural divides.[29] This book is not, in other words, about simply making leftist memory in the nineteenth century at once more audible and more visible in American literary studies; it is equally about the ways in which mainstream print and visual culture remembered the Commune even as they anxiously fixated on the radical cultures of memory embracing it in this period. As my book shows, remapping the borders of American memory requires us both to expand the print-cultural contact zones to which we attend and to rethink the margins we assign to radical cultural production in the long nineteenth century.

As historian Robert Tombs has recently pointed out, the "paradox" of the Commune lies in its vertiginous role in modern memory – at once famous and hardly known, for while it never lost its resonance for European Marxist thinkers, and received considerable attention from historians in the wake of its centenary in 1971, the Commune is both oft-written about and oft-forgotten.[30] Yet much as it has acquired renewed visibility in the political sense on both sides of the Atlantic, it has also garnered significant renewed scholarly interest of late with the publication of Ross's *Communal Luxury: The Political Imaginary of the Paris Commune* (2015), John Merriman's *Massacre: The Life and Death of the Paris Commune* (2014), and Alain Badiou's *Polemics* (2014). In examining the Commune as at once a social revolution and an international sensation refracted through US mass culture, *Sensational Internationalism* draws on that body of scholarship but does so to excavate the relationship between literary forms and extra-national memories, and to uncover dimensions of the Commune overlooked in studies of the event that focus only on its cultural aftershocks in France. In particular, my book reveals how the Commune's instant commodification and commemoration unexpectedly bring into relief the seismic epistemological shake-up that it represented in the nineteenth-century Franco-American imaginary, crucially unsettling the distinctions between metropole and periphery, domestic and anti-domestic figures, past and future, battlefield and home front, national and transnational memory. *Sensational Internationalism* thus adds to the conversation, begun by Gay Gullickson and Carolyn J. Eichner, on the gender politics of the event, but also crucially recontextualizes the degree to which the brutal reconquering of Paris by French troops should be understood as at once a civil war waged in France *and* a colonial war waged at home. For even as American novels in the 1890s surprisingly re-imagine Paris under the Commune as an imperial frontier where American boys might be made men, French writers vilifying the Commune in the 1870s had decried the spectacle of "Paris in the hands of Brutes and Negroes" and likened the Communards to "savages, a ring through their noses, tattooed in red, dancing a scalp dance on the smoking debris of society."[31]

Revolution Revisited: the Commune in '76

The Great Strike of 1877 is typically read as marking the watershed irruption of the Commune in postbellum US memory. In what follows, I turn instead to 1876, and the Paris Commune's spectacular presence at the Centennial celebration in Philadelphia, as a way not only of charting the instant commodification of the Commune in the US and exploring the archive of memory made possible by such spectacularizations, but also of opening up the larger material terrain of *Sensational Internationalism*.

The Centennial Exposition opened on May 10, 1876, in Fairmount Park in Philadelphia; by the end of its run that October, some ten million visitors had attended the fair, nearly one-fifth of the total US population.[32] While it most visibly commemorated the hundredth anniversary of the Declaration of Independence, the Exposition most often stands out in scholarly memory for its menagerie of things – typewriters were introduced at the fair, along with a mechanical calculator, Bell's telephone, Edison's telegraph, Heinz ketchup, and Fleischman's yeast – and its intricate controversies of exclusion: Frederick Douglass nearly barred from sitting on the platform on opening day; African American women's groups raising funds for, but receiving no official place within, the Woman's Pavilion; the "Southern Restaurant" that recreated life on the Old Plantation; and Native American participation limited to exhibits that showcased the "Vanishing American." But while the specter of the Civil War and the failures of Reconstruction hovered everywhere over the proceedings, there was another specter of revolution never too far from reach, the most spectacular example of which, "The Siege of Paris Cyclorama," was located just outside the gates of the main exhibition hall and garnered over a thousand Centennial visitors a day (Fig. I.1).[33] (The spectacle was such a success that it continued attracting crowds for twenty-six months straight, long after the Centennial itself had ended, before eventually moving onto Boston for an eight-month showing.)[34]

Indeed, in my reading, there were at least three Centennial sites spectacularly haunted by the Paris Commune: "The Siege of Paris" cyclorama, commissioned at the behest of an American for the Exposition;[35] "Paris By Night," a competing cycloramic view of Paris on display at the newly opened Colosseum building nearby; and the labor delegation that arrived from France to celebrate the hundredth anniversary of its "sister republic."

No American trade unions were allowed to participate in the Centennial festivities, but French trade unionists raised funds for an official visit to Philadelphia in July 1876. Although the suppression of the Commune – and the systematic repression that followed it – had done much to stifle the labor movement in France in the 1870s, reports of the delegation's impending trip spurred fears that these trade unionists might infect American labor, bringing with them "Commune-istic" ideas. As historian Philip Foner explains it, "American authorities reasoned the delegates had probably been Communards and certainly were sympathetic to the Commune."[36] In April 1876, *The New York Herald* warned readers in no uncertain terms that French workers were "nearly addicted to Commune-istic ideas" – joining the chorus of American newspapers who suggested the French delegation might inspire Americans "to model themselves after the Commune."[37] The irony, of course, was that a number of American radicals had already begun gathering yearly in cities like New York, Chicago, and Milwaukee to celebrate the Commune and keep its ideas alive. American labor, for its part, responded by appropriating that epithet to redirect the accusation: criticizing the vast numbers of immigrants employed in the construction of Exposition buildings in Fairmount Park during the deepening economic recession, the *National Labor Tribune* of Pittsburgh asked pointedly, "Are our authorities *cultivating* an American Commune?"[38]

The French delegation spent nearly twelve days touring the Centennial grounds, but they apparently made no stop at the Great Siege of Paris Building, perhaps purposefully missing out on the spectacle of the "Assassination of the Archbishop of Paris at the Hands of the Commune of 1871." [39] If their presence catalyzed fears of an impending "Commune" in the US, however, the panoramic spectacle housed on Elm Avenue and Fortieth Street signaled the way those fears were always already imminent in the US in this moment, for the cyclorama also points to the way that Americans, throughout the 1870s, consumed the spectacle of the Commune by way of guidebooks to Paris, popular histories, melodramas, widely anthologized periodical poetry, Pinkerton tracts, editorials, sermons, and magazine "remembrances."

But what was at stake in returning to this scene in 1876 by way of an immense, immersive visual spectacle, revisiting revolution at the same moment that the US was remembering its own?[40] To relive a moment that could not properly be called one's own, and further, to revisit a scene that one did not oneself live through, to inhabit – indeed, "try on" – someone else's memories is a paradoxical desire for both an impossible immediacy and a virtual reality most often associated with our own hyper-mediated cultural moment. Although Alison Landsberg specifically identifies such "prosthetic memories" with the rise of film, "experiential museums," and other more modern cultural technologies, I would argue the panoramic form similarly functioned as a technology that made available such experiential, *embodied* memory.[41] For if we follow Angela Miller's compelling suggestion that "the key to the panorama as a particular visual medium was a way of *seeing* – the panoramic," we can infer that the "panoramic" experience brokers a new technology of remembering as well.[42]

The two cycloramas mounted for the Centennial, "The Siege of Paris" and "Paris By Night," offered visitors, as their titles suggest, competing visions of Paris. Art historians such as Ralph Hyde have rightly noted this juxtaposition allowed viewers to glimpse a by then "old-fashioned panorama" alongside a cutting-edge version of the medium,[43] but in my reading these juxtaposing views did far more ideological and mnemonic work, for their opposing depictions of the city nevertheless proffered strikingly complementary visions of the Commune. Both spectacles notably billed themselves as intended to be *especially* of interest to Centennial visitors: "The Siege of Paris" was commissioned specifically for the event, while the *Colosseum Hand Book* details, "It was decided to place the 'Paris by Night' [rather than 'London By Night'] on view during the Centennial season, as a work which would probably be most pleasing to the greater number of persons congregated in Philadelphia during this festival time."[44]

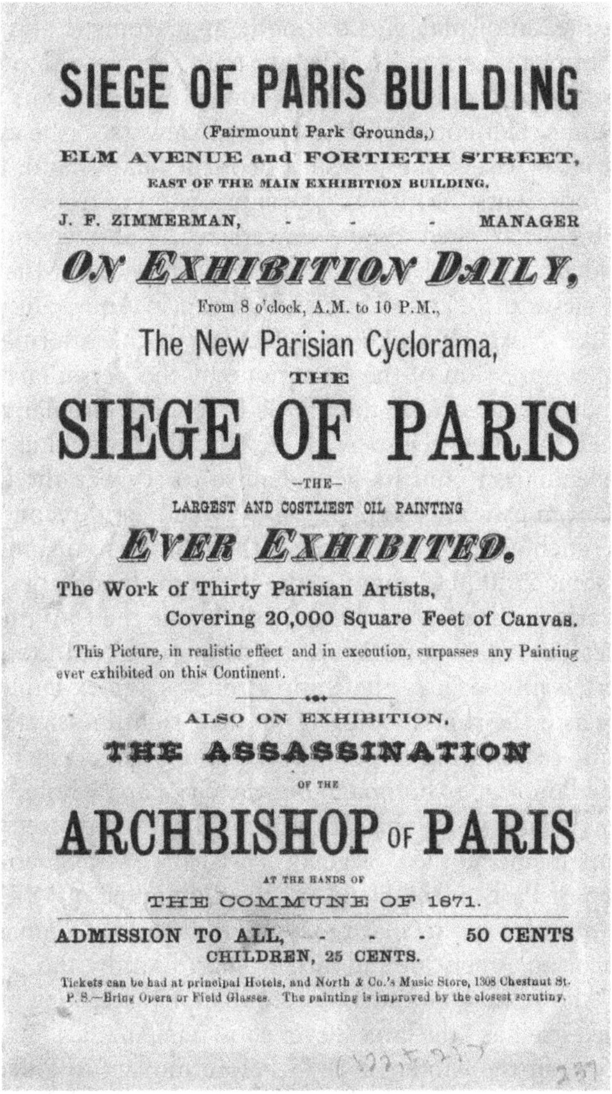

SIEGE OF PARIS BUILDING

(Fairmount Park Grounds,)

ELM AVENUE and FORTIETH STREET,

EAST OF THE MAIN EXHIBITION BUILDING.

J. F. ZIMMERMAN, - - - MANAGER

ON EXHIBITION DAILY,

From 8 o'clock, A.M. to 10 P.M.,

The New Parisian Cyclorama,

THE

SIEGE OF PARIS

—THE—

LARGEST AND COSTLIEST OIL PAINTING

EVER EXHIBITED.

The Work of Thirty Parisian Artists,

Covering 20,000 Square Feet of Canvas.

This Picture, in realistic effect and in execution, surpasses any Painting ever exhibited on this Continent.

ALSO ON EXHIBITION,

THE ASSASSINATION

OF THE

ARCHBISHOP OF PARIS

AT THE HANDS OF

THE COMMUNE OF 1871.

ADMISSION TO ALL, - - - **50 CENTS.**

CHILDREN, 25 CENTS.

Tickets can be had at principal Hotels, and North & Co.'s Music Store, 1308 Chestnut St. P. S.—Bring Opera or Field Glasses. The painting is improved by the closest scrutiny.

Figure I.1 "Siege of Paris . . . On Exhibition Daily" handbill (Philadelphia: 1876), The Library Company of Philadelphia.

When "Paris By Night" (Fig. I.2) originally debuted in London in 1848, audiences flocked to see a glimpse of the capital precisely at the moment that a revolution was unfolding in Paris; as Daphne A. Brooks has argued, some of that revolutionary fervor seems to have seeped into the panoramic experience, perhaps inspiring William Wells Brown to develop his own abolitionist panorama in the 1850s.[45] But by the time "Paris By Night" re-opened at the newly constructed Colosseum building in Philadelphia in 1876, the view of Paris it put on display was distinctly anachronistic and its charm was less "armchair travel" to the city than the fact that the Paris it allowed one to visit quite literally no longer existed. As its accompanying brochure self-consciously informed viewers, "[the cyclorama] recalls, in many cases, the pleasure of earlier days" and, more specifically, "represents the city as it was prior to the riots of the Commune."[46] It thus claimed to give viewers access at once to "the Paris of the guidebooks" and to a far more spectral one. Much like the bird's-eye views of "Paris in ruins" that ran in American illustrated weeklies like *Harper's* and *Frank Leslie's* in the aftermath of the week-long suppression of the Commune by the Versaillais army, the detailed map included with the "Paris By Night" circular repeatedly lingers over the sites "Destroyed" by the fire, invoking the Commune's incendiarism and its fiery demise to revivify the Commune as its end, even as it erases the "Bloody Week" and reconquering of Paris by French government troops – the fighting and summary execution of some 25,000 Communards – from the landscape. The move to show Paris "as it was" and implicitly blame the Commune for its ruin echoes broader transatlantic trends in visual culture: art historian Albert Boime argues the Impressionists, for example, painted city scenes as if the ruined buildings in their sightlines were invisible, symbolically recapturing these spaces for the bourgeoisie by filling in the missing landscape and imagining the cityscape whole.[47]

Whereas "Paris By Night" at once invoked and effaced the Commune from memory, the "Siege of Paris and Assassination of the Archbishop of Paris at the Hands of the Commune of 1871" offered visitors a far more spectacular re-laying of memory. Commissioned at the behest of an American and largely subsidized by the French government,[48] the static cyclorama – more than 400 feet long and 50 feet high – billed itself as "the largest ever shown in America" and debuted in New York in the winter of 1875 before moving to Philadelphia.[49] Ostensibly, the cyclorama depicted the courage of the French troops facing the Prussian siege of Paris during the Franco-Prussian War of 1870–1,[50] presenting shelled houses, collapsed walls, and broken bodies amidst scenes of "sorties" and actual fighting. Indeed, "The Siege of

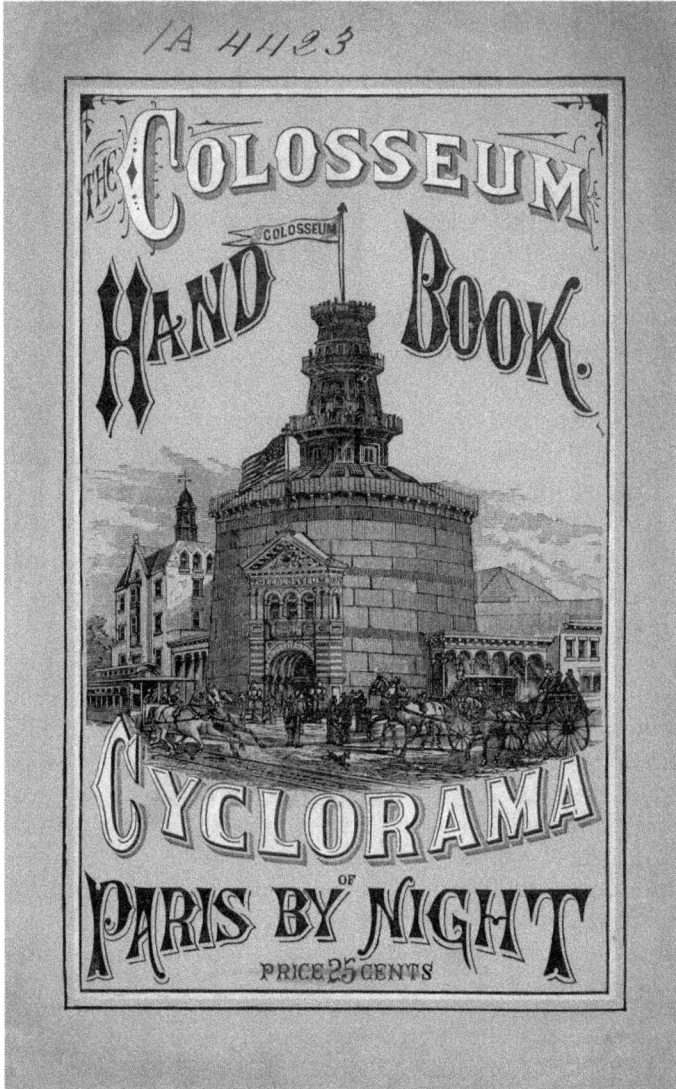

Figure I.2 Cover, *Colosseum Hand Book: Descriptive of the Cyclorama of Paris by Night* (Philadelphia: Allen, Lane & Scott's Printing House, 1876). Rare Book Division, Department of Rare Books and Special Collections, Princeton University Library.

Paris" registered the scars of war with such realism that its accompanying booklet claimed that "to realize this magnificent pageant is, after all, only an illusion requires a stronger mental effort than to accept it for reality"; but like "Paris By Night," the panoramic experience it afforded viewers enacted a spectacular displacement of memory.[51]

The original panorama entitled "The Siege of Paris" was painted under the direction of Henri Félix Philippoteaux in 1872 and seems a conventional case of panoramic memory invoked to facilitate nationalist fervor. As Hyde describes it,

> A renowned painter of military subjects, [Philippoteaux] was commissioned after the Prussian victory to record the heroism of the Parisian resistance in a new panorama for the Champs-Elysées rotunda . . . [it] provided a populace, stunned and embittered by the acceptance of Prussia's humiliating peace terms, with a source of solace for their injured pride.[52]

Showing the siege of Paris during the Franco-Prussian war from the perspective of the French lines, its popularity lasted for decades, and the spectacle remained on display in Paris at least until 1890.[53] The version commissioned by an American for the Centennial was, however, a view of the siege from the exact opposite vantage point, its line of sight shifted over to the Prussian lines menacing Paris in January 1870.[54] As one contemporary viewer describes it:

> The visitor ascends a stairway to the top of the mound of earth, representing a hill near Paris, and from the supposed high ground looks down upon Paris in the distance and the fight between Prussian and French soldiers in the earth works. The hill on which the visitor is supposed to be standing is covered with earth, littered with brushwood, debris of battles . . . forms of dead soldiers . . . At the foot of the hill, painted imitations of stones, debris, etc. on the immense canvas of the picture adjoin the palpably real earth at the visitor's feet, and they are such accurate representations that the dividing line between reality and illusion is not easily traced.[55]

The sensation of the line between reality and illusion "not being easily traced" effectively points to the panorama-goer's sensational experience of being transported outside of herself, into a space and time not her own, and this effect was particularly heightened here by Philippoteaux's innovation of three-dimensional *faux terrains* that helped to sharpen the realistic visual effect by diminishing the eye's ability to perceive the distinction between the three-dimensional and two-dimensional elements in the scene.[56] The "Siege of Paris" thus did not simply restage the past for visitors, but rather allowed them to imagine themselves able to recapture it, to experience a memory that is and is not their own, and the sensation of – as Griffiths aptly describes it – "the cognitive dissonance that comes from feeling like you're elsewhere while knowing that you haven't moved."[57]

The shift in perspective in Philippoteaux's Centennial cyclorama certainly allowed for a much finer view of Paris – no small selling point – and it would seem, paradoxically, to align American visitors with the Prussian perspective in order to better sympathize with the French. I would argue, however, that the move to place visitors outside Paris looking in actually functions as a kind of screen memory, summoning the once-rampant fears about a Prussian invasion of the city so as to counter the memory that it was actually to be the French government troops who bombarded, besieged, and eventually reconquered the city later that year (Fig. I.3). Even as the cyclorama spectacularly displaced the violence of the Commune's repression by the Third Republic, however, it also offered Americans the invitation to celebrate their own revolution while imagining themselves in the hills overlooking Paris, on the cusp of taking back the metropole from the red "savages" elected to govern it – and thus to reclaim revolution, in 1876, as uniquely our own.

Much as "The Siege of Paris" worked to subtly screen the brutality of the Commune's end, its sensational companion piece, "The Assassination of the Archbishop of Paris at the Hands of the Commune," painted by Jean Alfred Desbrosses specifically for the *US* edition of the cycloramic spectacle, further dispelled – or displaced – that event.[58] For in a calculus of memory that echoed much of the original transatlantic press coverage of the Bloody Week, to revisit the harrowing scene of Archbishop Darboy's execution by Communards on May 24, 1871, was conveniently to forget the unprecedented violence of the Third Republic's retaking of Paris, which in no small measure helped to incite it. The Philadelphia *Evening Star* notably insists that "The bloody scenes embodied in the picture representing the Assassination of the Archbishop should be seen by every Centennial visitor," while *The Evening Telegraph* went so far as to suggest that the spectacle was "quite as great a curiosity as the Exhibition itself."[59]

And yet it is, nevertheless, tantalizing to think that panoramic memory might be able to work otherwise, that invoking the Commune in 1876 might not simply re-lay the past but might imagine other, more radical futures. In a letter dated January 27, 1876, a twenty-one-year-old Eugene V. Debs wrote home from New York to ask his brother to "Tell Pa and Ma that I am going to see that great painting of the 'Siege of Paris' and the Franco Prussian War – which came from France and

Figure I.3 "They Are Doing Unto Themselves What They Would Have Done Unto Us," cover, June 10, 1871, *Harper's Weekly*, Annex A, Forrestal, Princeton University Library.

is going to be exhibited at the Centennial."[60] To imagine the future socialist organizer and leader of the Industrial Workers of the World (IWW) visiting this "curious" spectacle en route to Philadelphia is to begin to recapture, I think, the potential for reading articulations of memory against the grain, for seeking out contrapuntal notes embedded within even the most reactionary or vitriolic reconstructions of the Commune. But Debs's visit also forecasts the ways in which radical appropriations of the Commune often took spectacular forms, re-using and turning inside out the sensational tropes embedded within the most condemnatory commodifications of the Commune. Tracking the Commune's spectacularization in America, is, I argue, to chart the unlikely transit between radical and mass cultural forms, highbrow literary and radical print culture in the late nineteenth and early twentieth centuries.

Sensational Internationalism

In chronicling the Commune's longstanding and unlikely second life in America, the chapters that follow focus on key flashpoints in its circulation and remediation in the US. Chapter 1 turns to the 1870s, when fears of an American Commune were rampant and anxieties about the domestic threat posed by the incendiary women of the Commune were equally rife. Chapter 2 attends to the 1890s, which marked the high point of labor unrest, racist violence, and the Commune's spectacular transnational role in US leftist memory-making. Chapter 5 flashes forward to the late 1920s and early 1930s, which saw the Commune enshrined and reconfigured in post-1917 leftist memory by way of Communist Party of the United States of America (CPUSA) organizing and unparalleled growth in leftist print and performance culture, while my epilogue centers on the 1960s, when the high point of US student radicalism makes the Commune at once new and newly visible on US campuses. The chronology of this story is complicated, however, both by the fact that the time of revolution is "always out of joint," and by the way the culture of memory and international feeling I am charting here are cyclical and always already layered, with various Parises and visions of the Commune's past (and future) simultaneously circulating, impinging upon, and erupting from the present.[61] Thus Chapter 3 and Chapter 4 slide across the postbellum moment, charting the way the Commune came to feel in radical culture from the 1870s to the early 1900s, and the way it came to be sensed across postbellum tourism, transatlantic visual culture, and the writings of Henry James across this same swath of time. This chronological layering is, in turn, a mode of seeing memory and writing cultural history from a different angle, for, as Jordan Stein has recently argued, "Thinking reflexively about chronology . . . challenges us to see the multiple temporalities that history contains," shifting both the literary *and* the cultural histories we can perceive and adumbrate.[62]

In making that kind of cultural history sensible, *Sensational Internationalism* turns on a set of questions that have shaped at once the archive I amassed in writing this book and the reading practice I bring to the various mediums of viral memory and feeling I address in it. What are the specific affective and sensory relays between space and memory, international events, and national identities? In what ways do literary texts in particular archive and refashion collective memories and counter-histories? How are performances of memory peculiarly re-embodied across print, visual, and performance cultures, and what do these performances (and translations) in turn suggest about not only gender panic and imperial designs but also radical futures in the US in the long nineteenth century? And, finally, what forms of cultural and literary radicalism do extra-national memories shape?

Both during the 1871 uprising and in the wake of the Commune's fall, Americans encountered unsettling images of female Communards marching across the pages of illustrated periodicals. In turn, a variety of American sermons and editorials railed against the revolution and claimed its "overly emancipated" females might pose the most terrifying transatlantic threat of all. My opening chapter, "Framing the Pétroleuse," recovers the drama of that postbellum gender panic and resituates US periodical poetry written in response to it. Reading Sarah M. B. Piatt's 1872 periodical poem, "The Palace-Burner," alongside both *Harper's Weekly*'s pictorial coverage of the Commune and the subversive sentimentality of other postbellum poetic returns to the fiery "Women of the Commune," I argue that Piatt's reworking of the figure of the Parisian petroleum-thrower relies on and resists the ways the so-called "man–women" of the Commune were pictured in the US press, for in bringing the pétroleuse "into the parlor," Piatt crucially re-imagines both the fiery Communardes and the specter of the domestic firebrands they were so often used to portend.

Chapter 2, "Becoming Americans in Paris," charts the reconfiguration of the Commune's domestic threat in American popular fiction in the 1890s. I show how America's fin-de-siècle preoccupation with the revolution of 1871 consistently reframes Paris as a frontier of empire even as it critically re-imagines it as a site where American tourists – or, more specifically, Gilded Age American men – might be said to "find" themselves. Setting Edward King's 1895 boys' book, *Under the Red Flag*, alongside G. A. Henty's *A Woman of the Commune*, and two other immensely popular but virtually forgotten historical romances of the period, *The Red Republic* and *The American in Paris*, I argue that the 1890s were a particularly apt time to revisit the Commune because of the very real labor unrest plaguing the country, and more importantly because the "romance of the Commune" served to revise American conceptions of revolution at a moment when the US was re-imagining its role abroad and re-evaluating its attitude towards empire.

My third chapter, "Radical Calendars," moves from the specter of Paris under the Commune as a savage frontier for forging US imperial designs to an alternate terrain of spectacular postbellum memory, uncovering the Commune as the cornerstone of radical internationalism as at once a sensation and a lived practice of counter-remembrance in the long nineteenth century. Tracing the ways annual festivals and celebrations of the Commune, complete with oratory, tableaux vivants, and dancing, united an array of American radicals, I show how these performances of memory drew on the audacious internationalism of the Commune uprising to create both a counter-calendar and a counter-memory of the Commune's failure. Reading Lucy Parsons, Voltairine de Cleyre, and Emma Goldman's writings on the Commune alongside and against both this cycle of leftist remembrance and the cycle of anxious reprinting these festivals received in mainstream US newspapers makes, I argue, the remarkably vibrant and radically internationalist cultures of leftist memory in the long nineteenth century at once more visible and more audible, allowing us to hear beyond the limits of print as an archive of radical memory and lived feeling.

Chapter 4, "Tasting Space," moves from sights of Paris as a revolutionary underground to sites of Paris in ruin, from unexpected forms of imperial adventure or subterranean possibility to uncanny forms of affective possession. While *The American Scene* has been the privileged site to examine Henry James's fascination with – and affective responses to – lost landmarks and newly minted ruins, I excavate the sights of and detours around the post-Commune ruins of Paris in his writings and contemporary periodical culture. Situating James's attention to charred landscape and vanished tourist sights alongside their ongoing returns in US print and visual culture, I suggest, crucially reconfigures James's transformative and uncannily embodied "historic sense" even as it recovers the post-Commune ruinscape that came to function as an unexpectedly charged site of transnational memory in US literary, visual, and performance culture.

My concluding chapter, "Restaging Horror," turns from James's multivalent spatial memory to a series of radical texts that unearth precisely that "other" Paris for the Popular Front by exploring Guy Endore's 1933 bestseller, *The Werewolf of Paris*, a novel whose unlikely return to the Commune interrupts both its ostensible horror plot and its initial setting in 1920s expatriate Paris. Reading Endore's retelling of the Commune alongside both contemporary worker theater productions and agitprop that drew on the conventions of pulp fiction to reclaim 1871 for the American Left, I recover the way that radical pulp and radical theater in this period used the medium of horror to radically transform historical fiction and conventional histories of the Commune. Redeploying the sensational tropes so often mobilized in mainstream American narratives of the Commune so as to restage the horror of the Commune as its suppression rather than its existence, these texts escape the cul-de-sac of trauma by espousing what I term an "insurgent" rather than simply melancholic fixity on the past, refashioning the space of the Commune in Marxist thought and US memory.

Where my final chapter charts the Cultural Front's insistent returns to the Commune, my epilogue, "Barricades Revisited," examines the Commune's re-ignition in the 1960s. Returning to Endore's likening of the uprising to a "free-for-all," I argue that this conjuration – lacking the top-down organization of a party, prone to spring up anywhere unannounced – would survive the reign of McCarthy and the crackdown that did so much to dissipate radical memory and, with it, 1871's resonance in the US. I argue that the story of the Commune that would survive the 1950s offered future radicals not so much a program as a promise – a memory of a revolutionary future that might be "vomited up" at any moment. I anchor my discussion in two pivotal eruptions of the Commune on campus: Mario Savio's invocations of it during the Free Speech Movement demonstrations at the University of California at Berkeley as a model of campus activism and taking "only what is ours," and its more literal restaging five years later as student protestors at Columbia University turned to 1871 to make sense of their own cultural moment, dubbing themselves "Communards" as they reoccupied this once-again vital and viral revolutionary past.

Framing the Pétroleuse: Postbellum Poetry and the Visual Culture of Gender Panic

> La Pétroleuse! (petroleum-thrower): what a terrible significance has this newly invented name. Is it possible that those who belong to what is emphatically styled the gentler sex can perpetuate such atrocities?
>
> *Harper's Weekly* (1871)

> All her utterances, and especially her speeches at the anarchist gatherings, are wired throughout the country as fully and eagerly as though she were a Louise Michel or a Pétroleuse of the Paris Commune.
>
> *The Galveston Daily News* on Lucy Parsons (1886)

In perhaps the most climactic moment of *The Bostonians*, Henry James's 1886 novel of feminist agitation and tragicomic love triangles, Basil Ransom, having successfully snagged Verena Tarrant away from at once Olive Chancellor, the suffrage movement, and a life on the public stage, does *not* watch Olive as she contemplates replacing Verena by herself ascending the stage to face the increasingly mob-like crowd at the Boston Hall she had rented for her protégée's entrée into the public eye. Writes James,

> If [Ransom] had observed her, it might have seemed to him that she hoped to find the fierce expiation she sought for in exposure to the thousands she had disappointed and deceived, in offering herself to be trampled to death and torn to pieces. She might have suggested to him some feminine firebrand of Paris revolutions, erect on a barricade.[1]

Olive is imagined here as at once martyr and virago, poised to face the public rather than an onslaught of bullets, or, rather, about to face the hissing crowd *as if it were* an onslaught of bullets, the scenes melting into, or altogether overwhelming, one another. But what to make of the strange slippage here between mounting a platform and a barricade? For the connection is not quite as off-hand, or as strictly metaphorical, as James's conditional tense implies. While the plurality of the reference – summoning any, all Paris revolutions – dispels its curious particularity, the figure of the "feminine firebrand" nevertheless quite strikingly conjures one of the most terrifying remainders of the Paris Commune – namely, the figure of the female petroleum-thrower or pétroleuse laying waste to the city, even as it points to the way that this figure so often haunted that of the suffragist in the late nineteenth-century American imaginary: the danger that a woman on a platform *might be* a woman on a barricade, for both during the 1871 uprising and in the wake of the Commune's fall, Americans encountered unsettling images of female Communards marching across the pages of illustrated periodicals. In turn, a variety of American sermons and editorials railed against the revolution and claimed its "overly emancipated" females might pose the most terrifying transatlantic threat of all.

The Nation opined in 1871 that

> on the whole, the reign of the Commune must be pronounced the most extraordinary episode of modern times, and strikingly illustrates the truth of the observation that the barbarians whose ravages the modern world has to dread, live not in the forests but in the heart of our large cities.[2]

This formulation of what "the modern world has to dread" concisely points to the "Red" scare provoked by the Commune, and comments like it have led historians to attend to the domestic threat that the Commune was figured to pose to the twin realms of labor and capital in the 1870s, but that narrative flattens out – and quite strikingly forgets – the other fears that the Commune provoked at this moment about savages lurking not so much in the cities as in the home and the "unsexed" women who threatened at once property and ballot-box. While scholars have noted that references to the fiery women of the Commune circulated widely in coverage of the Great Strike, and that female trade unionists were often equated with the figure of the "unsexed female incendiary," the specter of the pétroleuse did not erupt out of nowhere in 1877.[3] Indeed, as James's reference to the "feminine firebrand" recalls, this terrifying figure repeatedly surfaced in sermons, editorials, and periodical literature throughout the decade, and signaled the way in which US feminist agitation was often figured to be as threatening to capital and the cult of domesticity as labor unrest well into the 1890s.[4]

Take, for example, *Frank Leslie's* March 16, 1872, cover story, "A New Order of Amazons." Even as the title summoned images of the "Amazons of the Seine" that splashed across American periodicals the previous spring, the editorial explicitly yokes the firebrands of Paris with the freewheeling free-love feminist (and vocal Commune supporter) Victoria Woodhull and "her shrieking sisterhood": "Events at home, as well as in France, must teach us the necessity of revising our old notions as well as our treatment of the sex which asserts itself so strongly of late on both sides of the Atlantic."[5] Insisting that the "crowing hen and the man–woman are equal anomalies and equally disgusting," it goes onto exhort American women to "shine in their own sphere" (and thus, promptly step back into it), leaving both the "revolver and the ballot-box" to men.[6] The editorial thus neatly invokes both the unruly women on the barricades in Paris and their spectacular incarnation in the figure of the female petroleum-thrower "shining" outside their properly domestic sphere, even as it signals the way in which the fierce furies of the Commune became an emblem of an emergent form of radically anti-domestic womanhood and a threat to gender categorization. (One French writer had refused to call these figures women at all out of, as he framed it, "respect for the women whom they resembled – when they were dead."[7])

But the Parisian firebrands blamed for brandishing revolvers and petroleum were also held responsible for a further affront to the transatlantic home front and, with it, the cult of true womanhood, for in the popular imagination, they were guilty not only of abandoning their homes to take up arms on a barricade, but also of recruiting children to join them in the struggle. As historian Gay Gullickson relates of the Bloody Week:

> It was common for children to be regarded as women's accomplices. [American Ambassador to France Elihu] Washburne, for instance, announced that "whenever it was possible, the pétroleuse . . . would find some little boy or girl whom she would take by the hand and to whom she would give a bottle of incendiary liquid" . . . Children who were deemed suspicious looking, like women, were arrested and executed on the spot.[8]

Such unprecedented scenes of summary violence directed at women and children in Paris elicited, at the time, little outcry in the American press, for these anti-domestic figures had, as *Harper's Weekly* would put it, "*generally brought it down upon themselves* by the ferocity with which they took part in the fighting and the terrible work of burning down the city."[9]

This chapter recovers the drama of the postbellum "gender panic" provoked by the spectacle of these female furies of the Commune and the visual–cultural landscape that textured it in the 1870s.[10] Chronicling the way that poets like Sarah M. B. Piatt at once relied on and resisted the ways "the women of the Commune" were represented in the mass-circulation pictorial press in her 1872 periodical poem "The Palace-Burner," I argue that postbellum American periodical poetry deployed forms of what I term subversive sentimentality to mobilize unlikely sympathy for the radically anti-domestic figures of the Commune, making the women and children who fought on the barricades and faced summary execution in Paris legible victims within precisely the system of bourgeois domesticity and republican motherhood they were most poised to threaten. In turn, I uncover how these genteel works of unexpected solidarity invited remarkably viral circuits of reprinting and remembering, with poems like Edward King's "A Woman's Execution" remaining vital to a variety of American publics as it crisscrossed highbrow and radical print culture into the twentieth century.[11] However, in reading Piatt's "Palace-Burner" alongside and against a series of emblematic illustrations of "the Women of the Commune," as well as Margaret Junkin Preston's "The Hero of the Commune," John Hay's "A Triumph of Order," and King's "A Woman's Execution, Paris, May '71," I aim simultaneously to trace the way that postbellum poets rewrote the story of the Commune as they struggled with the spectacle of unprecedented state-backed violence in Paris, strikingly meditated on the pedagogical possibilities and ambiguities of their periodical medium, and sought in various ways to reread the specter of the pétroleuse in the American parlor.

Picturing the Amazons of the Seine

The "Women of the Commune" marching across the pages of *Harper's Weekly*, fists upraised, posed a spectacular challenge to readers, breaking at once visual codes and social mores with their stridently masculine and insistently *public* presence. Indeed, their presence was all the more striking (indeed, terrifying) because the figures they presented and gestures they struck were, visually speaking, without precedent for *Harper's* readers, for despite American women's increased presence in the public sphere in the 1870s, representations of women assertively occupying public space were markedly absent from the illustrated weeklies. As feminist scholar Barbara J. Balliet has pointed out, "In the engravings of . . . weeklies such as *Frank Leslie's* and *Harper's*, women were typically represented as victims, criminals, workers of manual trades, denizens of the household, or shoppers" and the images themselves were most often "static" and "constrained."[12] Not surprisingly, the Communardes were also, quite often in the same edition of *Harper's Weekly*, set off against illustrations of the "other" (more properly bourgeois) women of Paris – women most often depicted as feminine figures cradling a child or publicly mourning a fallen husband or, when nestled at home, waving a handkerchief (rather than a firearm) to encourage passing troops from the remove of their Haussmannian balconies.[13]

The dynamic and not quite assimilable representations of the "Amazons of the Seine" stood in stark contrast with genteel characterizations of properly domestic American women and fit into no discernibly recognizable type, neither being hunched over their worktables nor inhabiting a discernibly domestic interior of the home or the department store. As I show, however, these engravings do not simply reveal the way in which the "Women of the Commune" presented an unassimilable female figure for American readers, or underscore how *Harper's* attempts to domesticate the "female firebrand" specifically falter over the problem of how to read her against her unsexed sisters-in-arms. Rather, they most crucially recover the way in which the emergent "man–woman" of the Commune, later condensed and retroactively re-embodied within the mythic figure of the pétroleuse, not only materially textured American readings of the Paris Commune as event and as revenant, but also rhetorically and visually layered images of American feminists – for example, *Harper's* later illustration of Victoria Woodhull (and her upraised arm) "asserting her right to vote" during her failed 1871 trip to the ballot box (Fig. 1.1).

In his landmark study of the Gilded Age "news image," visual historian Joshua Brown highlights the ways in which the wood-engraved graphics in the illustrated weeklies like *Frank Leslie's Illustrated Newspaper* instantiated rather than simply depicted the crises of the volatile era, and exceeded their scant textual descriptions – often relying, for example, on readers to recognize the figures in the illustration, and complicating or contesting the frame provided in the cut's title.[14]

MRS. WOODHULL ASSERTING HER RIGHT TO VOTE.—(FROM A SKETCH BY H. BALLING.)

Figure 1.1 "Mrs. Woodhull Asserting Her Right to Vote,"
November 25, 1871, 1109, *Harper's Weekly*, Annex A, Forrestal,
Princeton University Library.

While Brown, however, compellingly details the dynamic performance
enacted in the graphics, and offers rich readings of their visual and
typological codes, he rarely meditates on the tensions between pictorial and print reportage, the ways in which pictures jostled against –
rather than simply supplemented – the pictorial and print texts around
them.[15] In my reading, these illustrations were read in tandem with –
and cannot be separated from – either the "descriptive" or contex-
tual content of their titles *and* the texts – both print and images –
around them. In turn, the texts "around them" must themselves be
considered broadly, for the news images illustrated not only the print
reportage in the weeklies themselves but also "the events of the day"
covered elsewhere (namely, in the newspapers). (*Frank Leslie's* explicitly acknowledged this interaction between traditional print and pictorial reporting, describing its service to readers as a supplement to
the coverage of daily newspapers, "representing pictorially and vividly
those things and events which the daily press at best can imperfectly
describe."[16]) My aim here is, then, to read the engraving that inspired
Piatt's "Palace-Burner," "The End of the Commune – Execution of
a Pétroleuse," alongside and against both the text it most explicitly
illustrated and the host of images of – and texts on – "The Women of
the Paris" that ran in *Harper's Weekly* in the wake of the Commune.

The engraving entitled "Women of Paris" (Fig. 1.2) appeared in *Harper's Weekly* on May 27, 1871, above an article bearing the same headline. Printed in the midst of the French government's bloody week-long reconquering of Paris, the picture ran concurrently in *Every Saturday* and *Frank Leslie's Illustrated Newspaper* and captured a

Figure 1.2 "Women of Paris," May 27, 1871, 485, *Harper's Weekly*, Annex A, Forrestal, Princeton University Library.

group of women on the march, suggesting at once their movement and their number. Female figures crowd the scene, dissolving into the background and occupying most of the foreground; their number is uncertain, but vast enough to extend far beyond the frame of the illustration. These figures are notably unarmed but a Phrygian cap sits prominently on the head of the single figure whose fist is upraised as she flashes not a revolver, but a nevertheless brawny arm. Next to her another woman bears a flag, but it unfurls behind her and does not intimate its message beyond presumably gesturing to and implicitly echoing the redness of the Phrygian cap despite the black and whiteness of the image itself. The figures in the frame are recognizably female – costumed in working-class dresses and aprons rather than male attire – but their faces are rough and aged, their attention fixed on variously the flag, the Phrygian cap, or the distance ahead of them. Although the accompanying article describes them "shrieking the watch-cry, 'To arms!'," only a single figure has her mouth open (as if in surprise!), and the rest seem strangely silent. A male figure in military dress drums in the foreground of the image, as if to lead them into battle, but his gaze seems directed firmly at his drum and away from the marching women. This averted gaze brings into further relief the rapt captivation of a small boy, dressed in long blouse and dirty knickers with the hands-in-pockets pose of a street *gamin*, who lounges against a wall beside the marching women – his attention seemingly fixed entirely on the procession. His presence does not fit the scene and goes unmentioned in the article, but he registers a kind of failed domestic scene – the women do not recognize or meet his gaze – even as he foreshadows the cross-gender identification we will see in the "Palace-Burner"; he stands in for, in other words, the presence or participation of children in the march and on the barricades, a presence the illustrated weeklies do not otherwise pictorially depict.

The accompanying article suggests the illustration "represents a [shrieking] band of Vengereuses, or female avengers" marching down the boulevards with "a high priestess in the middle crowned with the orthodox red cap of Liberty."[17] The unruly redness of the cap comes to oddly link the women of Paris to a band of unruly "red Indians" – though *Harper's* raises that equivalence so as to suggest the women of Paris *might* in fact present a far worse threat: "the malcontent [in their path] would be *almost* safer in the hands of a tribe of red Indians than in the power of these infuriated Paris women."[18] While that threat is imagined finally to be one of body, it is also, in *Harper's* version of the story, figured to be one of *purse*, for while the article opines, "There is nothing more terrible, either in peace or war, than one of these *unsexed women*," it does so on the very heels of suggesting that, though "the ostensible object of these Amazons is to fight, it is whispered that these patriots . . . *have no objection to pillage.*"[19] These unsexed women pose, in *Harper's* formulation, a serious threat to onlookers – their bodies arresting the viewer's gaze and transgressing gender boundaries even as they augur a doubly "Red" threat to capital.

The cut, "'The Commune or Death' – Women of Montmartre" (Fig. 1.3), which appeared concurrently in *Harper's* and *Every Saturday*, echoes the marching masses in engravings like "Women of Paris," even as it displays martial women who seem far more imminently bound for battle. Although they are significantly *not* identified as petroleum-throwers, swirls of smoke billow in the background, even as fires rage and buildings burn in their wake. (While only one torch is discernible in the midst of a sea of upraised rifles and sabers, its smoke billows up and blends with the fire in the background, visually compressing the temporality of the frame – jumbling past and present in a single image.) The central figure in the engraving, a "brawny" woman – fist upraised, revolver at her waist, saber at her side – shouts upwards and bears aloft a flag in her other clinched fist. The flag is obscured by its fluttering, but seems to read "Vive la Commune." Beside her another female figure bears a flag whose words read unmistakably "La Commune ou la Mort." This other figure's face is turned away from us, but her precariously elongated stride visually underscores the unstoppable motion of the scene even as it suggests the uncontrollable nature of the mob as it moves outside the frame and onwards to the barricade. Although the central figure wears recognizably female attire, the women around her are dressed in markedly military caps and coats (a lone female figure at the front even appears to be wearing bloomers). With the exception of the central figure, their faces are roughly sketched and largely androgynous, and the figure directly behind the flag-bearer shouts monstrously, her face not quite human.

The accompanying text, "Women of Montmartre," suggests the sketch was made as the "band of women" marched to defend a barricade, and the article describes them as anything but sympathetic figures poised on their way to death. Instead, they are characterized as "defiant, jeering, shameless" and "the Amazons of the Seine," and the article further anatomizes so as to defeminize and dehumanize them, lingering on their "muscle, sinew, ferocity" – a ferocity that notably exceeds "the weaker vessel, man."[20] The text seems, in other words, explicitly bent on dispelling any "romantic"

"THE COMMUNE OR DEATH"—WOMEN OF MONTMARTRE.

Figure 1.3 "'The Commune or Death' – Women of Montmartre," July 8, 1871, 620, *Harper's Weekly*, Annex A, Forrestal, Princeton University Library.

pictures of the woman warriors that might make them sympathetic (or more "thinkable") figures for *Harper's* readers steeped in the rhetoric and visual codes of bourgeois domestic ideology: "These are the Amazons of the Commune, and they give us an idea of what the warrior-woman really is – coarse, brawny, unwomanly, and degraded; picturesque certainly, but by no means pleasing."[21]

Their "unwomanliness" is signaled here, however, not simply by their sinew, or the uneasy space they occupy in public – a space on the cusp of both petroleum-throwing and the barricade – for an "eyewitness" on the scene writes that "I fancied I recognized at the head of the company one of the favorite orators of the club at the Boule Noire, who seemed to take the place of an officer."[22] The uncertainty of the account is, perhaps, as suggestive as the addition of the eyewitness itself, for the presumably male speaker who here gazes on the march authenticates the illustration, despite the fact he cannot say for sure what he saw – thus standing in for the confusion of the "normative" male reader – even as his "fancy" sets off a chain of curious substitutions. The head of the company "seem[s] to take the place of an officer" – thus at once usurping and inhabiting a masculine role that he cannot fathom as rightfully or possibly her own – and therefore the speaker cannot quite believe what he sees, can only "fancy" what his eyes here register even as the face of the "head of the company" – the circumlocution itself registering the difficulty in saying, what, in the end, she might be said to be – finally assumes the features of "one of the favorite orators of the club at the Boule Noire."[23] Put simply, the struggle of the "eyewitness" is symptomatic of the larger trouble that the "Women of the Commune" posed for the *Harper's* reader: how to make sense of such "unthinkable" figures?[24]

The image to which Piatt most directly responds, "The End of the Commune – Execution of a Pétroleuse" (Fig. 1.4), was, spatially speaking, separated by nearly ten pages from "Women of Montmartre"; visually speaking, the cut is strikingly distant from both the treatment of the "Women of Paris" and the depiction of an execution of (male) Communards on the obverse page of the illustration itself. Unlike the other illustrations of the "Women of the Commune," this cut is a "close-up" that focuses our attentions almost entirely on the central figure, with only a hint of the crowd around her; it thus places us in uncomfortable proximity to the drama, our line of sight positioning us less as an observer and more as a member of the crowd itself. The wall behind the figure is pockmarked with bullets – a visual reminder of the battle that raged in the streets – but otherwise nondescript. A Versaillist soldier in the foreground keeps back an unruly crowd with a rifle, but a single figure's face – with a seemingly bonneted head – can be made out over the shoulder of the soldier, gnashing teeth, arm raised and hands out as if to grab the soon-to-be executed woman. A pair of hands in the foreground, both gripping revolvers, stand in for the soldiers carrying out the woman's summary execution, and the

THE END OF THE COMMUNE—EXECUTION OF A PÉTROLEUSE.

Figure 1.4 "The End of the Commune – Execution of a Pétroleuse,"
July 8, 1871, 628, *Harper's Weekly*, Annex A, Forrestal, Princeton
University Library.

barrel of the guns are so close to the female figure – a few steps at most –
that it is nearly impossible to identify the scene as one of summary
military execution rather than mob violence. The dramatic presence
of the hands clenched around revolvers and reaching upwards out of
the crowd visually underscores that the woman herself is "unarmed,"
hands tied behind her back, no revolver or milk pail of petroleum
in sight. (In her rereading, Piatt notably unbinds them.) As in King's

poem, the pétroleuse is thus figured here as unmistakably female – young, with long, unruly hair and simple dress – resting against the wall, leaning as if away from the angry crowd. She remains silent, and the angle of her gaze suggests that her eyes rest with some composure on the faces of the men about to shoot her. That grace is perhaps echoed too in her stance, which mirrors the feet of the soldier next to her – the positioning of her foot an ever so slight hint at her strength and a visual rejoinder to the rampant reports that pétroleuses were savages or altogether mad women.

Gullickson cites this illustration (which originally appeared in London in *The Graphic*) as a rare example of a sympathetic representation of the pétroleuse, but argues that such representations, in picturing the pétroleuses as "captured and afraid" and, most of all, as markedly *feminine*, stripped them at once of their horror and their power.[25] As she puts it, "These [figures] were not the furies of the bourgeois imagination but the innocent victims of the Versailles soldiers."[26] Such ambivalence is echoed in the engraving's accompanying article, "La Pétroleuse." The accompanying text begins by remarking on the "courage and ferocity shown by the women of Paris during the late insurrection," suggesting that the "fair sex" – in war and in peace – occupies a notably more "public" position in France. It goes onto explain – or, rather, to justify without justifying – the pétroleuse by reconfiguring her as a recognizably female type (in other words, as a victim).[27] Rather than explicitly alluding to the femininity of the figure in the illustration – nowhere does it "anatomize" her in the way it earlier lingered on the sinew of her sisters – it instead reframes her conversion to the Commune – and participation in the burning of Paris in the final week of fighting – as a kind of "fall": "Twelve months ago, probably enough, the Pétroleuse was an industrious, well-behaved woman, with a husband and children."[28] As if in response to the charge, in the *New York Herald* and elsewhere, that the pétroleuses were "debased and debauched creatures, the very outcasts of society . . . knowing no shame, dead to all feeling, without homes, without friends, no little ones to claim their attentions," *Harper's* insists instead that the pétroleuse is a "poor creature" driven into the arms of the Commune by want and desperation.[29]

Unsurprisingly, *Harper's* attempt to reconstruct the pétroleuse as a sympathetic, domesticated figure articulates the limits of traditional bourgeois sentimentality, for it requires first retroactively inserting her into her proper sphere (at home) and role ("well-behaved" mother and wife), and cordoning her off, rhetorically and visually, from her "unsexed" comrades. However, in attempting to narrate the genesis (or, rather, the fall) of the female incendiary, the article insists it has "no desire to extenuate the crimes of which many of the insurgent women in Paris ha[ve] recently been guilty," and the qualification immediately if unwittingly (re-)aligns the "poor creature" of the picture with the earlier image of the "insurgent women" of Montmartre and the "Women of Paris" more generally.[30] Moreover, while the article attempts to cordon her off from her peers by rooting her in a singular newness – "La Pétroleuse! (petroleum-thrower): what a terrible significance has this newly invented name. Is it possible that those who belong to what is emphatically styled the gentler sex can perpetuate such atrocities?" – its suggestion that a "well-behaved woman" can be "converted" to a petroleum-thrower – laying waste to capital and domesticity – points to perhaps the most vexing problem posed by this incarnation of the pétroleuse.[31] In attempting to contain or dispel her threat, *Harper's* might, in fact, inadvertently accentuate it.

Death in Public

The spectacular challenge that the "wild women" of the Commune posed to sentimentality and the cult of true womanhood is foregrounded in Edward King's elegy to a female Communard, "A Woman's Execution, Paris, May '71," which ran in *Scribner's Monthly* in September 1871.[32] King's work to remember the violence of the Commune's end is brokered by his subversive redeployment of sentimental tropes to "domesticate" the female Communard, and thus at once to memorialize her martyrdom and render her a more legible – indeed, "thinkable" – victim of the Versaillais juggernaut. In confronting the summary brutality of an execution that purportedly "saved Society," however, King must simultaneously work to reveal and contain the Commune's domestic threat.

Although Katz has suggested that King's poem was neither "distinguished as poetry" nor an "apolog[y] for the Commune," "A Woman's Execution" garnered immediate recirculation in a remarkable variety of American periodicals and crisscrossed highbrow and radical print culture into the twentieth century.[33] In the fall of 1871, for example, it enjoyed near-simultaneous publication in the genteel literary magazine *Scribner's* and such radical journals as *Woodhull and Claflin's Weekly* and *The National Anti-Slavery Standard*; within weeks of its original publication, it had been reprinted on the front page of a number of newspapers across the country, including the Little Rock

Morning Republican, the *Georgia Weekly Telegraph,* and the *Osage County Chronicle* in Kansas.[34] In 1880, King included the poem in his volume, *Echoes From the Orient,* and it received specific mention and none too little praise in both American and British reviews of the volume. (In its review, *The Nation* insisted, for example, that "A Woman's Execution" was "one of the best poems" in the collection.[35]) But even as King's poem was further recirculated and in a certain sense canonized by its inclusion in Edmund C. Stedman's influential anthology of American Literature, "A Woman's Execution" continued to be reprinted for an altogether other audience by way of labor periodicals. Through that alternate trajectory of reprinting, it came to pop up in Upton Sinclair's 1915 volume of social protest literature, *The Cry for Justice,* and found a final home in the Little Red Library's 1925 pamphlet-anthology, *Poems for Workers.* That a poem that first ran in *Scribner's* in the 1870s could be successfully repackaged as a worker poem on the cusp of the Popular Front is suggestive of how well it wielded its brand of subversive sentimentality and how readily that mode spoke across the various publics through which it circulated for some five decades. As Shelley Streeby has recently pointed out, sentimental and sensational culture continued to transfuse US literature, media, and visual culture in this period, and – even more importantly – "continued to shape the radical movements of the era, remaining primary modalities through which alternate worlds and near futures were envisioned."[36]

King's genteel execution poem sets the scene so as to invite the reader to witness, seemingly directly, a sensational spectacle of not quite assimilable violence, drawing our attention first and foremost to its subject's gender rather than her role in the Commune:

> Sweet-breathed and young –
>   The people's daughter:
> No nerves unstrung –
>   Going to slaughter![37]

The poem goes onto ventriloquize as it vindicates, returning to the final week of May '71, re-animating the now-dead woman and putting words into her dying mouth.[38] While King occasionally breaks the narrative continuity of that voice by interjecting descriptive parenthetical asides from the narrator ("women are snarling") and the crowd ("Give me your beams,/Liberty's darling!"), from the second stanza onwards the poem is framed as the soon-to-be-executed woman's *own* testimony.[39]

The move to allow a Communarde to speak from the highbrow pages of *Scribner's* is, in itself, quite astonishing. While the press often relayed the furies of the Commune meeting their death, it rarely allowed them to utter anything beyond the slogans "Vive la Commune" or "The Commune or Death!," which in turn captioned the illustrations of them reprinted in the pictorial press. Instead, their bodies spoke for them: as we saw, the "warrior-woman" of the Commune was typically characterized as "coarse, brawny, unwomanly, degraded," "unsexed," and "dressed in semi-masculine attire."[40] The poem thus draws on a repertoire of sentimentality to refeminize the Communarde, to not let her body, as it were, speak against her plight. She is thus figured as "young" with "hair to her waist/limbs like Venus" and as the "people's daughter" rather than the brazen child of Liberty or Revolution.[41] Like Piatt's "Palace-Burner," she faces her death with unflagging resolution and it is that singular presence of mind – "no nerves unstrung" – which most signals her innate grace – a certain classiness, if you will – even as it suggests she is not the mad woman or Fury she has been made out to be.[42] Her composure is, in fact, juxtaposed with the "snarling women" in the mob around her, a sleight of hand that arouses our sympathies by shifting the ferocity so often embodied within the figure of the female Communarde onto the bourgeois women who here so furiously condemn her. The poem further humanizes – or rather, domesticates – the figure of the Communarde by introducing her soldier–fiancé into the scene: "He at the front?/That is my lover."[43] As Lauren Berlant and Elisabeth R. Anker have argued, sentimentality often swerves into melodrama, and certainly the poem skirts that line here as it leaves ambiguous whether said fiancé stands in front of the line to be shot or in front to do the shooting, but the pathos of the scene – dying beside the man she intended to marry, dying at the hands of a soldier whose loyalties to the State supersede his private feelings – only amplifies the irony of such a young girl facing death in such a way, in such "bright weather."[44]

Yet for all that King's poem works to champion this woman as a sympathetic figure of the Commune, one who courageously goes to her death crying "Vive la Commune!" even as she participated in both fighting and caretaking during its final days, giving out "powder and bread," to do so it must simultaneously neutralize the threat posed by that very breakdown of the home front.[45] Banished, in other words, is any hint of the radical anti-clericalism of the Commune, as well as its radical gender politics (in particular, women's clubs that advocated for divorce and *"unions libres"*). Marie becomes, in King's reconstruction, a conventional figure of womanhood who looks forward to marriage and sees no shame in bearing "Christ mother's name."[46] Countering reports that painted the Amazons of the Seine as "mad with wine and the smell of blood," this woman of the Commune is sober and "sweet-breathed."[47] Her ideals are, however, intact and she remains, however tenuously, a true believer, driven to the Commune by faith rather than desperation; looking at the crowd, she is able to call them "friends" and urge them to "make us amends," reminding them that "we've burst your fetter."[48] Even her resounding anticipatory injunction to the crowd – "you'll love us better" – would seem to summon a future moment when she and the Commune she fought for will be acknowledged for having broken France's fetters – as if to echo another Communard's claim that "The only crime of the Commune . . . was to have anticipated the future."[49]

This raises, finally, the greatest tension within the poem. In asking the reader to identify with this now-executed woman, it invites us at once to occupy her speaking voice in the poem and to ponder her death against the wall at the hands of French government soldiers. Yet in asking us to question her treatment at the hands of the French government – and the American press – the poem works to make this unconventional sentimental figure a legible female body and conventionally domestic speaker. To do so is, however, to beg the question of how to square such utter conventionality with her role in the Commune, how to recognize a pétroleuse when you see one. More to the point – and herein lies the danger – if a woman of the Commune can register here as such a recognizably domesticated figure, how can her threat remain, for King's readers, altogether alien? It is exactly this terrain of liminality and unsettling identification that Sarah Piatt will take up as she restages the encounter with a Communarde's execution as a specifically *domestic* scene.

The Pétroleuse in the Parlor

Increasingly central to the critical understanding, and recent recovery, of Piatt's work, "The Palace-Burner" serves as the title for Paula Bennett's groundbreaking 2001 volume of *The Selected Poetry of Sarah Piatt*. The haunting image Bennett chooses for the volume's cover is in fact the *Harper's Weekly* illustration, "The End of the Commune – Execution of a Pétroleuse," which seems in turn to have inspired "The Palace-Burner," with the face of its soon-to-be-executed female Communarde shadowing our very entry into Piatt's verse. The illustration, along with the subtitle for the poem – "A Picture in a Newspaper" – immediately reminds us that Piatt was not only among the most published American periodical poets of the late nineteenth century, but also one whose work quite self-consciously meditates on her medium. In turn, the subtitle concretely illustrates the way in which the plaintive but fiery figure evoked in Piatt's poem entered the domestic scene by way of periodicals such as *Harper's Weekly*, *Every Saturday*, and *Frank Leslie's Illustrated Newspaper* – an event that the poem itself specifically dramatizes.

But while critics like Matthew Giordano have shrewdly pointed to Piatt's "manifestly public form of poetic authorship," and suggestively argued that "if we ever hope to understand the breadth and depth of her achievement, we must recover the periodical context of her poems and read them precisely *as* periodical pieces – that is, as literary works that are constituted by and that respond to the particular circumstances of their periodical publication," little work has been done to recover the dense political and representational intertextuality of "The Palace-Burner."[50] Rethinking "The Palace-Burner" and its relation to both the public sphere and American memory of the Commune thus requires that we attend to the way in which Piatt reconsiders that threat, mobilizing the genteel, domestic setting to stage a breakdown of the public and the private, of domestic and transnational space. However, in light of Paula Bennett's contention in *Poets in the Public Sphere: The Emancipatory Project of American Women's Poetry* that "resituating nineteenth-century American women's newspaper and periodical poetry within the tradition of social dialogue and debate from which it sprang and to which it belongs, will clarify this poetry's function as a form of *public* speech addressed to concrete, empirically identifiable others," it further requires digging into the particulars of Piatt's signature poem as a specifically "periodical piece."[51]

"The Palace-Burner" first appeared in *The Independent*, an influential Congregationalist weekly with close ties to the Republican Party and Henry Ward Beecher's Plymouth Church, nearly a year and half after the Commune's bloody week-long suppression. That a sympathetic portrait of a Parisian incendiary was printed in a progressive, abolitionist journal with a wide readership now seems altogether unremarkable. Critics, in taking any notice of the poem's publication history, point out that over the course of her career, Piatt placed "some sixty-nine poems" in the pages of *The Independent*, and more to the point, the New York paper was a direct rival to *Harper's*

Weekly; in responding to the image in *Harper's*, Piatt's poem is therefore taken to be simply all the more savvily self-conscious of its own (periodical) milieu.[52] But while Piatt's connections with Henry C. Bowen's paper no doubt made it easier to place "The Palace-Burner" there, *The Independent*'s own coverage of the Paris Commune would seem to make it a rather unlikely spot for the poem: only a year before the paper had detailed in elegiac terms the damage to public buildings and monuments wrought by the savages of the Commune and its mythic band of petroleum-throwers. Unlike the illustrated weeklies, *The Independent* could not offer readers a "bird's-eye" view of the fires or the charred landmarks, but it soundly condemned "the savages who have laid in ruins the great and beautiful city."[53] While *Harper's* mustered some sympathy for the dying pétroleuse (if not for the women and children who died fighting on the barricades), *The Independent*'s editorial on the Commune's end could not have more firmly stated its case: "The Commune has gone down in blood and we hope may never have a hideous resurrection."[54]

What to make, then, of Piatt's resurrection of this "fierce creature of the Commune" within the pages of *The Independent*? I will propose two answers to this question, both of which reframe the way we might read the poem's wielding of irony and public speech.

As with so many of her poems, Piatt couches her remembering and rereading of the Commune in an explicitly domestic setting, and therefore strategically relies on the conventionality of the scene – a mother and son perusing old newspaper clippings – in order to "slip in" her lesson. Indeed, the poem turns on the undoing of those readerly expectations: rather than being a poem about the lesson the mother teaches the boy, as we might expect it to be, it actually seems to unwork the maternal scene of disciplinary instruction altogether. Or, as Mary Wearn so aptly puts it: "The critical message of the poem concerns not what the mother teaches the boy, but what the boy teaches the mother."[55] In this reading, the boy's sympathetic identification with the unruly woman – his desire not so much to feel her pain as to be, like her, "a palace-burner" and in turn see his own mother as a "palace-burner" too – momentarily maternalizes the pétroleuse and radicalizes the mother, and in doing so forces the mother to "reread" the picture in the newspaper through her son's eyes.[56] While critics (most notably Bennett) have suggested this rereading puts the mother and, by extension, bourgeois domesticity on trial, I argue the poem simultaneously takes aim at another target, for while the irony of the poem has often been read as directed at the mother (for failing to read as the boy does) or the boy (for naively identifying with a soon-to-be executed woman), it also seems quite strikingly directed at its own periodical readers.

Take, for example, the mother's initial reaction to her son's desire to burn a palace in stanza three:

> You wish that you had lived in Paris then? –
> You would have loved to burn a palace, too?
> But they had guns in France, and Christian men
> Shot wicked little Communists like you.[57]

Wearn compellingly suggests that the harsh rebuke that some critics finds here – "*But they had guns in France, and Christian men/Shot wicked little Communists like you*" – is tempered by the playfulness of the mother's tone, but much as Janet Gray has argued of Piatt's "A Child's Party," I want to suggest the poem speaks on several registers here, addressing at once the child, the mother, and the reader.[58] Thus, the potential rebuke to the child is turned back on the mother in the final line of the poem, as she comes ultimately to find in this woman who has been burning palaces "a being finer than [her] own soul."[59] However, the threat of the child sharing the petroleum-thrower's fate if he steps into the "role" of the palace-burner cannot be regarded as simply the fanciful stuff of nineteenth-century conduct books for children, for it was by no means an empty threat.

Indeed, the introduction of "Christian men" with guns directly invokes the violence of the original *Harper's* illustration – the way it captures the woman on the cusp of her death, back to the wall, facing a mob of guns – even as it signals the specter of another picture that never ran in the illustrated weeklies: namely, the summary executions of children who fought alongside their parents on the barricades, or stood accused of burning houses. The specter of such executions literally and spatially faces the pétroleuse in the newspaper; on the obverse page of the original illustration, *Harper's* ran a far more graphic engraving of the shooting of several male Communards, and below it another of row upon row of dead (male) bodies. In the text between them, the article "Bloodshed in Paris" alludes to and evinces a certain horror at the unprecedented slaughter and summary executions of women and children in the streets of Paris, but argues finally they "*generally brought it down upon themselves.*"[60]

Piatt's poem does not, then, simply raise the threat of such violence, but rather strikingly underscores its reality: while in this stanza the boy's desire to "be" a pétroleuse remains still in the safely subjunctive mood – here he wishes only that he *could* have been in Paris, only *desires* to have burned a palace, the speaker's turn to the concrete past tense again reminds us what the men in Paris had (guns) and did (shoot children). But the speaker's invocation of "guns" as a threat seems here excessively unnecessary. The boy, after all, has been looking at the picture. The pétroleuse facing execution might be her own best object lesson – *to step into her shoes is to take your place against the wall, young man,* as it were. The reminder that "they had guns in France, and Christian men/Shot wicked little Communists like you" seems not, then, for the boy so much as for the reader.[61] If the poem, through the eyes of the mother, passes judgment on the pétroleuse, "a wicked little Communist," and finds her finally "a being finer than my soul," it does so by, in turn, echoing the irony of good Christian men who participated in the slaughter of women and children, but so too, I would argue, by wielding that irony against the good Christian men reading *The Independent* who condoned these executions. In so doing, Piatt also echoes and reworks two periodical poems by Margaret Junkin Preston and John Hay that earlier restaged the spectacle of a boy Communard facing execution.[62]

Preston's "The Hero of the Commune" appeared in *Scribner's Monthly* in April 1872 and, like the "Palace-Burner," it immediately foregrounds its own periodical milieu with the subtitle "An Incident of the Siege of Paris," which echoes a headline even as it immediately situates the scene the poem pictures and performs. Preston routes the drama of the boy and the pocket watch – an anecdote that began life in the "Home and Foreign Gossip" section of *Harper's Weekly* and was reprinted in the US hundreds of times thereafter – through the dialogue of two isolated speakers – "the garçon" and the "National."[63] In her retelling, the boy is notably younger – "scarcely ten years old" in the "National's" estimation – and unlike his predecessor in *Harper's Weekly*, the poem allows the young Communard to explicitly express his *willingness* to face the execution that never comes:

> We're here to be shot;
> And there by the pillar's very spot,
> Fighting for France my father fell.
> – Ah well!
> That's just the way I would choose to fall,
> With my back to the wall![64]

The boy hero thus identifies with the "cursed crew" around him, and subtly aligns the cause of the Commune with that of France even as he imagines he will take the place of his father at the wall.[65] The boy's identification with the Commune is further solidified by the poem's title, which quite explicitly draws on *Harper's Weekly*'s characterization of him as a "little hero"; unlike *Harper's*, however, the poem insists the boy is a "hero of the Commune" rather simply than a heroic child of France, but while the poem rather remarkably asks its readers to imagine that a Communard could be heroic, its title also functions to contain that rereading; the child hero may be, in fact, the only hero in the bunch.[66] (The suggestion that his father died there as well perhaps brokers the possibility that "the hero of the Commune" might not be as absolutely singular as the title implies, however.)

Drawing out the anecdote's own latent unease about the act of shooting a child, in Preston's version of the story it is the soldier who, recognizing the boy to be a child, first calls out to him: "Do you hear? Do you know?/Why the gendarmes put you there, in the row?"[67] The poem's admiration for the boy Communard is thus highlighted and complicated by its vantage point: we see the boy largely through the eyes of the "National" soldier. Much of the poem is, in fact, the "National's" interior monologue, and though we are positioned to hear the boy's words, we are given no access to his thoughts. While the soldier does not immediately spare the boy upon recognizing his youth, it is the soldier, rather than the boy, whose asides condemn the summary executions: "(. . . Who wants wolfish work like this to do?/Bah, tis a butcher's business)"; "I hardly think I could have braved/The ardor of that innocent eye."[68] The poem, in turn, positions us to condemn the "wolfish work" while sympathizing with both the boy hero *and* the French soldier ordered to shoot him. While the poem powerfully begs the question of who is responsible for turning the sympathetic soldier into a monstrous figure – part animal, part butcher – let loose in the streets of Paris, the boy is, as Preston's original readers no doubt would have expected, ultimately spared. Yet French writer and diarist Edmond de Goncourt famously writes of the Commune's suppression during what came to be called the "Bloody Week":

> It is good that there was neither conciliation nor bargain. The solution was brutal . . . the bloodletting was a bleeding white; such a purge, by killing off the combative part of the population defers the next revolution by a whole generation.[69]

In the logic of Goncourt, then, a logic echoed in editorials that ran in *The New York Herald* and elsewhere on this side of the Atlantic, no Communard could safely be allowed to live. Goncourt's nightmare is averted by the future the boy hero represents, the promise Preston here offers of a happy ending to come: "France will hear of him some day!"[70] The glorious vision of future assimilation that the poem makes possible for its American readers allows them to forget that Communards who lived to stand trial were being shipped off to permanent exile in Nouvelle Calédonie, their bodies, like the scarred landscape, marking an irremediable rupture point in the "body politic" of France. But in so doing, it allows the exemplary boy of the Commune to stand in for the possibility that our own fractured nation might be made whole through the glorious future re-absorption of a rebel boy who was spared, and with him a defeated South, into the annals of future American memory. Perhaps this explains the poem's continuing resonance in American culture: among Preston's most anthologized poems, "The Hero of the Commune" was reprinted in her 1875 collection *Cartoons* and later appeared in numerous anthologies, among them E. C. Stedman's influential volume, *A Library of American Literature from the Earliest Settlements to the Present Time* (1889, 1894, 1900, 1927), *Library of Southern Literature* (1909), *Southern Writers: Selection in Prose and Verse* (1905), *Three Centuries of Southern Poetry* (1908), *Children in American Poetry* (1930), and the *Oxford Book of American Verse* (1931).

Hay's "A Triumph of Order" ran in *The Atlantic Monthly* in April 1872, four months after Preston's appeared in *Scribner's*, and seems explicitly in conversation with "The Hero of the Commune" – echoing key details of its reworking of the anecdote but crucially rewriting the happy ending of both Preston's poem and the story in the newspaper that inspired it.[71] While "A Triumph of Order" is not written in Hay's signature "dialect" style, it draws on the ballad form that made him famous and remains one of his most frequently anthologized poems. By no means simply periodical ephemera, it was cited among Hay's poems "with continued appeal" into the 1980s, and garnered specific mention in, for example, John Hollander and Eric Harlson's *Encyclopedia of American Poetry*.[72]

Unlike "The Hero of the Commune," Hay's ballad precisely locates its scene as "by the wall of Pere-la-Chaise," the site where the Commune made its last stand. The poem thus explicitly yokes the boy's end with the Commune's, and allows him to stand in for that other story.[73] While the original anecdote offered no sense of the surrounding scene or vision of the Communards fighting and dying around the boy, and "The Hero of the Commune" leaves the company a largely undifferentiated mass of "wretches," Hay's poem opens by listing and lingering over the details of the scene:

> There were desperate men, wild women
>   And dark-eyed Amazon girls
> And one little boy, with a peach down cheek
>   And yellow clustering curls.[74]

Like Preston's "hero," the boy is a notably singular presence – the only child of the Commune facing death at the wall. His steely resolution is juxtaposed to the desperation of the men and women around him, but the poem's iteration of his downy cheek and "clustering curls" not only mark his youth but also dreamily link him to the "dark-eyed Amazon girls" in the stanza and such figures of sacrificial sentimental childhood as Little Eva. These Amazons, moreover, are not the brawny warrior-women of the Commune; this romanticization, together with the rhythm of the ballad meter itself, would seem to distance the reader from the horrors of the scene much as the diction – the captain, echoing Preston's rather than *Harper's*, asking, "What dost thou here?" – would seem to relocate the story into the mists of a far less recent past. Yet such distancing works, I would argue, to heighten both the drama of the boy's heroism and the irony of the poem's ending. In Hay's version of the story, the boy self-identifies as a Communard – "I'm a Communist, my dear!" – and notably refers to the captain in the parlance of the Commune as "Citizen."[75] In turn, the poem, in ventriloquizing the captain, makes clear that, given his loyalties, the boy's youth will not save him: "Very well! Then you die with the others!"[76]

Most importantly, however, the ballad's final stanza repurposes the originary anecdote even as it strikingly rewrites the ending of "The Hero of the Commune": while the boy will no doubt be heard about in the future, it will not, in Hay's vision, be because he was allowed to live. This reworking of the end – and deeply ironic – consummation of the "triumph of order," conveyed not simply through the willing death of a Christ-like (or, shall we say, Little Eva-like?) child but rather through the unmitigated force of a firing squad, bears, I think, specific pause:

> "Now blaze away, my children!
>   With your little one – two – three!"
> The chassepots tore the stout young heart,
>   And saved Society![77]

As if to reinforce the synecdochal (if not quite allegorical) work of the poem itself – the substituting of the boy's brutal end for the Commune's and vice versa – the boy is represented metonymically by his most characteristic feature, "the stout young heart," while the "children" in the stanza point not to the boy but rather to the "chassepots" that shoot him. The elongated caesura between the counting off – visually underscored by the repeating dashes – conjoins the blazing of the guns all the more sonically to the enunciation of "society," even as the brutal death of the boy Communard, like the suppression of the Commune, is rebranded here as a singularly ironic salvific act. It is crucial, in other words, that the poem catholicizes the end or, rather, breaks through the explicit national borders of the poem – the boy's death is not figured here as the death that saved France but rather the one that redeemed "Society" – and while the critique may have been most trenchantly directed at the French government, the poem begs the question of what republic can be built on such ashes.

"A Triumph of Order," like the watch in the poem itself, acts, then, as an unlikely elegy for both the boy and the Commune, one that mourns even as it questions the necessity of the boy's death and also the presumption, on this side of the Atlantic, that the Commune's suppression in fact saved "society" the world over. To do so, it rewrites Preston's poem and the *Harper's* anecdote from which it originated so as to capture the death so neatly averted in both narratives. Two decades after it appeared in *The Atlantic*, W. D. Howells would remark of the poem's continuing sentimental power, "[It] is something that still makes the heart bleed as if the boy communist had *just been shot in Paris.*"[78] Howell's articulation of the reader's response, while suggestive of the curious "immediacy" of the poem's narrative, also strikingly points to the limits of sympathetic solidarity (and introjection) underlying such "bleeding-heart" sentimentalism. The reader's heart does not, in Howell's formulation, simply bleed as if the boy is executed in front of our eyes, but rather as if the bullet that tears the boy's "stout young heart" leaves the reader's own heart rent and bleeding. Hay's biographer would, however, liken the poem's "almost photographic closeness to life" to the realism of "one of Manet's drawings."[79]

While I am not sure that I entirely agree with that reading, the formulation of the poem's "almost photographic" realism – a realism that might otherwise seem uneasily contained within the ballad form – is suggestive. For it gets at the way that the final stanza, not unlike a photographic close-up, "captures" and suspends the moment of the boy's death in a way that recalls the link between the shot of a gun and that of a camera, the way that Communards, as their critics rather gleefully noted, lined up to be photographed as they would later line up to be shot. In so marking (or re-marking) the boy as the emblem of the Commune, however, and calling on the reader to mourn at once his death and the "triumph" of order, Hay's poem also quite strikingly displaces the other Communards in the final scene. With its line of sight trained on the boy, in other words, the poem, for all its unexpectedly radical sympathies, nevertheless occults the reader's final view of the scene around him. In doing so, it displaces the boy's comrades – those "desperate men" and, quite strikingly, the "wild women" and "Amazon girls" – even as the boy's watch, returned home to his mother, neatly re-establishes the spheres of the private and the public so spectacularly dissolved by and embodied within these otherwise anti-domestic figures of the Commune.

By contrast, in raising the pétroleuse from her ashes, both literally and figuratively, Piatt's poem does not simply recuperate this woman of the Commune and, more pointedly, does not actually absolve her of the guilt of the crime for which she is executed. While the poem works to maternalize "this fierce creature of the Commune" – "Ah! In the dusk and distance sweet she seems/With lips to kiss away a baby's cry" – this "domestication" of the pétroleuse largely echoes *Harper's* own narrative of the fallen housewife (who turns, out of desperation, not to prostitution but rather to house-burning) but it does so with a significant twist. For Piatt's palace-burner is not a woman driven to petroleum-throwing by desperation: she is instead a figure resolutely "bright with bitterness" and "serene."[80] Moreover, unlike the illustration, the poem begins by pronouncing her guilty of the worst crimes of the Commune, immediately labeling her not a "pétroleuse" – the term coined in 1871 specifically for the Parisian incendiaries that circulated widely in the US well into the twentieth century, and one that could have registered the guilt of "simply" burning homes or private property – but rather a "palace-burner," thus signaling her direct participation in the destruction of the Tuileries and the Communard's "vandalism" of Paris.

In turn, under the guise of a child playing with pictures, the poem goes onto resurrect and re-enact the worst fears about the female incendiary: namely, that she would, in fact, recruit children to her cause, and that her "madness" might, after all, be communicable. In the dangerous scene of reading that Piatt stages in the parlor, the boy's captivation with the pétroleuse in the picture leads him at first to want to be like her ("You wish you had lived in Paris then?") and then to want not simply to emulate her but rather to "be" her, for the flexibility of the term that Piatt coins for the Parisian petroleum-thrower – and in particular its gender neutrality – allows the term to slide seamlessly from the picture to the boy and briefly from the boy to the mother.[81] The danger here seems doubled, summoning at once the corrupting influence of the pétroleuse and contemporary fears about the effects of boys' reading. Glenn Hendler, for example, details the "explosion in the 1870s of articles and conferences on the reading of boys and young men," and argues that these fears "almost replaced the worries over women's reading that had pervaded literary criticism in the first half of the century."[82] Misplaced sympathy could lead boys, in other words, to behave like the bad boys they read about, it was feared, and on the surface of it, one would be hard pressed to find a less sympathetic figure for a boy to wish to be. As literary critic David A. Zimmerman explains,

> For most Americans, the image of the pétroleuse setting buildings and homes ablaze . . . confirmed the connection between feminist agitation, political revolution, economic conflict and cultural catastrophe. "Pale, frenzied . . . [and] . . . fierce," as a poet in *Harper's Weekly* described them, the pétroleuses presented a nightmarish specter of women aggressively repudiating bourgeois norms of womanhood.[83]

Yet it is the boy's "naive" sympathy for and identification with the "palace-burner" – his assertion that he would burn palaces and his mother would too – that leads his mother to reread both "the picture in the newspaper" and her own subjectivity. However, in bringing the pétroleuse into the parlor, and more crucially in, as Wearn suggests, briefly "melding" the speaker and the palace-burner in the boy's eyes, the poem does not simply leave us with the unexpected lesson that the Communard is a "finer soul" than the bourgeois domestic subject. Such a suggestion would itself be an admittedly significant (and largely unprecedented) "lesson" – a far different "picture" to circulate in an American newspaper. Of even more moment, I want to suggest, is the ironic insinuation that the pétroleuse and the mother might not, after all, be diametrically different: that, as Havelock Ellis would later put it, "every woman carries a slumbering pétroleuse in her bosom" – that, in other words, the pétroleuse may always already have been in the parlor.[84] While it is a possibility that the speaker herself tries to contain in the final stanza – "The child has seen/. . ./A being finer than my soul, I fear" – this ironic reversal is not, as it were, complete, for while the speaker "fears" she would not be like the palace-burner, her final question – "Would *I* burn palaces?" – remains forever open.[85]

Let us turn again to the subtitle with which I began: "a picture in a newspaper." Unlike "A Lesson in a Picture" and "From North and South: A Lesson from the Newspaper," poems Piatt placed in journals as varied as the youth-oriented *Wide Awake* and as influential as *The Atlantic Monthly*, "The Palace-Burner" quite markedly does *not* signal itself as a poem with a message. Instead, it points to and aligns itself simply with an illustration set demurely beside – even as it jostles against – the texts around it. That it does so suggests the poem's own "shadowy power," for its most subversive act is not, finally, its lesson but rather the domestic scene it manages to get printed in a newspaper.[86]

Figuring the New Woman

Twenty years after "The Palace-Burner" appeared in *The Independent*, the Episcopal Rev. William Croswell Doane, a man *The New York Times* characterized as "one of the most prominent anti-women's rights men in the country," addressed the 1895 graduating class of young ladies at St. Agnes's School of Albany, New York.[87] That he chose on that occasion to denounce the New Woman and rail against woman's suffrage is, in itself, less than remarkable. It is, however, striking that his denunciations summon the specter of Piatt's poem, and with it the uncanny slippage between the parlor, the platform, and the barricade:

> One gets sick and tired of the way that the talk of woman's vocation fills the air, not merely in the wild vagaries of its blatant assumptions, but in the parade and push of its claims for recognition ... Meanwhile, when constitutions shall have been altered, to disturb the equipoise of the relation between man and woman, when motherhood shall be replaced by mismanaged offices ... when "woman," as has been well said, "once the superior, has become the equal of man," then the reaped whirlwind of some violent political reaction will be gathered in tears by those who are sowing the wind in the mad "joy" of the Pétroleuse of the French revolutions.[88]

Like the figure of James's "feminine firebrand," the pétroleuse of the Commune has here multiplied, the female fiend that torched the city of Paris merging with earlier visions of bacchanal women revolutionaries in France. The slippage is, however, anchored in the name specifically coined for the female incendiaries of the Commune, as if this final incarnation of the Parisian revolutionary could safely signal and outdo all its progenitors. Perhaps this is why, in Doane's speech, the work of organizing for legislative rights can collapse so easily into "the mad joy" of petroleum-throwing. Although the term itself originally, albeit oddly, disarmed the Communardes – a hideous woman with a milk pail full of petroleum was not, after all, a brawny Amazon fighting the Versaillais army shot for shot – the myth of the pétroleuse largely sprang from a vision of Communard women who did their fair share of both organizing and barricade fighting.

Doane's pluralizing of the Pétroleuse thus serves to blur the boundaries between the pétroleuse and the domestic firebrand – or, rather, to insinuate the way those boundaries were, as Piatt shows us, always already artificial. It also serves to summon and translate her threat for an audience of potentially home-grown pétroleuses. Some two decades after her "ashes" had grown cold, the radical sympathies and domestic scene invoked by Piatt's "Palace-Burner" continued to haunt the landscape of the American imagination. As *The Bostonians* reminds us, a woman speaking from a platform was quite often figured to be as terrifying an emblem of postbellum US radicalism as the now more familiar image of a bushy-haired anarchist wielding a home-made incendiary device, collapsing the distance between the stolidly bourgeois suffragist Olive Chancellor and fin-de-siècle anarchist activists such as Lucy Parsons and Emma Goldman, who were routinely labeled "petroleuses" in the US press for their incendiary rhetoric and "blood-thirsty harangues."[89] In the following chapter, I explore how that domestic threat is reconfigured in a series of bestselling boys' books and historical romances that return to the scene of the Commune to reframe Paris as an imperial frontier where American men can be made in the 1890s.

Becoming Americans in Paris: The Commune as Frontier in Turn-of-the-Century Adventure Fiction

> What America means is the gospel for which his life stands, his only *tant-mieux* to show for his time in Paris.
>
> Eugene Savidge, *The American in Paris* (1896)

In the late 1990s, PrestonSpeed Publications began re-issuing the adventure fiction of popular fin-de-siècle British boys' writer G. A. Henty for an American homeschooling audience. Several more small presses followed suit, and soon the "smashing success" of Henty's sales in the homeschooling market began to garner attention in such prominent publications as *The New Criterion, The Wall Street Journal,* and *The New York Times* even as the books themselves became the centerpiece of the popular "Robinson Curriculum" for homeschoolers.[1] This resurgence of Henty mania in America was itself marketed as and fueled by an investment in déjà vu; publishers like Robinson Books and Lost Classics take pains to remind parents that these boys' books were wildly popular with US readers at the turn of the twentieth century, while Evangelical ministry sites like the Vision Forum, as if taking a page from Theodore Roosevelt, claimed to "rebuild a culture of courageous boyhood" through, among other things, the reading of Henty.[2]

However, Henty's appeal for US homeschoolers also has its roots in the successful packaging of his formulaic historical fictions *as* history; indeed, as one publisher puts it, they altogether "alleviate the need for [history] textbooks" – a claim that itself rehashes Henty's own turn-of-the-century marketing schemes.[3] Although much critical work remains to be done on Henty's renewed purchase for American boys, the case of cultural déjà vu surrounding his fictions runs still deeper, for as a rising generation of homeschoolers turn to Henty to learn about history, we seem to be revisiting many of the debates about democracy and revolution, manliness and empire, that originally framed the popularity of – and often were explicitly enacted within – the genre of historical romance and boys' adventure fiction in the US in the 1890s.[4]

In this chapter, I read Henty's recently re-issued but altogether critically overlooked 1895 title, *A Woman of the Commune*, alongside several now-forgotten American bestsellers of the period: Edward King's boys' book, *Under the Red Flag: Or, the Adventures of Two American Boys During the Paris Commune* (1895), Robert W. Chambers's *The Red Republic: A Romance of the Commune* (1895), and Eugene Savidge's *The American in Paris: A Biographical Novel of the Franco-Prussian War, the Siege and Commune of Paris from an American Stand-point* (1896). My interest in Henty's boys' book is, then, not simply that it garnered a significant fin-de-siècle American audience and is increasingly popular today. Instead, I will focus on the way in which *A Woman of the Commune* sheds light on another, little-remembered, US literary resurgence: namely, the unlikely afterlife of the Paris Commune in American fiction of the 1890s. Henty's choice of subjects was far from an anomalous one for the 1890s. In fact, by tracing the transnational historical context for his work to its origins, we find an array of popular adventure fiction revisiting precisely the same scene. Indeed, although now virtually forgotten, the US literary resurgence of interest in the Commune was one of particular intensity, prompting one *Literary World* reviewer to lament, in 1896, "we have had the Commune from the perspective of the novelist *ad nauseam*" even as America's appetite for yet another "story of the Commune" continued unabated.[5] In what follows, Henty's boys' book serves as a crucial counterpoint to the romance of revolution that American fictions of the Commune packaged for US readers because it dispels its own fears about the Commune by embodying them within an American who "falls" for the Commune in precisely the manner that the American romances render altogether invisible or impossible, even as it showcases a strikingly similar imperial template for re-emplotting Paris.

Replotting the Romance of Paris

Thomas Gold Appleton famously suggested in the 1850s that "good Americans, when they die, go to Paris," but by the turn of the twentieth century, it was already a commonplace that most Americans need not die to go: "innocents abroad" and would-be bohemians alike flocked to, as one American writer put it, "the capital of pleasure and happy hunting-ground of the Cook's tourist."[6] Even as middle- and upper-class Americans looked to the City of Light for a taste of culture and corruption, however, another memory – or more precisely, another Paris – repeatedly resurfaced, not only in seemingly anodyne remembrances of "life under the Commune" that ran in periodicals like *The Century* and *Munsey's* but also in bestselling American fiction of the 1890s.[7] Returning over and over to the Paris of 1871, these boys' books and historical romances recycled an ostensibly conventional plot – sending their heroes to the City of Light to be painters or tourists – so that Americans, in turn, could be privy to and participants in the brutal reconquering of Paris by French government troops. These Commune romances thus reworked both "the International theme" and the appeal of Paris for Americans by consistently re-imagining the city not as the seat of civilization, however fallen, but rather as a frontier of empire overrun by "red" savages. In turn, the City of Light is again and again figured in these novels not as a locale of sexual or high cultural awakening (or disillusionment), but rather as a site of political contamination or conversion for Americans – the terrain where, quite literally, men become "Americans" in the political sense. That their republicanism – or "Americanism," as one novel puts it – is born by the witnessing of, and in some cases the direct participation in, the decimation of a nominally republican uprising seems a particularly apt fiction in the decade leading up to the Spanish–American War and the US intervention in the Philippines – for, in other words, an America contemplating its role abroad and its own burgeoning imperial ambitions. As literary critic Amy Kaplan and historian Gail Bederman have so persuasively suggested, America's relationship with its diminishing frontier and expanding role abroad was a deeply vexing preoccupation for fin-de-siècle Americans.[8] But so too does it archive at once the lingering anxieties about the Commune's unruly feminine firebrands, which I explored in the previous chapter, and concerns about the ongoing appeal of the Commune's 'universal republic' – and the American radicals embracing the red flag and left-wing internationalism in this moment, which I take up in greater detail in the following one.

Recovering America's romance with the Commune in the 1890s thus significantly reconsiders the cultural work of Paris – and what it meant to be an American there – in fin-de-siècle US fiction, but it also critically revises our notion of the role the Commune played in America's cultural memory during this period. Put simply, the story that historians have come to tell about the Commune's "afterlife" in America suggests that it had largely faded from the cultural scene by the 1890s, and more to the point, that as touchstone and epithet it became synonymous with – and cipher for – only the very real labor unrest of the Gilded Age.[9] These novels tell another story, insisting not simply that the Paris of 1871 was far from dead in the 1890s, but also that it resurfaces so frequently because the Commune served as a crucible for redefining American democracy even as it provides a crucial terrain for forging both American men and their imperial ambitions.

Remembering to Forget

Ernest Renan famously argues in "What is a Nation?" that it is selective amnesia rather than collective memory that most holds a nation together. Yet even as he elaborates the nature of that very forgetting, which has allowed France to become a nation – "no French citizen knows whether he is Burgundian, an Alan, a Taifale, or a Visigoth, yet every French citizen has to have forgotten the massacre of Saint Bartholomew, or the massacres that took place in the Midi in the thirteenth century" – Renan demonstrates that all forgetting is not equal, and some lapses of memory are far better left unsaid.[10] When this lecture was delivered at the Sorbonne in 1882, what *citoyen* would not have remembered – or rather, would not have had to forget – the "Bloody Week" that consolidates the rise of the Third Republic? Perhaps, for all that MacMahon and Thiers had done to eradicate and then banish the Paris Commune, it had not yet been laid to rest in the way that those other, more speakable, massacres had been.

In her work on the role of the 1878 Exposition Universelle in effacing the Commune from public memory, Colette Wilson similarly foregrounds the spectacle of forgetting that France stages around the Commune, pointing out that when general amnesty finally was granted to the exiled Communards in 1881 by the centrist republican government under Gambetta and Grévy, the act signaled not a political remembrance but – however paradoxically – a willful forgetting. Indeed, in Gambetta's own words, the Amnesty was intended not to re-open the question of the Commune but rather finally to set "the tombstone of oblivion over the crimes and traces of [it]."[11] In his formulation, then, the living body of Communards would return to France so as to lay the event of the Commune firmly to rest, and in an inversion of Hugo's phrase, the body would be resurrected to show the world that the idea is now safely *à terre*.[12]

G. A. Henty, British boys' writer extraordinaire, and Edward King, a respected American foreign correspondent for the *Boston Journal*, experienced the Paris Commune first-hand, and in a move that oddly, if inadvertently, echoes at once Gambetta and Bram Stoker, both choose to resurrect so as to re-inter the Commune in the 1890s for an audience of British and American boys born too late to remember the event themselves.[13] That almost a quarter-century after the Commune's brutal demise both writers manage to revive it in often elaborate and exacting detail – description not seen since the flurry of memoirs and diaries published in the US and Britain in the wake of the Commune itself – seems only to under-score their very desire to lay the events of March to May 1871 to rest once and for all. The Commune is dead, the novels insist – "[It] was crushed. The serpent of the insurrection was dead at last."[14] Yet, as both Henty's *A Woman of the Commune* and King's *Under the Red Flag* symptomatically demonstrate, its specter needs nevertheless to be put back in the ground, remembered into oblivion, as it were – not least because of the remarkably vibrant role the Commune con-tinued to play in leftist memory culture in this period. As I show in Chapter 3, the yearly commemorations and celebrations of the Commune by American radicals of all stripes garnered coverage in mainstream newspapers across the country, a cycle of remembrance and reprinting that began in the 1870s and reached its apogee at the turn of the century. Significant continuing anxiety about the Commune's return and ongoing domestic threat thus overlays these boys' books, which would write history so as to occlude memory, and in their respective restagings of the event of the Commune, both novels work to exorcise contemporary anxieties of impending polit-ical change by confining the threat firmly within the geographical space of France even as they re-imagine Paris as a colonial space, rather than cosmopolitan metropole – as, in other words, a frontier where boys might be made men.

Empire Boys

The publication of Thomas Bailey Aldrich's *Story of a Bad Boy* (1869) sparked what Steven Mailloux has dubbed the postbellum "Bad Boy Boom" in America, and the popularity of, or contempo-rary concerns about, "Bad Boy Books" continues to dominate recent scholarship on the nineteenth-century US boys' book.[15] Indeed, the "Bad Boy Book," which allowed its boy hero – and, by extension, its boy readers – to be "gentle and temporary savage[s]," has largely come to define our sense of the boy-book genre.[16] As Lorinda B. Cohoon persuasively suggests, however, the trouble with this conflation is the way it privileges a select set of texts as the "definitive site[s] for explaining American boyhood in the nineteenth century," overlooking, for example, the surging market for boys' imperial adventure fiction on both sides of the Atlantic beginning in the 1880s and fueled in part by the rise of "global magazines" like *Beeton's Boys' Own*.[17] Offering readers formulaic tales of "boys participating in the projects of Empire," these fictions afforded their readers not an escape from civilization, but rather the experience of direct participation and initiation into it.[18]

While his initial transatlantic appeal and recent resurgence have received scant scholarly attention, Henty was the premier purveyor of British adventure fiction in the nineteenth century on both sides of the Atlantic. Penning over a hundred boys' books between 1868 and 1903, his sales were unprecedented: "No other author could with equal success sustain the attention of boy readers. His adventure fictions . . . outnumbered even Haggard's, as do their sales figures, which may run to a total of 25 million copies."[19] Henty's US sales were no less impressive; although Scribner & Wolford of New York was his official American publisher, some fifty-eight others sold pirated editions until the International Copyright Act of 1891.[20] Indeed, by 1899, J. P. Lippincott hailed him as "the most popular living writer for boys."[21]

Yet, as Joseph Bristow notes of these formulaic fictions, Henty's among them, British boys' books tirelessly presented their readers with a "fearless endeavor in a world populated by savage races, dangerous pirates, and related manifestations of 'the other' to be encountered on voyages towards dark and unexplored continents."[22] The critical attention that has been paid to the genre has therefore primarily centered on how these books sought to underwrite the British imperial project. That project was never conspicuously veiled, however, in the books themselves: as Henty himself once boasted of his works, "I know that very many boys have joined the cadets and afterwards gone into the army through my stories."[23]

While Henty's recent resurgence in the American homeschooling market seems to have largely flown under the critical wire of Henty scholarship, the critical attention paid Henty as an imperial writer has focused exclusively on some twenty novels of his that explicitly adopt a colonial theme and locale, with the bulk of his canon going mostly unremarked upon – despite their ongoing popularity and continuing claims to historical authority.[24] In categorizing Henty's work, then, the critical line dividing his role as the writer of historical adventure fiction for boys from that of a propagandist of empire has so far been nearly impermeable; Gail S. Clark thus asserts in a landmark essay, "Imperial Stereotypes: G. A. Henty and the Boys' Own Empire," that "[Henty] is identified with the aggressive imperialist sentiment of the last quarter of the nineteenth century, even though fewer than one-fourth of [his novels] had imperial settings" before drawing our attention only to those twenty-three novels of empire.[25] As we might expect, Henty's explicitly imperial fictions suggest empire is quite literally where men are made: "In virtually every story, the hero leaves England to seek his fortune abroad. After achieving great success in his endeavors the hero then retires young and returns to England to live out the rest of his days in quiet prosperity."[26] In this tried and true formula, empire no doubt also provides, as Bristow details, a place to encounter – and usually subdue – the Other, allowing Henty's intrepid Englishman to return home further emboldened by his cultural chauvinism and faith in the imperial project.

While Paris and its bohemian Quartier Latin at first glance might not seem the ideal frontier for trying an Englishman's mettle in the Henty vein, *A Woman of the Commune* nonetheless closely follows the plot of his more traditionally regarded empire fiction. Cuthbert Hartington, after suffering the loss of his father and a rejection at the hands of his proto-feminist British sweetheart, Mary, duly sets out to seek his fortune and become something more than a dilettante, if only to prove said sweetheart wrong. So he finds himself in the Paris of 1870–1 – the terrain upon which he solidifies his vocation as a painter, sorts out his finances, joins the military offensive against the Prussians, and wins the newly demure and domesticized girl; by book's end, readers are assured in turn that he will eventually return to London with Mary, his once opinionated and now duly submissive bride.[27] Even the Dark Continent of imperial imagination has resurfaced in the novel, here resituated firmly in Montmartre and populated by workers-cum-savages who briefly commandeer control of the city before being crushed by the oncoming Versaillais army. Indeed, Cuthbert, awaiting the chance to strike out at the Prussians during the Siege, insists that he would much prefer to take on the *racaille* of Belleville and Montmartre instead: "I would rather fight against the *savages* than level my rifle against the honest German lads who are led here against us. I should think no more of shooting one of these [Belleville] roughs than of killing a tiger."[28]

In reconstituting the frontier, *A Woman of the Commune* would seem, then, to unwork the Henty critical divide, embodying adventure fiction of both the historical and the imperial varieties. That it might do both is indicative of larger generic shifts of the 1890s, albeit across the Atlantic, for, as Amy Kaplan has argued, the wildly popular historical romance genre served in this decade as a vehicle to forge and foreground masculinity while expanding the geo-temporal frontier at precisely the moment when the American frontier was diminishing, its heyday exactly coinciding with expansionist debates about where authentic masculinity would be made in an America without wars to be fought or territory to be gained.[29] Thus, in these major, if formulaic, bestsellers, "settings from European and American history function as the fictional equivalent of the Philippines for Beveridge . . . where a man can reassert his 'militant manhood.'"[30]

It is perhaps not altogether surprising, then, that *Under the Red Flag* – Edward King's only attempt at boys' adventure fiction – closely echoes this imperial–historical formula, with a touch of Henry James for good measure.[31] In search of a prodigal son corrupted by Europe, Grandpa Drubal – "the affectionate appellation given to Mr. Hasdrubal J. Corners, a prominent citizen of St. Joseph, Mo., by his grandsons" – carries young Frank and Will to France.[32] With their arrival in Paris timed to coincide with the opening days of the Commune, the American family is immediately privy to life "under the Red flag," even as young Frank is granted unlimited access to the military battles with the Versaillais by an unlikely friendship he strikes with the Communard General Dombrowski.[33] Ultimately, the family finds itself mixed up in the Bloody Week, before finally welcoming the dawn of a "liberated" Paris under Marshal MacMahon – a celebration tempered only slightly by the sight of piles upon piles of the dead.

While King's plucky American boys are – at six and fourteen, respectively – too young for a marriage plot in the Henty fashion, there is space enough in the text for libidinal energies to be discharged otherwise. Frank thus chivalrously saves Laurette, a young *cantinière*, from death by a Versaillais soldier, before finally lending a hand in the suppression of the Commune. (Early in his Parisian meanderings, Frank befriends Sny, a fellow American boy who, as it turns out, is actively spying for the Versaillais.) Paris, in other words, yet again becomes the frontier where men are fashioned: "The few weeks of adventure had transformed [Frank] into a resolute and purposeful youth, who had almost the strength of a man."[34] By book's end, the lost father has been found, having repented his former ways, while Marcelle, a newly reformed female Communard, "no longer seem[ing] 'the warlike virago,'" will be carried back to, as Sny so aptly puts it, the "land of the free and the home of the brave" with the newly reunited Corners family.[35] As in Henty, *Under the Red Flag* closes by assuring readers that life will go on – elsewhere.

One of the hallmarks of the genre of historical fiction, as Lloyd Pratt has pointed out, is its "temporal copresence" – its uncanny ability to archive "synchronic and diachronic simultaneity."[36] Such a layering of disjunctive time – but also conflicting memory – can be seen in the way King's novel most immediately immerses its readers in life "under the red flag," but does so in tandem with allusions to a by 1895 far-removed but in 1871 still-recent past: the frontier back home, the gallantry of Grandpa Drubal during the Civil War, and the way in which the boys are born horsemen during the Commune because of their pioneering lifestyle back in the States. Sny, in setting his imperial sights on the city, looks out over Paris-as-frontier and confides to Frank that "[he] could lead an army or found a colony. Where shall we go to-day?"[37] Yet, even as *Under the Red Flag* recalls the frontier and invokes the American Civil War back into the present, it is vigilant never to link the situation in Paris directly with the situation at home; indeed, the bloody civil war they are witnessing in France pointedly summons no memory of the internecine warfare Grandpa Drubal participated in, even in those moments when the novel explicitly frames the Commune in terms of a fraternal, if not exactly civil, war: "Here and there were piles of dead bodies, regulars and Communists, in the fraternal embrace of death."[38] Moreover, though the Communards immediately hail the Americans as representatives of *l'Amérique*, "land of freedom," no reciprocal sentiment can be entertained by Americans in the novel.[39]

Indeed, much as we will see in the historical romances aimed at adults, great care is taken to prevent any such affective or historical identification, for these imperial adventures are equally dramas of anti-internationalist feeling. When, for example, the Corners family encounters Jules Raisin, a Frenchman they had known formerly in Missouri, he immediately questions "General Corners" about his failure to support the Commune's fight by invoking an uncomfortable kinship between the Commune and the American Revolution: "We want the same liberties for Paris that American cities have always enjoyed . . . and we will fight to the death to secure them. America revolted against unjust government; we have done the same thing."[40] Such a relationship is quickly quashed, however, by Grandpa Drubal's rejoinder – "Yes, but America didn't raise the red flag; which means pillage and abolition of private property" – after which point no further consideration of Raisin's argument can be accommodated by the novel.[41]

Under the Red Flag's reticence towards – if not repression of – any significant parallels between the "Red Republic" and the republic across the Atlantic is brought into greatest relief when read against Henty's novel. *A Woman of the Commune* entertains exactly this connection, distancing it from the British hero by embodying it within a convenient double, Arnold Dampierre, a fellow artist and, in the words of the Communards, a "representative of that great Republic across the seas."[42] Henty makes Dampierre a Southerner, metonymically linking his passion for the Commune to time spent with slaves and his swarthy, vaguely mulatto complexion; the fraternity Arnold feels with the Commune is, in other words, racially suspect from the outset.[43] The novel somewhat over-determines his "fall," at times attributing his political conversion to the Commune to his fatal love for Minette, the working-class model turned fiery priestess of the Commune, who echoes Louise Michel in her devotion to the Commune and affords the only view of working-class Paris that Henty's novel will tolerate.[44] (Communards are otherwise represented primarily as crouching, scurrying vermin or dismissed simply as *racaille*.) Yet for all that Henty does to banish the dynamic spatial and social changes occurring in Paris during the Commune by focusing Cuthbert's line of sight on the military events of April to May 1871, the single window onto the Commune's political dimension is proffered by Cuthbert's American friend, who passionately, if naively, relates that

> the people are fairly roused now and will soon sweep away the butchers of Versailles before them, and a reign of perfect freedom and equality will be established, and the world will witness the spectacle of a free country, purging itself from the tyranny of capital and the abuse of power.[45]

Dampierre's words are quickly reduced by the novel to the ramblings of a madman who has been seduced by a Communarde. Moreover, Arnold is given the right to speak for the Commune only because he is of noble birth and therefore, the novel insists, the only one of any consequence or sense that is party to it. (René, a fellow artist at Cuthbert's studio and a supposedly raging republican, thus confides that, "Although I hate tyrants I should be tempted to take up a rifle and . . .

defend them if they were menaced by scum such as this," before elaborating that "there is among them, save Dampierre, a single man of birth and education, if only, perhaps, you except Rochefort. There are plenty of Marats, but certainly no Mirabeau.")[46] Yet the very fact that this identification between the vaguely aristocratic Arnold Dampierre and Minette, the fiery woman of the Commune, is made by Henty rather than King underscores the latent tension of America in the 1890s over what revolution and republicanism would constitute and which people could be determined worthy of self-determination. Cuthbert, in the early days of the Commune, admits from the outset an uneasy parallel between the two governments before admonishing Arnold for not seeing their great difference: "I can, of course, understand your predilections for a republic, but between your Republic and the Commune, for which the organs of the mob are already clamouring, there is no shadow of resemblance."[47] Yet it is the "shadow of resemblance" that both novels most disavow, even as the grounds on which Cuthbert dismisses the parallels between America and the Commune – namely, on the social inclusiveness of the Commune rather than on its relationship to private property – only summons further contradictions within the "Republic across the Seas."

The irony of America's stance towards the Commune was not lost on all its contemporary witnesses: the American sculptor, Olin Levi Warner, for example, returned to the States in the 1870s to lecture on the Communards. Reacting to the initial onslaught of negative press coverage, he points out the uncomfortable parallels between the two peoples:

> Here in America we are supposed to be a freedom loving people. This is regarded as the great home of freedom. Then why is it that we who are such a liberty loving . . . people are so willing, as we seem to be, to decry and brand as assassins and incendiaries a band of men who fought for the sovereignty of the people, but not being as fortunate as we were when we struck for our liberties, they lost their cause?[48]

This position is marked, moreover, by *Under the Red Flag*'s absolute identification of – and insistence on – America as the land of the free and home of the brave, words sprung from the mouth of Sny, the young American who, in spying for the Versaillais, most proactively fights to bring the Commune to its bitter end. (It seems telling that Henty's British hero, for all his spouting off about game-hunting Bellevillois, is never more than an avid observer of the demise of the Commune.) King's resolute dismissal of the Commune – and eventual characterization of MacMahon's government as republican – only accentuates the shift in American thinking towards revolution that Kaplan details.

This dismissal is all the more telling, for unlike Henty's, King's novel is invested in giving the boys – and its readers – an insider's view of the Commune, epitomized by Frank's relationship with Dombrowski. Yet the novel makes clear that the General, while heroic, does not hold out any faith in the Commune per se: "I will be frank with you, my boy. I hope the insurrection will succeed but I know that it will not."[49] Dombrowski's resignation to the failure of the Commune parallels – and once again draws attention to – both novels' curious sense of disjunctive timing: their view of the Commune, while always in the present tense, seems oddly always already retrospective. In an early occasion of the historiography of "it could not have been otherwise," there is never, in other words, a sense in either book that the Commune would, or could, succeed.[50] This narrative certainty only serves, however, to heighten the brutality of a suppression that would seem at once overdone and unnecessary. As if to compensate, the books employ a strategic blend of foresight and hindsight. Both insist, for example, that the streets of Paris will run with blood because of the Commune. (Grandpa Drubal is keen to say they might be killed in their beds, while Cuthbert's future bride, Mary, repeatedly alludes to the streets themselves being awash in blood.) Certainly the intuition is correct – but reworks an intimation of the Bloody Week as, in fact, the rationale for it, with the Commune's suppression rescripted as a pre-emptive strike against a Terror that never materializes.

In thus reviving to re-inter the Commune, the boys' books find themselves on most perilous ground, then, in their showcasing of the day-to-day experience of the Commune's suppression. For, as we have seen, the week of May 21–9, 1871, was far bloodier than any Paris had yet experienced, and as historian Gay L. Gullickson emphasizes, the Versaillais slaughter of Communards in that final *Semaine Sanglante* was as ferocious as it was unrelenting:

> Those who fought were shot; those who surrendered were shot; those who hid in houses were dragged into the streets and shot, until the last barricade fell on Monday, May 29, at eleven o'clock in the morning. Even then, the killing did not stop; prisoners continued being taken, lined up in parks and cemeteries, and mowed down by machine guns. Not everyone died immediately, of course, and, at night, screams of agony could be heard from the piles of bodies.[51]

For all that *The New York Herald* might editorialize, from the other side of the Atlantic, that "our advice is no cessation of summary judgment and summary execution. Devils let loose from their own place cannot be too soon sent home . . . Root them out, destroy them utterly, M. Thiers, if you would save France. No mistaken humanity!,"[52] said paper need not (and did not) elaborate for its readers an exacting daily accounting of the horrific spectacle unfolding under these very auspices. The boys' books, on the other hand, thrust their young heroes into the thick of things, making readers an eyewitness to the Bloody Week even while working to contain the ghastly sight that they retroactively summon for display. Both novels are ultimately unequivocal in their condemnation of the Communards, and do much to detail and in turn tailor the events so as to mitigate against any inadvertent readerly sympathy for – or identification with – the Commune. Yet even in choosing when to avert the eyes, or from what slant of light to view the mounting death toll, the novels nevertheless make the demise of the Commune available to readers in often-grisly detail – detail that might turn against its makers, and cannot always be scripted so as to be contained.

In a prophylactic mode, Henty adopts a pronounced strategy of aversion in narrating these events: despite its title, *A Woman of the Commune* allots a mere fifty of its nearly 300 pages to the experience of the Commune itself. While roughly half of these pages are devoted to the Bloody Week, in keeping with the novel's overall revision of the Commune as primarily a military event rather than a radically socio-political one, the sight it grants its readers of the week itself is mostly obstructed. The novel's reticence to "see" the piles of bodies – to hear the screams of agony – is complicated, however, by its swaggering hero's earlier posturing. Cuthbert has, in other words, no qualms about wanting to shoot the workers of Belleville and Montmartre like big game in the midst of the Franco-Prussian War – but when the moment arrives in which Communards are hunted down in just such a fashion, he is consuming the spectacle from the remove of a rooftop.

Appropriately relegated to the bourgeois quartier of Passy, the novel's initial rooftop view permits Cuthbert to describe and re-imagine the Versaillais' entrance into the city. It hails the troops as liberators rather than invaders, and their entry precipitates a marked linguistic shift in the novel: whereas the troops under Thiers have so far been principally denoted as Versaillais, the moment they break through the fortified walls around Paris, they are rechristened the "Loyalists." Thus, "at one o'clock in the morning the Loyalists were in possession of this important position [in the Trocadero]."⁵³ The shift in registers allows the novel to revision the Communards – rather than the Versailles government – as the "capitulards" in the Franco-Prussian War debacle, and in turn retroactively condemn them for their initial cowardice.⁵⁴ As Cuthbert tells his future bride, "I have no sympathy for the Communists . . . not one spark. They would not pull a trigger or risk a scratch for the defense of Paris against the Germans, now they are fighting like wild cats against their countrymen."⁵⁵

This failure of memory facilitates another radical re-imagining of the Bloody Week. Upon entering Passy, the Versaillais put down their arms to a jubilant welcoming, with the neighborhood rushing to meet them:

> at two o'clock the head of the French column came down the street. In an instant . . . the inhabitants poured into the street and welcomed their deliverers with shouts of joy. The troops piled their arms and fell out, and as soon as they did so men and women brought provisions of all kinds.⁵⁶

The staging of such an encounter, with the army evaporating into the people by laying aside their weapons, seems a strikingly unmarked re-enactment of the first moments of the Commune itself. Indeed, the scene closely echoes the energetic accounts of the March 18 encounter between the people and the army on the Butte Montmartre given by Lissagaray and others (here filtered through Henri Lefebvre):

> All the people of Montmartre are there. Who are among them? Certainly, there are men with guns, but above all there are women. They arrive from everywhere, [and] cry, "Long live the soldiers!" "Long live the army!" They hold out bottles of wine. Did [the soldiers] not march all night without food or drink? And all of a sudden, something extraordinary happens: in one hour or so, the army disappears, dissolving [into the crowd] like sugar in water.⁵⁷

Such a reworking of the Commune's birth is in keeping with the novel's overall refusal to recognize or remember any Paris that is not explicitly bourgeois; while the workers might be spoken of, and promptly written off as *racaille*, they rarely find a space in the novel. (Cuthbert suggests from the outset that all you need to know about them can be found in the novels of Balzac.)

It is perhaps all the more fitting, then, that when *A Woman of the Commune* ultimately grants Cuthbert a means to witness the street fighting safely, the pass is signed by no less a personage than Marshal MacMahon himself. Yet Cuthbert's walks and expressed desire to see the fighting do little to bring the ghastly spectacle into focus, instead offering readers an account of the military's sweep through Paris that is riddled with amnesia; despite the mass summary executions occurring throughout the city, hostages are everywhere in Henty's novel, but bodies are nowhere to be found. (The text eventually estimates that 20,000 will fall before Paris is conquered, but nowhere does it represent for its readers a sense of the scale of that number.) Indeed, the economy of violence is orchestrated so that it is the burning of the city and the killing of hostages by the Communards that unleash the violent reprisals of the Versaillais:

> The fury excited by such a deed will be so great that the troops will refuse to give quarter, and the prisoners taken will have to suffer to the utmost for the crime committed by perhaps a handful of desperate wretches.[58]

While such a restructuring of the chronology of the Bloody Week is in general keeping with the contemporary vitriol leveled at the Commune for its vandalism of Paris, it conveniently glosses over the fact that it was Thiers's refusal to allow prisoners of war that initially prompted the Commune to take hostages many weeks before the Bloody Week. (*Under the Red Flag*, on the other hand, acknowledges the case matter-of-factly: "The conquerors were instructed to shoot first and apologize afterward. And in nine out of ten cases they obeyed their instructions to the letter."[59])

A Woman of the Commune ultimately condenses the violence overwhelming the city into a single scene of summary execution, with Arnold and Minette standing in for all those other, unseen bodies. (Their tombstone appropriately closes the novel.) Minette crystallizes the terror of at once the figure of the pétroleuse and the Commune in Henty's reading of it, and her death signals the wiping out of its threat; the soldiers at her execution assure Cuthbert that "[the Communards] are not human . . . and their women are worst of all."[60] Indeed, throughout the novel Minette has been characterized as a tigress in waiting, seducing Arnold to his ruin even as she is eventually held symbolically responsible for the literal ruination of Paris by fire. She pointedly enacts, in her highly public political role within the Commune, the rights for women that her English double, Mary, early on espouses before finally giving up altogether.[61] And she is a female fiend – of the variety Cuthbert wants thoroughly to mark off as uniquely French: "It is well for you that your country does not breed such as these," or so the soldiers assure the Englishman.[62] As the summary execution of Minette is characterized as summary justice – she has been caught torching houses – her incendiarism almost too neatly collapses the imagery of the "overly emancipated" female with the destroyer of homes. Her treatment parallels the way in which the adventure plot of *A Woman of the Commune* is ultimately subsumed by the Woman Question in the novel; Cuthbert watches the suppression of the Commune from afar, but Minette's double, Mary, demonstrates the threat of the Commune that has not (entirely) been averted. Resettling in England and wedded out of any further ideas about women's rights, Mary neatly exorcises the incendiary figure of the emancipated female. The novel thus draws to a close on an almost impossibly happy note:

> Cuthbert has often declared that the most fortunate event in his life was that he was a besieged resident in Paris through its two sieges. As for Mary, she has been heard to declare that she has no patience whatever with the persons who frequent platforms and talk about women's rights.[63]

King's novel assumes what would seem – by contrast – a more neutral stance towards the events of the Bloody Week, for it not only looks the violence in the face, but also brings its young hero into closest proximity with the Versaillais juggernaut. Indeed, for a moment, even Frank is a hair's breadth from losing his life to a Versaillist bayonet. *Under the Red Flag* thus allows its readers to meet and mingle with Communards, befriend Dombrowski, and see the brutality of the Versaillais army, even offering an unflinching look at the horror of the Bloody Week; Henty's jubilant portrayal of the Versaillist entrance into Paris is tempered by King's characterization of one Versaillais in the early stages of the army's entrance into Paris: "Is the fellow dead or asleep? he said. Oh, asleep is it? Well, begin with him, so that I can take his chair."[64] However, while the Communards are, for King, never simply *racaille* and the reprisals of the Versaillais never go unacknowledged, much is done to keep the reader on the "right" side – which requires quite a bit of narrative maneuvering.

Dombrowski, while a hero for the Commune, thus becomes in King's narrative one of its harsher critics, so that Frank ultimately realizes that "the general had a deep contempt for the gross and vulgar errors of the insurrection for which he was fighting."[65] No sympathy, in other words, can be meted out, finally, and MacMahon is characterized as both liberator and republican – another re-laying of memory and willful forgetting: "On Sunday at four o'clock all was over, and Marshal MacMahon's proclamation announced the deliverance of Paris. 'Order, labor, and tranquility will now revive,' wrote the Marshal, who was a few years later to be President of the French Republic."[66] The most elaborate staging of strategic amnesia in the novel is, however, the clearing away of "true" Communards in order to leave behind only the worst elements in society:

> wearied by the incessant fighting, the poor Communards, finding that they had been misguided – that the uprising which they had made in the name of liberty and local self-government had been slowly per- verted to a Socialistic revolution – melted away . . . [leaving behind] only the desperate and resolute – the men who had vowed a terrible vengeance upon society – remained.[67]

It is an evacuation all the more curious because it implies that some vestige of recognizably republican sentiment once provided the impetus for the Commune – an impetus that might have appealed to American readers – despite having never elaborated this as a pos- sibility in its account of the Commune's earliest days.[68] And in keep- ing with the move to redefine republicanism, the novel duly recodes Thiers, a man of dubious republican sentiments who had built his career as a royalist, who, "ever contemptuous of 'the vile multitude,' had long had a plan for dealing with them – a plan he proposed to Louis Philippe in 1848 [but could only enact in 1871]."[69] In King's version, however, Thiers is both patriot and republican: "Slowly the old patriot, Thiers, who had worked so vigorously for the young republic when it was under the heels of the Prussians . . . was mass- ing a large army, ready to be hurled into Paris" – a hurling that would result in, as David Harvey puts it, "one of the most vicious of bloodlettings in an often bloody French history."[70]

Although a female Communard with torch in hand graces the spine of its original 1895 cover, *Under the Red Flag* assiduously leaves aside "the Woman Question," seeming instead most preoc- cupied by the liberty question. The novel affords, for example, a Frenchman with Versaillais sympathies a moment to regret the scene outside his window and lament the summary judgments, but a hard- ened Frank, our American boy hero, turns a cold eye to the bodies piling in the streets, the mass executions, and the seemingly endless processions of men on their way to internment and exile. The lesson the boys have gained – and thereby impart to their readers – is both that the American Revolution is exceptional and that revolution is never, under any circumstances, justified. Extemporizes Sny,

> If anybody is to be judged harshly, I think it is the man who turns against his country, his city, his nation, just to gratify a miserable ambition or whim, in the hope of establishing some petty doctrine. I have not got any sentimental objections to thinking that such men deserve exactly what these fellows . . . are going to get.[71]

It is a lesson that echoes Kaplan's contention that historical romances of the 1890s culminated in reproductions – and restagings – of the American Revolution that effaced any trace of politics or conflict out of it in order to "repossess and . . . neutralize it": in fine, "these novels whitewash the Revolution as an exclusive inheritance against both the influx of immigrants aspiring to national identity and the claims of colonial subjects, such as Cubans and Filipinos, to revolution and self-government."[72] *Under the Red Flag* no doubt dramatizes lingering anxieties over the degree to which revolution needs to be reclaimed from workers. (The eight-hour workday is briefly introduced – only in jest – at the beginning of the novel, though the need for passage of such a law would prove the touchstone of labor unrest in America in the 1890s.) But its work to reconstitute Revolution in the minds of its boy readers serves more crucially to reclaim it from immigrants, radicals, and colonial subjects. (In Henty, the worker and the colonial subject would be nearly interchangeable.) For King's novel is most shrewd, perhaps, in its reading of the threat of the Commune, and in the elaborate distinction it wants to draw between the respective revolutions.

A Woman of the Commune, on the other hand, explicitly insists – quite notably before the Commune takes place in France – that it could *never* happen in England:

> Thank god such a thing is never likely to happen – at any rate in my time . . . Our workmen have sense enough to know that a mob rule would be ruin to them as well as the rich and, were it needed, in twenty-four hours half a million men could be sworn in as constables, and these would sweep the rabble in the Thames.[73]

Perhaps the novel protests too much: the outburst betrays a certain hesitation, as its certitude lies finally only in the fact – or is it hope? – that in Cuthbert's lifetime it would be an unthinkable event. (Given that the novel appears some two decades later, Cuthbert's outburst seems most directly leveled at Henty's young readers.) And the urgency of mobilization in Cuthbert's scene – the speed with which the rabble would be swept into the Thames – only further gestures toward the possibility that such an insurrection might not be, anymore than with the woman of the Commune herself, uniquely a product of France.

Yet both books contend, in varying ways, that their work is done. No one is left to speak on the Commune's behalf by novel's end, and its specter seems safely laid to rest: "Paris was conquered, the Commune was stamped out, its chiefs dead or fugitives, its rank and file slaughtered."[74] Arnold and Minette lie in peace at "Père La chaise," Mary has been weaned of her heterodox gender ideas, and Marcelle recants any lingering faith in the Commune. In turn, France is left behind and readers are assured, to varying degrees, that the Republic has come to stay: Paris is, after all, liberated, and such things could never happen at home. The cost of the peace and its tenuousness, however, are – even in only a sidelong glance – a vexing remainder.

New Designs of Empire

The cost of the Commune's suppression and the problem of the potential parallels between the respective revolutions are explicitly addressed in the popular American romances of Robert W. Chambers and Eugene C. Savidge. Indeed, the motif of Paris as the site of "republican" conversion and frontier of empire is put into further relief by these fictions, which retell the Commune for an adult American audience in the 1890s. Their work at once to domesticate the Commune – often by repopulating the scene with Americans – and in turn to "nativize" it – both in the sense of primitivizing the Communards and in redefining the American man as "native-born" – not only reconstitutes revolution, but also more thoroughly defines American republicanism and manhood as inextricably coterminous.

Chambers, one of the most popular American historical romance writers in the late nineteenth century, titles his bestselling novel of the Commune, somewhat ambiguously, *The Red Republic* (1895) and suggests "the separation of the romance from the facts would leave the historical basis virtually intact."[75] His assertion that the artifice of the romance plot can be separated from the historical narrative does not simply privilege the latter, however; it also suggests the ready-made audience for yet another fiction that seeks to refashion the history of the Commune in elaborate detail. A *Dial* reviewer of Chambers's novel writes, later that year, "The Paris Commune of 1871 is likely in the course of time to yield as many good stories as any episode in modern history. Perhaps the best of them that has yet been told is 'The Red Republic.'"[76] Indeed, contemporary reviewers of *The Red Republic* often focused their attentions most on the value of its historical plot: the 1897 *Encylopaedia Britannica*, for example, hailed it as "a vivid, realistic, and in some ways the most valuable, account of the Commune that has been written," while the *Dial* review most applauds the novel's attention to detail – as if it had been an act of reportage rather than fiction: "The day to day happenings of those terrible weeks are chronicled with the attention to detail *of a newspaper report.*"[77]

The popularity of *The Red Republic* is, in my reading, part and parcel of its effectiveness at packaging itself as the inside story, as if Chambers (like Henty and King) had been there to see the events himself.[78] Savidge, on the other hand, offers readers "a biographical novel" – though one most interested in relating the biography of an event rather than a personage. Like Chambers's romance, *The American in Paris* establishes its authority by textual allusions – in this case, by layering each chapter in epigraphs by famous historical players in the drama unfolding within the novel. The novel thus allows the historical actors to speak for themselves, while nevertheless suggesting that the body of the novel allows them to voice their opinions in their own words as well ("Liberties have obviously [only] been taken with the time and connection").[79] While both *The Red Republic* and *The American in Paris* warranted notice in *The Bookman* for their sales, Savidge's novel was taken to task by a *Dial* reviewer, who suggested that the novel could not be adequately separated from its historical rather than literary ambitions:

> *The American in Paris* may be best described as an anecdote history of the Franco-Prussian War, the siege of Paris, and the Commune, interspersed with numerous quotations from state papers and personal memoirs . . . the story, aside from this, is hardly worth mentioning.[80]

The American in Paris enjoyed, however, at least three print editions.

Given their reliance on – and claims to – historical immediacy and veracity, it is all the more important to focus our attentions on the way *The Red Republic* and *The American in Paris* specifically mobilize a selective history of the Commune in the service of dramatizing American identity formation in Paris. The history they forget is a telling one, particularly in light of the fact that it often ignores or de-emphasizes details that, as we have seen, figure prominently in both anti- and pro-Communard histories and memoirs published on both sides of the Atlantic. For example, *The Red Republic*, for all its attention to day-to day-life under the Commune, offers a limited portrait of it, making no mention of the felling of the Vendôme Column, and – in perhaps the strangest act of narrative revision – entirely overlooking the prominence of women during the Commune. That a single Frenchwoman, Faustine, is the sole *vivandière* and barricade-rouser pictured in the novel – and she is armed only with words – is all the more odd, given that a female Communard, complete with rifle and red Phrygian cap, figured so prominently on the book's original cover (Fig. 2.1). The fierce and fiery female incendiaries of the Commune otherwise make no appearance, and the Bloody Week – while alluded to only via its death toll (as in Henty) – is nowhere put

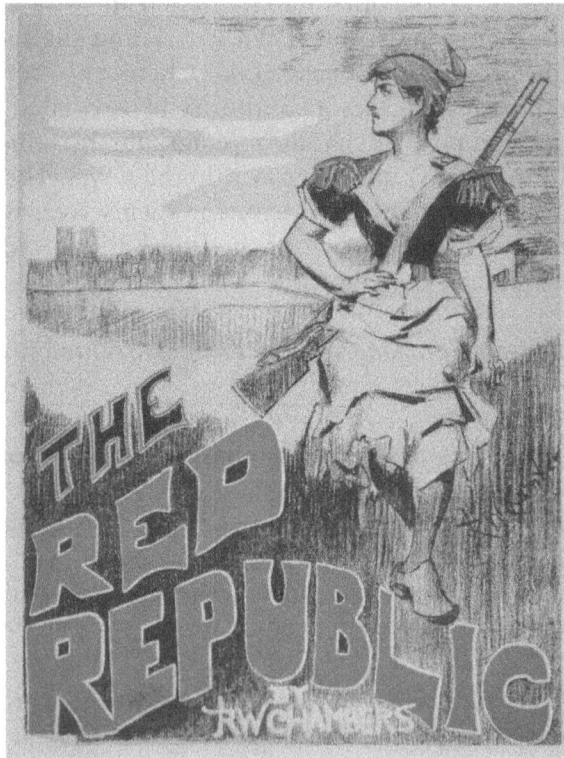

Figure 2.1 Cover, *The Red Republic* (1895). The Miriam and Ira D. Wallach Division of Arts, Prints, and Photographs: Art and Architecture Collection, New York Public Library.

on display in a novel that regularly indulges its readers in spectacles of acute violence. (Characters are routinely shot in the back, and a fatal stabbing is the catalyst for the marriage plot.) And though the text labels the Commune a "republic," it aligns its narrative energies absolutely with the forces that will eventually crush it. (We witness, for example, the birth of the Commune on March 18 from the perspective of French government troops, rather than of Parisian bystanders or American tourists.)

In a novel that allows the Commune to be called a republic, albeit a "red" one, it seems all the more glaring that Communards in the text are rarely – if ever – allowed to voice their political aims. Faustine is permitted to cry "Vive la République" – and make clear the elision between *la République* and *la Commune* in many Parisian minds – but the workings of the Commune are otherwise reduced to thievery and murder rather than daily administration or even, as in Gribble's *The Red Spell* (1895), an ineffectual propensity for meetings. The political clubs – and politics of everyday life – are nowhere discussed. (There is no mention of the clearing of rent, of the closing of night bakeries, or of the changes in the educational system.) This clearing away of the revolutionary politics of the Commune is all the more important, given the novel's reception as an authority on the event; a reviewer in *The Atlantic Monthly* writes, for example, that "the tale depicts with exceeding vividness and truth the Paris of the Commune and *the sort of men* who ruled therein."[81]

Romancing the Revolution

Chambers's narrative revolves on the marriage plot between Jeanne de Brassac, a young Frenchwoman from an aristocratic military family, and Philip Landes, a young American come to Paris to be a painter. This narrative draws on the vaguely incestuous love plot most associated with the domestic novel, with Landes, a close friend of Jeanne's deceased brother and essentially Jeanne's protector after the death of her father at the opening of the novel, seeing Jeanne as both "little sister" and lover, and Jeanne often slipping in her reference to him.[82] This nominal slippage between *amant* and *frère* functions somewhat to underscore the powerlessness of Jeanne; by infantilizing her, the plot emphasizes her essential fragility ("She was so gentle, so winning in her innocence, so helpless, so dependent.")[83] While Faustine, her lower-class contemporary, spends time with rabble-rousers and works tirelessly for the cause of the Republic, the domesticated

Jeanne is quite content to stay at home and Landes loves her for it. In a novel that so conspicuously evacuates women from the scene of the Commune, Jeanne's demurring presence cannot be read as simply a function of the romance plot itself. Indeed, the historical romances of the 1890s often presented readers with a New Woman-type heroine.[84] But Jeanne can reek here of neither the New Woman nor the pétroleuse. Chambers's choice of heroines is, in my reading, at once political – Jeanne wards off, even as she contains, the peril of the emancipated female – and strategic, for the active forgetting of "the Women of the Commune" seems to work in the service of the novel's decided interest in the development of its American hero.

Landes is an inadvertent hero who unwittingly becomes a spectator at (and at times unwilling soldier of) the Commune, but while the narrative emphasizes his heroism, it takes pains to emphasize as well that, as an *American*, he fights only those fights forced upon him. Though the novel does not neatly fit the imperial romance genre, it nevertheless draws heavily upon it. Much like *A Woman of the Commune*, *The Red Republic* recasts Paris as a frontier where Landes can prove his mettle, subdue the natives, and win his lady. However, even as the population of Paris is, in turn, "nativized" – with Communards rendered as essentially primitive – the Commune itself is curiously Americanized.[85]

Americanizing the Commune and Nativizing Americans

Chambers's romance immediately sets up an antagonism between "the red republic" and the American one; indeed, the narrative opens with its initial speaker, Isidor Weser, suggesting, "I'm not fond of Americans."[86] In turn, Weser is central to both the historical and the fictional narrative threads, and is immediately identified in the narrative as party to the Commune. (The novel's opening is positioned at the eve of the uprising, and Weser, as confidant to the Commune's future head of police, Raoul Rigault, is part of the movement to bring it into being.) The enmity between the Commune and America is stated, then, explicitly and early on, and is further woven into the fabric of the romance plot by making the persecution of Landes for personal reasons (he prevents Weser from robbing Jeanne de Brassac's family diamonds) central to the actions we see taken by the Commune – with the origins of the Commune thus rescripted from a call to municipal government to a direct attack on private property. Put simply, although the narrative dwells at length on the events of March 18, it implicitly makes robbery and enmity towards an American the "real" originary moment of the Commune. It thus quite effectively neutralizes the Commune's political ends, and works in turn to recast any allusion or attention paid to the day-to-day workings of the Commune entirely in the light of pillage, greed, and personal grievance.

This narrative repurposing forgets the Commune's amity towards both the American Minister to France and American citizens, and further the affinity many Communards saw between themselves and Americans – an affinity that we saw, for example, fictionalized in both *Under the Red Flag* and *A Woman of the Commune*.[87] More crucially, it brings into relief the way in which *The Red Republic* "Americanizes' the Commune – making the actions of the Commune's central characters *about* America (in the figure of Landes) and their personal enmity towards him, *and* in the more obvious sense of repopulating the ranks of the Commune with a number of American citizens.

Given that American anarchists in this period actively embraced the Commune and directly identified their struggle with that of the Communards, it is not surprising that in her 1897 three-part history of the Commune for *Munsey's Magazine*, Molly Elliot Seawell wards off the possible contamination – or contagion – of the Commune in the 1890s by insisting that no American fought for it, excepting General Cluseret (who, after all, was only a naturalized one). She further contains the Commune by emphasizing its fundamental foreignness; in her account, few French participated in it. Although she thoroughly overstates the case, many foreigners did in fact take part in the Commune, and yet the number of Americans who did so remains uncertain.[88] While only naturalized French–Americans appear in King's text, and Henty offers only a token Anglo-American as part of the fray, in Chambers's novel Americans are everywhere during the Commune. Wilton, a fellow painter in the Latin Quarter and friend of Landes, gets swept up in the idea of a good fight and the enthusiasm of Faustine, his *grisette* turned Communarde, while a host of Irish–American immigrants fresh from New York fill a battalion on the Commune's behalf. (New York is also specifically marked as the home for Communard exiles, Weser among them.)[89] This Irish–American presence in the text is particularly perplexing because the narrative explains neither their enthusiasm for the Commune nor how they came to be in Paris to fight in the first place. This American presence in the novel complicates Landes's assertion – a few pages after he encounters these foreign compatriots – that

Americans cannot identify with the Commune, for when asked by a Communard, with some disbelief, "You do not care for the Commune?," Landes replies only: "Care for it! *I'm an American!*"[90] While the phrase implies that, fundamentally, an American must be opposed to "the red republic," the novel has already suggested Americans have been swayed – or taken in – by it. The phrase itself could be read against the grain to imply that because of being American, Landes would care for it (or, rather, feel some identification with it), for even *within* the novel, there is some slippage between the two republics.

The novel works to ward off the threat of that identification (or mis-allegiance) by most thoroughly embodying it within the New Yorkers voluntarily fighting for the Commune, and thus more clearly marking off the term "American" for the native-born only. The text thus works, in other words, to primitivize the non-native-born Americans in the text, while at the same time defining American manhood and republicanism through the figure of Philip Landes, the "native" American. Indeed, these Irish–Americans become, for Landes, more foreign and more primitive than the "evil" Communards:

> When he first heard the familiar sound of his own language he had felt for a moment comforted and hopeful, but now, the ruffians at the next fire seemed more distant and foreign to him than the worst ragamuffin in the battalion.[91]

Savidge's "biographical novel," on the other hand, quite explicitly grapples with the vexing possibility that the Commune and its excesses are themselves the progeny of American democracy set loose upon the world. This anxiety is embedded in both the American protagonist's political *Bildung* (or conversion) in Paris – it is there that he realizes what it is to be an American, the "gospel" of Americanism referenced in my epigraph to this chapter – and in his doomed love plot with the court *cocodette*, Hortense.[92] It is Hortense, half-French, half-American, who, in the opening pages of the novel, questions Kent about the evils of democracy. (At their first meeting, she teasingly says, "The tendency to rich uncles is the only redeeming feature in democracy," before going onto add, when asked if democracy required "redemption," that "the whole race needs rescuing from the mediocrity entailed by this era of equality.")[93] In turn, it is she who is converted to its cause by Kent's own enthusiasm, but while Kent leaves Paris – and the corrupted love affair – to go home and spread the gospel of "Americanism," that gospel is fissured by his experience of the Commune. Hortense goes to her death because of Kent's enthusiasm for America, and dies not only fighting for the Commune but also crying out "My darling! My angel! See what I have done for your love and for your cause! . . . Vive l'Amérique, Vive—."[94] While the phrase is cut short by a bullet, her death marks the unmistakable elision between the Red Republic and the American one. The "lesson" of Savidge's text is further complicated by the multiple American viewpoints it seeks to offer on the Franco-Prussian war and the Commune – while it does not populate the Commune with Americans, it largely populates the novel with Americans of various stripes (Hortense is half-American; her other suitor, Jaeger, is a naturalized German–American; and Kent is converted to his absolute faith in the cause of America by Clarke, an American doctor he meets in Paris). Each of them is meant to eventually adopt the properly American idea – Jaeger, who fought in the American Civil War before returning to participate in the unification of Germany, is perhaps the most striking case of being forever touched by his American experience (even as he tries to reconcile it with his German identity and faith in the monarchy).

Yet Hortense is not the only example of the failure to properly comprehend the meaning of the American "gospel" in the novel. The most potent spectacle of miscomprehension (or, rather, re-imagining) of that idea is born of the entrance of General Cluseret, that naturalized American, into the text. He enters the scene as Kent is forcibly conscripted to build barricades for the Commune. As an American, Kent refuses to participate (much as Landes does in *The Red Republic*), but Cluseret fought in the American Civil War and calls on Kent to work for the Commune explicitly in the name of his nationality:

> I too am an American citizen . . . and that is all the more reason why both should fight for France. Get back to your place, or I will have you shot as a recreant American who refuses to fight for liberty, equality and fraternity.[95]

Hortense is, in one sense, then, simply a stand-in for Kent: her death prevents his "fall," and preserves his properly American view of democracy. Yet Kent, in witnessing Hortense's execution, cannot help but reflect on his own role in her misplaced enthusiasm: "Oh, those misinterpreted phrases which had made Hortense one of the infuriated crowd; and his well-meaning phrases, too!"[96] The effect of Kent's "well-meaning phrases" taught Hortense the "wrong" lesson – and fatally so, but while the novel insists that Kent leaves Paris with the "right" gospel, the narrative everywhere suggests the instability of such gospels and the troubling, irrepressible contagion of well-meaning phrases. During the final days of the Commune, the narrator observes, "And yet among these wild beings were thousands transported in their frenzied exaltation, believing honestly that they were giving their lives for France and for humanity."[97] The text thus destabilizes such hopes, even as it allows its hero to claim them in the name of a republic with which the Communards – those "half-frenzied" enthusiasts – cannot be identified.

Kent leaves France, in other words, as both avid enthusiast for American democracy and staunch critic of self-determination in practice. He thus amplifies the young boy American's sense, at the end of *Under the Red Flag*, that revolution is no longer possible, and its Parisian enthusiasts received what was coming to them. Indeed, both protagonists resolutely carry that lesson back to America with them. That they must do so seems intimately bound up with America's own larger struggle to imagine its revolution as at once exceptional and no longer fathomable as it grappled with the prospect of, in Kaplan's phrase, "the anarchy of empire." Perhaps Twain, writing on the US intervention in the Philippines, put the conundrum best: "There must be two Americas: one that sets the captive free, and one that takes the once-captive's new freedom away from him."[98] However, if, in light of Kaplan's work, we have come to read historical romances in this period as primarily representing and rendering invisible the politics of empire as they work to masculinize their readers and sanitize the American Revolution, I would argue that we have not yet fully accounted for the ways in which they exist in equally uneasy suspension with ongoing domestic anxieties about the "anarchy" of international feeling, the continuing specter of the fiery anti-domestic "women of the Commune," and – perhaps most acutely – the claims US radicals were making on American revolutionary traditions at this moment. In the following chapter, we turn from sites of Paris as frontier to sites of Paris as international underground, from unexpected forms of imperial adventure to affective and material forms of radical repossession.

Chapter 3

Radical Calendars: The Commune Rising in Postbellum Internationalism

You need not be surprised, my friends, if you hear very soon that, I too, have been condemned to death for the cause. I will carry the red flag of the Commune and plant it everywhere in New England.

Lucy Parsons (1886)

On June 24, 1891, over 10,000 Coney Island "pleasure-seekers" attended the debut of a lavish pyrotechnic spectacle, "Paris, from Empire to Commune," on Manhattan Beach. Billed in local newspaper advertisements as "a grand, living, moving tableau of history," James Pain's newest pyrodrama offered its audience an immersive sensory experience that merged the outsized visual technology – and modes of seeing – of the panorama with the innovations of late nineteenth-century pyrotechnics while also tapping into the ongoing popularity of historically inflected melodramas.[1] Claiming to exceed Pain's previous historical pyrotechnic shows in scale, interest, and ingenuity, "Paris, from Empire to Commune" involved not only a diverse display of fireworks, reputedly costing over $1,000 an evening, but also a live performance of colossal dimensions: a cast of over 300 costumed actors, acrobats, and circus performers, a 400 foot-wide stage, scenery of immense proportions that recreated Paris's monuments and streets in intricate detail, and a 120 foot-wide waterway situated between stage and crowd that represented the Seine and "afforded still greater opportunities for magnificent [pyrotechnic] effects."[2] This spectacular visual performance was accompanied – and, indeed, sensationally illustrated by – a noless thrilling sonic experience, with dialogue and theatrical tableaux filled out by music from Gilmore's military band and the incessant whooshing and crashing of the hundreds of fireworks dancing across the sky above Manhattan Beach's newly opened 15,000-seat amphitheater. As the *Rocky Mountain News* later put it, "the crash of falling walls, the roar of explosions, the thunder of artillery and the blaze of the flames combined to form an impressive panorama."[3]

"Paris, from Empire to Commune" remained the hit of the season, with *The Sun* describing it as a "remarkably strong magnet" for Coney Island visitors and the *Brooklyn Daily Eagle* reporting that the nightly pyro-spectacular was continuing to draw crowds of "not fewer, at the lowest estimate, than eight thousand people" two months after it opened.[4] But its continuing pull on Coney Island audiences had as much to do with the Paris it put on display and the history it spectacularly repackaged for its viewers as with the bravura of its fireworks. For what "Paris, from Empire to Commune" offered Coney Island crowds that summer was a chance to revisit Paris's lost landmarks, to immerse themselves in scenes of Napoleon III and Empress Eugénie being entertained by acrobats in the final days of the Empire, but most of all to relive as sensation what *The Ohio Democrat* would describe as "the most exciting period in the history of France" by way of scenes and pyrotechnics "depicting in the most vivid manner the terrible scenes of fire and carnage in connection with the days when Paris lay helpless in the grasp of the terrible Commune."[5]

The poster advertising the amusement further underscored this sensational history by compressing the narrative sweep of "From Empire to Commune" into a single moment conveyed by an arresting, if by then familiar, visual image – Paris in flames – accented by a single female figure, torch in hand, appearing in the upper left-hand corner above the caption "Vive la Commune" (Fig. 3.1). What the poster telegraphs by visual shorthand and Pain's pyrotechnic show writ large was, then, a mode of seeing red, of collapsing the Commune into the "destruction of the beautiful city" (as the South Carolina *News and Courier* later dubbed Pain's show), and equating the Commune's flag with the terrors of pillage, anarchy, and female petroleum-throwers. In turn, the short-lived revolution's bloody demise could be safely rewitnessed as pyrotechnic entertainment.

This performative distillation of revolutionary uprising as sensational shorthand and outsized commodity speaks, in turn, to the way the Commune as frontier continued to sell (and sell well) in American culture in this moment. As I have taken up at greater length in the previous chapter, boys' adventure fiction set during the Commune became an instant bestseller in the 1890s and an article such as "What an American Girl Saw of the Commune" garnered copy in *The Century Magazine*,

Figure 3.1 "Paris and the Commune" (New York: Sackett & Wilhelms Litho. Co, 1891). Theatrical Poster Collection, Library of Congress Prints and Photographs Division.

even when it offered such a limited parlor-side view of the events that it might more fittingly have been titled "What an American Girl *Didn't See* of the Commune."[6] But it also points to the Commune's continuing appeal for mainstream US audiences across the country.

The success of "Paris, from Empire to Commune" at Coney Island led Pain to take his show on the road, with multi-week stops in Charleston, Richmond, Cincinnati, and Denver over the next three years. Promising in local advertisements "a thrilling and realistic reproduction of one of the most terrible revolutions that has ever occurred in the world's history," the traveling pyrodrama of the Commune continued to garner immense crowds along its tour.[7] Of its visit to Richmond *The Times* relates, "At 7 o'clock every seat was taken and still the people came. The scene for fifty yards around the entrance was a wonderful one, indeed. Such a solid mass of humanity is hard to conceive of."[8] The pull this pyrotechnic production was figured to have for audiences capitalized on the surprising "magnetism" of the Commune's story – as *The Ohio Democrat* emphasized in a front-page article in advance of the spectacle's opening, "it will be a production of most thrilling interest to all."[9] But this magnetism was figured squarely along national lines, with the newspaper suggesting Pain's pyrodrama would be of "particular interest to Germans, French, and Americans," and "appeals especially to the interest of all patriotic Germans," who are presumed to be poised to recall the defeat of the French during the Franco-Prussian war and the Commune's toppling in rapid succession with particular relish.[10]

That Americans would be encouraged – indeed, be expected to already want – to line up to see the Commune and its demise restaged as an immense, immersive spectacle and that this spectacle could be so easily imagined as a specifically *patriotic* one is all the more striking given the spectacular ongoing role the Commune occupied in the postbellum radical calendar, the cycle of lavish festivals, complete with oratory, tableaux vivants, music and dancing, that postbellum radicals staged each year to celebrate the start of the uprising.[11] This chapter explores these celebrations alongside and against the Commune's pivotal (if now largely forgotten) role in postbellum radical print and performance culture, in particular the essays and lecture tours of three of the most prolific and yet still under-examined American women radicals of the postbellum era: the Russian émigrée and anarchist publisher Emma Goldman, who J. Edgar Hoover dubbed "the most dangerous anarchist in America"; longtime labor activist, publisher, and Haymarket biographer Lucy Parsons, who Robin D. G. Kelly identifies as "the most prominent black woman radical of the nineteenth century"; and, finally, influential anarcho-feminist Voltairine de Cleyre, who Paul Avrich describes as "one of the leading figures in the American anarchist movement," not least for her knack of bridging the gap between "native-born libertarians" and "Jewish immigrant revolutionists."[12] I focus on these figures because they spoke yearly on the Commune and were themselves pointedly derided in the US popular press as pétroleuses for their incendiary speech and "wild blood-thirsty harangues."[13] Reading these annual cycles of commemoration and speechifying as at once counter-spectacles and radical acts of counter-cultural memory, I show how postbellum US radicals drew on the spectacular repertoire and sentimental modes embedded in Pain's pyrodrama of the Commune, but did so to reclaim the crushed uprising as a living blueprint for revolutionary agitation and a key locus of international feeling rather than a failed radical past.[14]

In the past decade, increasing attention has been paid to the 1886 Haymarket bombing as a mass-media event of global dimensions – Oscar Wilde was among those who petitioned for clemency for the eight Chicago anarchist activists put on trial and sentenced to death for their "incendiary speech" at the demonstration where the bombing had occurred, though they themselves played no part in the bomb-throwing – as well as an under-explored cornerstone of leftist literary production, from pamphlets and numerous working-class elegies to plays and commemorative speeches.[15] Building on this work by Kristin Boudreau and Shelley Streeby to expand the radical canon beyond and before the Popular Front, this chapter aims to make the Commune and a broader cross-section of postbellum leftist print and performance culture both more visible and more audible in American literary and cultural history by piecing together that vibrant movement culture by way of posters, newspaper articles, pamphlets, announcements, broadsides, periodical advertisements, and other ephemera produced by postbellum US radicals and their critics. In theorizing and analyzing this archive, I draw on Daphne Brooks's work in *Bodies in Dissent* "to present a more vibrantly textured landscape of black performance," as well as Britt Rusert's method and provocation towards "a necessarily creative approach to the archive" in the face of archival opacities and the ephemerality of performance itself.[16] In so doing, I crucially counter the assumption that the Commune had limited (or even negligible) purchase for the US left after the failure of the Great Strike of 1877, and that, as historian Philip M. Katz puts it, "the only workers in the US who still celebrated the Paris uprising after 1877, or even consistently remembered it, were foreign-born workers – *and not even all of them.*"[17]

What little attention that has so far been paid to the Commune in US leftist memory has focused almost exclusively on German, Yiddish, and Italian immigrant communities in cities such as New York, Detroit, Providence, and Chicago.[18] In tracking the Commune's memory culture across the country and various radical circles, and through cross-national festivals, I tell a different story, chronicling how these celebrations sustained extra-national memory and brought together radicals across ethnic and ideological divides rather than simply consolidating ethnic or political enclaves. In fact, what often made these celebrations so newsworthy – reports of them were circulated and widely reprinted in mainstream newspapers and mass-circulation periodicals – was precisely the way they affiliated groups that otherwise would not be expected to mingle. As the Philadelphia *North American* described it in its coverage of a March 1884 Commune festival held in New York City, "Only mischief of the worst kind could bring French, Germans and Russians into fraternity, and in this case the mischief is a criminal combination against the best interests of society."[19]

But if the alarm caused by these celebrations centered on their multi-national invocation of the Commune as "Universal Republic," it gravitated also to the way these festivals figured themselves as extra-national festivities that stood in place of – or threatened altogether to supersede – national holidays, national affiliations, and national memory for US radicals, and Anglo-American participation in these decidedly non-national events garnered equal amounts of scrutiny (and hyperbole) from US newspapers. As the *Rocky Mountain News* opined in 1887, "the celebration of anniversaries of bloodshed and unexampled exhibitions of human ferocity in foreign countries, by organized bodies of American workingmen, is certainly remarkable."[20] To celebrate the Commune in the late nineteenth- and early twentieth-century US was, in other words, to live by and through a radical calendar whose sense of alternate time and subversive affiliation provided the grounds for extra-national feeling as an embodied practice of radical memory-making: internationalism as at once temporality *and* sensation.

Radical Cultures of Memory

In April 1918, nine months after she had been consigned to the Missouri State Penitentiary for sedition and a year and a half before she would be forcibly deported from the US, Emma Goldman authored her final letter as publisher and editor of *Mother Earth Bulletin*, a recent offshoot of the tremendously successful anarchist monthly magazine, *Mother Earth*, which she had published for over a decade. In it, Goldman reflected on the "incessant grind" of her daily work in prison and the conditions experienced by her fellow prisoners. Yet she closed her letter, and by extension her magazine, on a note of typically steely resolve:

> But I am fortunate in having the Babushkas, the Louise Michels, and the other great ones to draw from . . . This is the month of the Commune. They said it was dead when they slaughtered thirty thousand, but it lives forever.[21]

Goldman's invocation of past revolutionary touchstones at this, the seeming nadir of her career as a left-wing publisher, speaker, and agitator, could be taken for a bout of nostalgia – a triumphant if misguided backwards glance in the face of prison, a burgeoning Red Scare, and continuing war-time press censorship that sought to keep her message (and her magazine) out of readers' hands. In our own moment, such nostalgia has been critiqued as an essentially self-defeating and necessarily limiting affective relationship with the past. In her now-landmark 1999 essay, "Resisting Left Melancholy," influential political scientist Wendy Brown argued that, in the wake of Thatcherism, the rise of Reagan, and the fall of the Berlin Wall, "what emerges is a Left that operates without either a deep critique of the status quo or a compelling alternative to the existing order of things" – a left enamored with its own "impossibility," given over to "a structure of desire that is backward looking and punishing."[22] The term Brown applies to such backward glances (or wayward political desires), "left melancholy," was, as she points out, borrowed from Walter Benjamin, and reflected his disdain for the "revolutionary hack" too devoted to past ideals to see or harness the grounds "for radical change in the present."[23] Her clarion call was thus both to eschew our sense of leftist defeatism and to resist melancholic nostalgia for ever-receding glory days and timeworn tactics in favor of political hope that wrestles with the contradictions of our own historical conditions, but as José Muñoz argues, by way of Ernst Bloch, in his study of queer pasts and queer futurity, *Cruising Utopia*, "the past, or at least narratives of the past, enable utopian imaginings of another time and place."[24] And as John Funchion has recently reminded us, the past was not a psychic cul-de-sac but rather a vital affective and political resource for turn-of-the-century US radicals. As he points out, in the aftermath of the failure of the Great Strike of 1877, "interest in alternatives to the United States' brand of republican capitalism reached unparalleled heights" and a variety of "radical intellectuals, labor organizers, and politically committed novelists [sought] to recover estranged histories and places" in ways that galvanized social change precisely by "recasting their agitation as an effort to rehabilitate the revolutions of the past" – an affective structure and activist tactic that he suggests we might best reread, in light of Brown and Benjamin, as productive "left nostalgia" rather than melancholy.[25]

Yet what is perhaps most remarkable about Goldman's invocation of the revolutionary past is that it is, in her formulation, neither lost nor finished. More to the point, the past that is, in this moment of defeat, most usable is one that had not, in its own moment, succeeded. Her formulation of "the month of the Commune" underscores both its continuity – residing in the present tense – and its continuing centrality to radical calendars and radical modalities of feeling. She thus deftly aligns her own situation with that of the

Commune's struggle and makes both grounds for further fighting rather than ineffectual backward glances or defeatist navel-gazing. Such an affective and material attachment to what Social Gospel proponent and later Socialist George Herron described, in his 1903 address on the Commune at Faneuil Hall in Boston, as the "splendid and fruitful failure" of the 1871 uprising seems a structure of revolutionary feeling and mode of reliving the past that is neither melancholic nor exactly nostalgic.[26] For this remembering *within* and *beyond* the present – a mode I term insurgent memory – is equally a form of living within and beyond the nation state.

If Goldman's parting letter archives the sensational contours of internationalism as a material and affective practice, and the Commune's vital role in sustaining it, it also highlights the uprising's underappreciated ongoing role in leftist print culture and cultural production. *Mother Earth* devoted ample annual coverage to the Commune in its March issues, both in its editorial letter and in essays by influential anarchists such as Voltairine de Cleyre and Peter Kropotkin, which theorized the Commune for contemporary anarchist ends, as did its nineteenth-century precursor, *Liberty*. These essays give some indication of the speeches Goldman, de Cleyre, surviving Haymarket anarchist Oscar Neebe, and other anarchist leaders gave at turn-of-the-century Commune festivals across the country, allowing readers who did not attend to participate in an ongoing culture of remembrance. Together with the festival advertisements that ran in *Mother Earth* and Alexander Berkman's *The Blast*, they point to the way such celebrations became a cyclical fixture of US radicals' alternate, non-national calendar well into the twentieth century, a foundation of counter-cultural memory-making and radical community-building as well as energizing. As IWW leader N. L. Griest put it to a Los Angeles crowd in March 1902: "Other men may have their days, but to the American workingman the anniversary of the Paris Commune will be the greatest celebration in the calendar."[27]

But if these annual Commune celebrations served to keep the uprising in cyclical circulation, they just as importantly flew in the face of wider condemnations of the uprising in mainstream US culture. As historian Tom Goyens points out, "Since the events of 1871 in Paris were reviled by respectable society, a Commune festival was truly a subversive statement, something the anarchists exploited by marking it with excessive imagery."[28] In turn, these "subversive" celebrations played a key role in keeping radical periodicals in circulation: much as the *Arbeiter-Zeitung*, the anarchist newspaper edited by future Haymarket martyr August Spies, launched itself as a daily

Figure 3.2 "Commune Festival" advertisement, March 1912, *Mother Earth*, Miriam Y. Holden Collection, Rare Book Division, Department of Rare Books and Special Collections, Princeton University Library.

paper in 1879 through funding raised by its Commune festival, *Mother Earth* often linked the magazine's own birthday festivities to its annual Commune celebration, promising readers the event would offer the by-then requisite recipe of festivities – speeches and dancing (Fig. 3.2).

The liveliness of this birthday party – linking the start of both the Commune uprising and Goldman's magazine – speaks back to the larger message postbellum radicals posited about the event they commemorated each year: it was, they insisted, anything but dead. As Goldman herself explained to an audience of a thousand at a Commune celebration in Milwaukee in 1908, and as the *Los Angeles Times* anxiously recirculated in wire coverage of the event, "The spirit of the Commune is now in existence stronger than ever and soon, if conditions don't change, the red flag of anarchy will float in every corner of the globe."[29]

The global reach of the Commune's red flag – its unfinished role in an international circuit of extra-national revolutionary memory – was a cornerstone of early twentieth-century anarchist theorizations of the ongoing nature of the event. As Peter Kropotkin put it in a 1912 commemorative essay for *Mother Earth*, "Under the name *Commune of Paris* a new idea was born, to become a starting-point for future revolutions."[30] However, the Commune itself was, from the start, a radically non-national event, as Kristin Ross has recently argued:

> An insurrection in the [Parisian] capital fought under the flag of the Universal Republic, the Commune as event and as political culture has always proved resistant to any seamless integration into the national narrative. As one of its former members recalled years later, it was, above all else, "an audacious act of internationalism."[31]

Moreover, as she demonstrates, the Commune's non-national orientation can be measured not simply by the number of foreigners who were elected to it and fought in its name, or by its commitment to toppling symbols glorifying empire and nationalism, as seen in its destruction of the Vendôme Column, but rather in the global working-class political imaginary it enabled.[32] And it was exactly this "audacious" internationalism that early US celebrants both hailed and enacted in their gatherings.

Take, for example, the December 1871 parade organized by Victoria Woodhull and New York City's newly splintered International Workingmen's Association (IWA) in honor of the recently executed Communard general, Louis Rossel, who was tried a full six months after the insurrection had been officially suppressed. An event that has been described as the largest march in the city's history, and which made headlines across the country, it was also a landmark moment of cross-racial and cross-national working-class collaboration, comprising the African American Skidmore Guard, suffragists holding red banners calling for "Complete Political and Social Equality for Both Sexes," Communard refugees, Irish nationalists, members of the Garibaldi Guard, Cuban and Venezuelan revolutionaries, various societies and unions, and the Association Internationale des Travailleurs (among others) in the cause of remembering the "martyrs of the Universal Republic" (Fig. 3.3).[33] *Frank Leslie's Illustrated Newspaper* suggested the memorial procession attracted "an unusually large crowd of spectators" (by its estimation, nearly 6,000 assembled in Union Square) and remarked in particular on the fact that "all nationalities and colors were represented" among the

NEW YORK CITY.—FUNERAL PROCESSION OF THE INTERNATIONALS ON SUNDAY, DECEMBER 17TH, IN MEMORY OF THE COMMUNISTS EXECUTED IN THE PRISON, GOVERNMENT OF FRANCE.—SEE PAGE 264.

Figure 3.3 "New York City: Funeral Procession of the Internationals," *Frank Leslie's Illustrated Newspaper*, January 6, 1872: 264-5. Library Company of Philadelphia.

marchers, while Kansas's *Lawrence Daily Journal* took note of the banner that proclaimed "The World is Our Country, To Do Good Our Religion."[34] While many US newspapers took aim at exactly the brazen internationalist bent of the parade, expressing concerns over "an association of Foreign and American Communists in New York styling themselves 'internationals' and setting forth principles akin to, if not identical with, those of the Paris Communists, who succeeded in making themselves both notorious and infamous by a public parade on the Lord's Day,"[35] labor activist and founder of the Women's Typographical Union, Augusta Lewis, described the scene instead as "the most genuine democratic affair that was ever witnessed."[36]

The inclusive spirit and defiant internationalism of the memorial parade continued to animate the Commune's annual anniversary festivals celebrated in New York throughout the postbellum era. As an advertisement for the ninth anniversary "Grand Festival, Concert, Banquet and Ball" suggests, the event was held at Germania Hall, a working class German–American assembly room in the heart of the Bowery's "Little Germany," but was sponsored by a broad assortment of radical groups: the Société des Réfugiés de la Commune, the Socialistic Labor Party, the Freethinkers, the Women's Socialistic Society, the Socialistic Liedertafel, and the Arbeiter Liedertafel (Fig. 3.4). The multi-national constellation of the event was further signaled by the poster's lengthy enumeration of the event's roster of speakers, including the honorary President, exiled Communarde Louise Michel, "now prisoner at New Caledonia," as well as the Vice-Presidents, including leading American labor journalist John Swinton, Communard refugee Edmund Mégy, German anarchist Justus Schwab, Italian labor leader Guiseppe (*sic*) Traversa, and Spanish radical Antonio Gonzales. Yet if the red flag prominently displayed on the poster specifically summoned images of the Commune – and the "Vive la Commune" emblazoned across it further underscored that the event was embracing this radical ensign – the framing of this celebration made it at once about then and now, suggesting the festivities were a call not simply to remember 1871 but also to "Strike for the Universal Commune!" The redness of the flag in turn presaged the subversive embrace of red at these festivals, a color scheme so provocative that it consistently merited mention in mainstream newspaper accounts of the events. *New York Times* coverage of the 1884 celebration at Germania Hall notes, for example, that "over a thousand people . . . had met to celebrate the thirteenth anniversary of the Paris Commune" and frets that the entire hall and the audience were bedecked in the Commune's color of choice:

Figure 3.4 "Strike for the Universal Commune!" poster (New York: 1880), Poster Collection, International Institute of Social History (Amsterdam).

> Flaming programmes, deep scarlet entrance tickets, boutonnières of red immortelles and ribbon worn by nearly all present, and an unlimited number of flags . . . children wore red sashes, red dresses, and red hats, and men adorned themselves with satin neckties of the approved roseate hue.[37]

If the hall and the attendees thus telegraphed their embrace of the red flag and counter-cultural memory of the Commune, the "stirring" speeches in French, German, and English further cemented the point. In turn, the music and dancing that followed these addresses served as a continuation of, rather than a digression from, the program at hand, as they signaled communal celebration rather than elegiac commemoration, a radical jubilance that consistently served to generate consternation in the reports from the hall sent by wire across the country. The message of these evenings can perhaps be best summed up by labor leader Edward King, whose address at the 1884 festival celebrated the Universal Republic by calling on Americans "to imitate the Paris Commune, vindicate the memory of the gallant communists, and commemorate the anniversary of the great social revolution."[38]

What is perhaps most astonishing, then, about this annual cycle of celebrating the Commune is the way in which it represented leftists equally across radical ideological divides, from influential postbellum activists like Victoria Woodhull and Wendell Phillips, and Social Gospel proponents like George Herron, to Socialists like Daniel De Leon, anarchists like Benjamin Tucker and Emma Goldman, Wobblies like Big Bill Haywood and Eugene V. Debs, labor organizers like B. G. Haskell and W. C. Owen, and thousands of other Americans in cities as various as Cincinnati, San Francisco, St. Paul, Detroit, Providence, Indianapolis, St. Louis, Hartford, Louisville, Boston, Milwaukee, Denver, Philadelphia, Los Angeles, and Chicago. These celebrations, as well as the essays that preceded and sometimes encapsulated them, also appeared in the full spectrum of postbellum leftist print culture, uniting readers of *Woodhull and Claflin's Weekly*, the *Arbeiter-Zeitung*, *Liberty*, *The People*, *Appeal to Reason*, *Mother Earth*, and *The Blast*, as well as various immigrant papers. Though radical print and performance culture is often studied in isolation, these anniversary celebrations elicited substantial coverage in a variety of local and major metropolitan daily newspapers in the 1870s and well into the turn of the century, both in the sense of announcements now otherwise buried in the "local miscellany" section of papers such as the *St. Louis Globe-Democrat*, the *Rocky Mountain News*, the *Indianapolis Journal*, and the *Milwaukee Daily Sentinel*, and in the detailed reportage from celebration halls featured in *The New York Times*, the *Los Angeles Times*, and Chicago *Daily Inter Ocean*, which were in turn telegraphed across the country and reprinted in, for example, the *Poughkeepsie Daily Eagle*, the Kansas *Atchison Champion*, the Raleigh *News and Observer*, the Philadelphia *North American*, and the *Galveston Daily News*.[39] As I will argue, traversing these circuits of memory opens up new ways of reading radical culture and reseeing "red" in the postbellum US.

Seeing Red in Black and White

Although Chicago police famously labeled Lucy Parsons, who was likely born a slave in Texas and routinely described as a "mulatto" in the press, though she admitted publicly only to her mixed Mexican and Indian heritage, "more dangerous than a thousand rioters," her sixty-year career as an activist, orator, journalist, and Haymarket archivist has until recently received scant scholarly attention.[40] As Angela Y. Davis argued in her seminal early study of women in the US labor movement, *Women, Race, and Class*, this was in part because Parsons was for too long relegated to being "simplistically identified as the 'devoted wife' of the Haymarket martyr Albert Parsons," despite the fact that "[her] involvement in labor struggles began almost a decade before the Haymarket Massacre and continued for another fifty-five years afterward."[41] But Parson's relative obscurity, given her pivotal role in late nineteenth- and early twentieth-century anarchist, labor, and later Communist organizing, and the sheer volume of her speeches and writings, points also to what Shelley Streeby has aptly termed "the limits of print as an archive for radical memory" in the face of ongoing police raids and de facto censorship, as well as to the limits of literary studies in recognizing radical print and performance culture as worthy of study on their own terms.[42] As Streeby observes, the speeches, pamphlets, and periodicals Parsons wrote or edited during her lifetime would be unlikely to appear on a syllabus, and most likely "would be viewed as belonging, like history, with those 'others' of literature – those texts that the literary apparatus cannot or decides not to value within the category of literature."[43] I turn to Parsons to think through the ways she drew on and reformulated the Paris Commune in her work to internationalize the Haymarket struggle and agitate for radical social and economic change in the US. Reading *The Life of Albert Parsons* alongside and against her invocations of the Commune and her speeches at annual Commune celebrations, I show how Parsons mobilized both the specter and the spectacle of the not-forgotten 1871 uprising to reclaim defeat as the spark for future revolution, even as she herself was characterized as a female Communard in contemporary mainstream coverage of her lecture tours.

Such a task is harder than it might seem. Although Chicago anarchists' yearly commemorations of the Commune at times garnered as many as 40,000 attendees in the 1870s and 1880s, advertisements for such festivals continue nearly into the 1920s in anarchist periodicals, and Parson's biographer, Carolyn Ashbaugh, notes that Lucy spoke at dozens of Paris Commune Celebrations in the final decades of her life alone, we have not a single full transcript of her speeches at any of these events nor an extant authorized published essay version of what she said at these gatherings. Such a gap in the paper trail of her activism reflects the effects of near-constant police raids on her newspaper offices during her lifetime and the seizure, after her death, of her papers as well as her collection of more than 1,500 radical books and periodicals.[44] These archival opacities make *The Life of Albert Parsons*, which Lucy published in 1889 at her own expense and which went into at least three more print editions, an invaluable resource as well as counter-archive for understanding the way she wanted to challenge the US media portrayal of her husband, internationalize their struggle, and wrestle with what insurgent forms might be born from a defeat and execution that was recast as martyrdom.

Yet for all that the gaps in her archive point to the limits of print in giving us access to the full range of radical cultural production, her spectacular ongoing presence in mainstream US newspapers is a vital, if largely unexamined, mode of reconnecting us with her electrifying performances during otherwise ephemeral lecture tours. While it is fair to question the accuracy of the reporting of these gatherings, the circulation and wide recirculation of her speeches across the country nevertheless index some measure of the exhilaration she provoked in radical audiences and the trepidation she unleashed even at second hand for readers consuming these events from the safety of their parlors. The sheer "virality" of her presence alone provoked outraged commentary in US newspapers – the medium most responsible for keeping her in constant circulation. As the *Galveston Daily News* put it acidly, "All her utterances, and especially her speeches at the anarchist gatherings, are wired throughout the country as fully and eagerly as though she were a Louise Michel or a Pétroleuse of the Paris Commune."[45] In splicing together this circuit of radical memory and memory-making by way of mass-cultural, even hostile, sources, my aim, then, is to recover the surprisingly center-stage role Parsons played both in and beyond radical culture in this moment. While Parsons is now viewed as a "minoritarian" subject – to use the term Dana Luciano and Ivy G. Wilson employ in *Unsettled States* – in a "minor" field within American literary studies – namely, labor studies – she occupied a far more central one in her own day, crisscrossing radical and mainstream forms of US print culture.[46]

Take, for example, Parsons's speech at an 1889 Paris Commune festival in Chicago, which was covered at length in the *Chicago Daily Tribune*, the *San Francisco Chronicle*, and the *Los Angeles Times*, and immediately reprinted in abbreviated form in dozens of newspapers across the country, with headlines ranging from "The Dusky Anarchist Delivers Tirade" to "Loud-Mouthed Lucy."[47] Although the slant of the *Chicago Daily Tribune*'s coverage is evident from the article's subtitle, "West Twelfth Street Turner-Hall Packed with

Eager Listeners to Wild Talk by Mrs. Lucy Parsons," it nevertheless archives some trace of the sway Parsons held over the crowd
of nearly 3,000 men and women gathered that night to celebrate
the eighteenth anniversary of the Commune, and the way "the clink
of beer glasses had become less frequent" the moment she took to
the front of the stage, as well as the reactions her speech elicited
over the course of its performative arc, from "quick and significant
exchange of glances," and "shouting and stamping of feet" to rapt,
silent attention.[48] Coverage of her earlier lecture tour in New York,
New Jersey, and New England in defense of her husband similarly
emphasized how Parsons captivated large crowds – and at times even
hostile audiences – with the sheer composure of her stance and the
flair of her performance:

> With her heavy ear rings, topaz buttons, and shining silk gown she
> has an air of old Egypt [on the platform] . . . and speaks with a grace
> and force that held her auditors' closest attention to the end . . .
> She is an exceedingly good, wonderfully impressive speaker. Her
> audience follows her to the climax without an instant's weariness.[49]

If the thrill of Parsons's performance in Chicago lay in her sar-
torial flair and the virtuosity of her voice's hold on the audience,
it also owed something to her placement on the stage "within a
foot of the bust of Spies, decorated with the reddest of sashes."[50]
For this visual proximity further merged Parsons's own reflections
on the Commune with the memory (and threat) of Haymarket, a
carefully staged spectacle that drew on the rich visual and performance tropes already embedded in these celebrations, particularly
the use of elaborate costumes and tableaux vivants to retell the
story of the Commune. This visual shorthand in turn underscored
the embrace of the red flag by the anarchist leader the *Cincinnati
Enquirer* dubs an "agitatress." Such spectacular ensigns of insurgent memory – and leftist stage props – heightened the incendiary
nature of Parsons's speech and the extra-national celebration of
which it was part but they also highlight the important aural and
visual dimensions of her radical performance of memory on the
platform. Indeed, these emblems were regularly the outraged focal
points of coverage of her Commune speeches, often garnering as
much copy as the words she uttered from the platform. In an article
on "The Dangerous Classes," published in the March 1887 issue of
the Spiritualist monthly *Buchanan's Journal of Man*, which echoes
reports "by special wire" that ran in cities as various as Chicago,

Cincinnati, Fort Worth, and Oshkosh, Parsons's "inflammatory" address on the Commune in Cincinnati is described as "the most revolutionary gathering ever seen in this city," not least because "the entire hall was profusely directed with large red flags. There wasn't an American flag in the hall, and above the stage was a picture of the condemned anarchists."[51] Echoing earlier coverage of Commune celebrations across the country, the distinctly non-national character of the event – down to the Marseillaise being substituted for any "national airs" that otherwise might have played – generated substantial mention in national coverage, while local coverage pointed out the celebration had been organized by the "Anti-National Society" of Cincinnati, and suggests advertisements for the event had specifically exhorted "Comrades, men and women, rally round the red flag!"[52]

Parsons herself would dramatize this incendiary international rallying point in her speeches, proclaiming in 1886 to a crowd of 3,000 at New York's Clarendon Hall that she would "carry the red flag of the Commune and plant it everywhere in New England."[53] Three years later, she suggested in her Commune address in Chicago that the 1871 uprising had in fact been the catalyst of her own political coming-of-age, much as the Haymarket trial would later be cited as the conversionary turning point for radicals such as Emma Goldman and Voltairine de Cleyre. As Parsons put it, "It was the Commune that first directed my attention to the study of the social problems."[54] What is perhaps most startling about this assertion is not the revelation that the Commune might be capable of radicalizing Parsons – certainly mainstream papers had warned of its contagion from the start, and her conversionary narrative and yearly celebration of the uprising effectively underscore its continuing threat – but rather that she suggests it was precisely mainstream condemnations of the Commune rather than radical defenses of it that were most responsible for her political awakening: "I heard Mr. Washburne, who was our Minister to France, speak on the subject, and I thought his view was a bitter one."[55] In my reading, Parsons here invokes the Commune and her conversion to convince her audience of the radical spark ever present in this defeated revolution, and the necessity of radical memory within and beyond the nation-state; even more importantly, though, her framing of her first encounter with the Commune suggests that insurgent forms of memory might be sparked from unlikely sources and, indeed, from altogether antithetical press coverage, which in turn speaks to her anticipation– and even defter mobilization – of the vitriolic circulation of her speech far outside the walls of that Chicago hall. Certainly, her work that night to keep the Commune in the present tense – her reiteration that she and her audience were living through "stirring times" – as well as the sensational final line of her speech, "We want a revolution. Whether it is peaceful or bloody makes no difference. A revolution must come!" – circulated across the country, far beyond the reach of radical print networks alone.[56] And that call for revolution – whether described as shouted, shrieked, or simply stated by Parsons – was itself so incendiary it was the most oft-repeated line of her address, with many papers transforming it into a kind of refrain, opening and closing their articles with its insistent clarion call.

For all the radical possibilities of the mass dissemination of her message, it well might be asked whether we ought to trust the *Chicago Daily Tribune*'s account of her remarks on the Commune on this or any other occasion, given its overwhelming (and admittedly not at all veiled) hostility to her cause. Certainly, Parsons crafted *The Life of Albert Parsons* as a platform to critique media misrepresentations of the labor movement and her husband, as when she quotes Helen Wilmans, an influential Chicago journalist who edited the radical reform paper, *The Woman's World*, on the "distorted and outrageous pictures, purporting to be portraits of these men," as well as of "Mrs. Parsons," that ran in the pictorial press.[57] Yet Parsons just as savvily repurposed media coverage in her hybrid biography, which brought together essays, autobiographical sketches, letters, speeches, newspaper accounts of the trial, and her own commentary on that coverage, in a way that recalls the model of nineteenth-century media mining and "database" creation that, Ellen Gruber Garvey argues, antebellum reformers such as the Grimkés had employed in their 1839 abolitionist magnum opus, *Slavery As It Is*.[58] In teaching us how to reread media coverage, Parsons significantly underscores the radical work this reportage might do in spite of itself by choosing to highlight in her prefaces and footnotes the fact that several of the speeches by Albert Parsons she chose to include in the volume are the versions as they appeared in the mainstream press, rather than, say, from working-class newspapers.[59] In this way, she not only creates a counter-archive of radical memory but also underscores the way in which mainstream print culture already functioned, albeit unwittingly, as a crucial transcript of otherwise ephemeral moments of radical oratory and performance.

Parsons's indictment of the trial and execution of her husband, as well as her repurposing of print material she termed "all the more valuable from the fact it is from disinterested parties," in *The Life of Albert Parsons* sought most explicitly to ask Americans to resee the history of the American labor struggle and the role the Haymarket anarchists played in it,[60] a project Streeby suggests is most concerned with "disrupting" the spectacle of Haymarket in US culture. What has received little attention is, however, the way Parsons accomplishes this critical work of revisioning by way of a no less crucial revisiting and resignifying of the Paris Commune for the reader and, in turn, of Haymarket in light of the legacy of this earlier uprising. Parsons thus opens her biography of her husband with a "history of the American labor movement" penned by Joseph Greunhut, a Socialist leader best known for his editorials and columns in *The Progressive Age*, immediately suggesting the arc of the story of Albert Parsons continues after his death and expands beyond his life – encompassing a movement rather than a moment.[61] This biographical sketch of the labor movement in Chicago in turn frames the rise of the Socialist Labor Party in that city in terms of its success at organizing the 1879 Commune festival:

> One of the most notable incidents showing the growth of the party was the celebration of the Paris Commune during this same spring. The committee of arrangements secured the Exposition building, with a capacity of 40,000, but so great was the jam that it was impossible to carry out the program of singing, dancing, and drilling. It was estimated that at least 60,000 people visited the Exhibition building that night, while thousands, after waiting on the outside for hours, unable to gain admission, returned home.[62]

The allusion here to the dancing and singing, as well as the "celebration" rather than commemoration, recalls the lack of elegiac feeling at these yearly festivals; as historians Hartmut Keil and John B. Jentz point out, the events were marked by an overriding note of optimism, as well as by speeches, theater, music, and marches.[63] And Parsons, by way of Gruenhut, notably archives here the remarkable scale of the event – a testament to what Gruenhut describes as "the boldness of our propositions in demanding collective (Governmental) control of land, means of transportation, communication, and production, and the *dash* which characterized our efforts in making converts to this scheme of social and industrial emancipation."[64]

The scale of the event's "dash" and audacity is further evidenced by press coverage of this 1879 Commune "fest" that consistently emphasized the troublingly multi-national nature of the gathering. The *Chicago Daily Tribune* described the scene acerbically: "In short, it was such a gathering as only a Socialistic community could bring out or would tolerate," emphasizing the crowd hailed from "bohemian socialistic slums" as well as "Scandinavian dives," and included "the worst specimens of feminine depravity," – among them, "red-headed, cross-eyed and frowsy [Irish] servant girls."[65] The internationalist bent of this festival is not surprising; as we have seen, cross-national anniversaries were being held across the country since the early 1870s and well beyond the turn of the century, and coverage of later Chicago festivals – for example, reports on the 1891 celebration that ran in *The Atchison Champion* and Raleigh (North Carolina) *News and Observer* – similarly observed, "The Paris Commune anniversary was celebrated yesterday by half a dozen nationalities of Chicago."[66] Its inclusion in the volume, however, signals an extra-national affiliation and culture of memory that highlights long before Haymarket and its aftermath how the history of American labor is a story at once within and beyond national borders.[67]

The jubilant internationalism and anarchic embrace of the Commune's memory crystallized in this 1879 festival are further underscored across *The Life of Albert Parsons*. In his autobiographical sketch, entitled "The Story of His Life," Albert himself interrupts that life narrative by inserting within it the manifesto of the Pittsburgh Working People's Association Congress, a manifesto addressed to "The Workingmen of America," which nevertheless set as its initial aim "destruction of class rule by all means – i.e., by energetic, relentless, revolutionary and international action," and closes by echoing Marx's exhortation that "Proletarians from all countries, unite!"[68] Parsons would return again and again to that exhortation in his speeches, emphasizing that the cause of the American workingman was, in no small measure, the cause of workingmen everywhere, and the archive of these speeches in *The Life of Albert Parsons* in turn works implicitly to signal the international stakes of his own trial and execution. Parsons's commitment to internationalism as a material and lived practice is further highlighted by the inclusion of "Under the Red Flag" and "Observing Thanksgiving Day," two of the few non-Haymarket-related speeches that Lucy selects for the volume. In the former, Albert suggests that "We meet to-day beneath the red flag, that flag which symbolizes an equality of rights and duties, the solidarity of all human interests; that flag which has . . . been the emblem of 'Liberty, Fraternity, Equality.'"[69] In so doing, Parsons neatly resignifies a flag linked to images of pillage, anti-clericalism, and incendiary political belief in US sermons and editorials, and links the struggle for the eight-hour work day in Chicago to the international struggle for liberty, fraternity, and equality; he thus makes the American labor movement's fight part of 1789 and 1871, much as he would work to cement the connection between 1886 and 1871 by quoting a poem about the Commune's future rise as he was being taken to the gallows. Even more resoundingly, Albert argues in the address he gave at a counter-Thanksgiving event in 1885, a protest against working people being asked to "return thanks for the miserable existence they were compelled to endure," that "the flag of America has . . . become the ensign of privilege and the guardian of property, the defender of monopoly. Wage-slaves of Chicago, turn your eyes from that ensign of property and fix them upon . . . the red flag."[70] This radical substitution of one flag for all others invokes the worst fears that Commune festivals – with their overabundance of red flags and red sashes – yearly provoked for media commentators, and its inclusion in the volume echoes the visual and rhetorical resignification of the red flag that Lucy herself engaged in during her lecture tours. The centrality – and vitality – of the red flag's internationalism are further crystallized in Albert's final speech in court, which recalls an earlier address he had given in Cincinnati that lingered on the red banner carried during the procession, a banner that spoke of, as he described it, "liberty, fraternity, equality and labor all over the world," whereas every other national flag "repudiated [or] outlawed the workingman."[71] In this way, *The Life of Albert Parsons* works, finally, to "resee" red by directly linking the struggles of the 1870s and 1880s to the 1871 uprising in Paris, at once archiving and performing working-class affiliation within and beyond the nation-state.

Communal Feeling, International Risings

If the Commune was a source of anarchic jubilation and anti-national feeling for American radicals in the decades immediately following the uprising, it was a no less potent site of insurgent memory and occupied a no less central place in the radical calendar after the turn of the twentieth century. Yet for these later radicals, its splendid defeat seemed most to augur lessons for their struggle and glimmers of a glorious rebirth in their lifetimes. As influential Michigan-born, Philadelphia-based anarcho-feminist Voltairine de Cleyre puts it in her May 1912 anniversary piece for *Mother Earth*, "We do not stand to-day as mourners at the bier of a Dead Cause, but with the joy of those who behold it living in the resurrection."[72] I turn to de Cleyre's reflections on the Commune as a key archive of pre-Russian Revolution/pre-CPUSA memory-making, as well as a vital index of the way the Commune's memory continued to animate radical feeling and speak to contemporary revolutionary struggles some four decades after its sensational demise.

In *The Selected Works of Voltairine de Cleyre*, the 1914 collection published two years after her death, fellow anarchist Hippolyte Havel offered an overview of de Cleyre's life that centered on her remarkable productivity in the face of ill-health, twelve-hour teaching days, and extended lecture tours:

> One wonders how, under such circumstances, she could have produced such an amount of work. Her poems, sketches, propagandistic articles and essays can be found in the *Open Court*, *Twentieth Century*, *Magazine of Poetry*, *Truth*, *Lucifer*, *Boston Investigator*, *Rights of Labor*, *Truth Seeker*, *Liberty*, *Chicago Liberal*, *Free Society*, *Mother Earth*, and in *The Independent*.[73]

And as literary critic Eugenia C. DeLamotte points out, de Cleyre associated with the most famous revolutionaries of her time, including Goldman, Kropotkin, Louise Michel, and Ricardo Flores Magón, while her lecture circuit took her across New England and the Midwest, as well as England, Scotland, and Norway.[74] Her international reach was such that, in 1902, the *New-York Tribune* relayed with concern that "her writings are said to be known by anarchists all over the world."[75] But perhaps because de Cleyre was not blessed with, in the words of Paul Avrich, "Emma Goldman's notoriety or dynamic vitality," she has so far received much less critical attention than Goldman and her male contemporaries, despite being one of the most prominent homegrown American radicals of her time.[76] Avrich's 1978 biography, *An American Anarchist*, and work over the past decade by DeLamotte and Sharon Presley to re-issue collections of de Cleyre's letters, essays, and speeches have, however, invited us to re-attune ourselves to the full significance of her political thought and the sheer dexterity of her literary corpus – her forays into an array of genres, from poetry and short fiction to essays, translations, and speeches.[77] Although we have no transcripts of de Cleyre's annual speeches on the Commune, the artfulness of her re-articulations of the legacy of 1871 for her own political moment can be seen in the anniversary essays she published in *Mother Earth*, as well as in the undated piece on the uprising that Alexander Berkman included in his 1914 collection of her writings.[78] And de Cleyre's abiding interest in the Commune's ongoing legacy was such that, before her untimely death, she had begun a translation of Louise Michel's 1886 account of the Commune,

Mémoires de Louise Michel. That it would take another seventy years before this history of the Commune by a female Communard would be available in translation for American readers speaks to just how ahead of its time was de Cleyre's attempt to make Michel's account accessible to early twentieth-century US radicals.[79] Her work to tell the Commune's story in her writings and by way of this unfinished transla- tion grew out of her exasperation with the way that story continued to be told in mainstream American culture. Much as Herron, the Social Gospel proponent turned Socialist, observed in his 1903 anniversary address at Faneuil Hall that "the novelist and the historian, the politi- cian and the priest and the king, and all the retainers of the ruling class have stamped the Commune with infamy,"[80] de Cleyre would evoca- tively proclaim "what false colors they give [the Commune's] light, the preachers and teachers who have miswritten history, and lied, and lied, and lied."[81]

Yet, unlike many of her contemporaries, de Cleyre saw the issue of retelling the Commune's history and reclaiming its light as a prob- lem that did not just stem from the way its enemies had portrayed it, for she pointedly suggested its friends (and yearly commemorators) were equally to blame for misrepresenting it. As she put it in "The Paris Commune," the undated anniversary speech Berkman included in his collection of her writings, "Which is the real Commune – the thing that was, or the thing that our orators have painted it?"[82] In particular, she expresses concern over the way contemporary radi- cals – "our Commune commemorators," as she calls them – figure the uprising as a "spontaneous assertion of independence" rather than the work of a small, committed body of agitators, many of whom had already spent time in prison for their efforts.[83] Similarly, she foregrounds how, despite the great affective investment she and these misguided commemorators have in the uprising – "One almost catches the redolence of outbursting faith, that rising of the sap of hope and courage and daring, like an incense of spring; almost feels himself there, partaking in the work, the danger, the glorious, mis- taken assurance which was theirs" – she argues that this sensation makes them prey to the Communards' own blind spot: namely, the failure to see how much of Paris "did not attend public meetings, who sat within their houses or kept silent in the shops, were not converted or affected by their teachings."[84] What is perhaps most striking about de Cleyre's critique coming in the form of a com- memorative essay is the way that she wrests the Commune's legacy from its detractors, and also from those who would fail to see its lessons for the present struggle. Contemporary radicals should not be blinded by their own enthusiasm, in other words: revolution is a full-time occupation.

If, however, de Cleyre's commemoration of the Commune is tempered here by her anxiety that its memory might lead the radicals around her to lose sight of either the sheer amount of work that must go into overturning the social and economic structures around them, or the fact that, in her reading, the Communards failed because "They attempted to break political chains without breaking economic ones," her writings nevertheless archive the uprising's continuing centrality in the radical calendar and as a vital touchstone of insurgent memory.[85] As she observes, "There are times and occasions which reduce all men to direct, primitive feeling . . . to me, the commemoration of the 18th of March is one of those times."[86] Her rendering of the sensation that underlies her yearly remembering as "direct, primitive feeling" roots that cycle of memory squarely in her body; in turn, de Cleyre goes onto invoke both sentimental and sensational modes to transmit that sense of memory as bodily "possession" to her readers as she relates "what they did to the thousands of men, women, and little children who filled the graves, the prisons, and the exile posts in the Commune's name."[87] The horror of this scene flashes up for de Cleyre as a living, moving picture, a spectacle she can neither forget nor unsee, and describes as "distinct and lit with a white, awful clearness, as in the paralysis of a lightning flash,"[88] but that horror is not the ultimate light she instructs her readers to see. Instead, she goes onto conjure a glorious vision of the Commune that at once invokes and transplants Winthrop's "city upon a hill" across the Atlantic: "She [Paris] sought deliverance where only deliverance can be found, within herself. And though she struggled and was conquered, she set that day a beacon light upon a hill – a light they could not drown with all the blood they spilled."[89] Such a conjuration and migration deftly relocate the promise of the Massachusetts Bay Colony – the touchstone of American exceptionalism – across the waters, thus shifting the locus of American revolutionary memory at once to Paris and, more specifically, to 1871 as past as well as present.

The image of the Commune not as red flag but instead as "light upon a hill" suggests de Cleyre's commitment to commemorating the Commune in the present tense and celebrating both its legacy and its lessons: where a flag would still require a standard-bearer, the light she invokes is sufficient unto itself and, more to the point, cannot be put out. The resilience of this figuration speaks to an era where American radicals are faced paradoxically with, on the one

hand, a sense of their own belatedness – the forty years separat-
ing them from the Commune's rising, the sixty-some years since the
abolitionist fight, the prospect of, as de Cleyre puts it, "the long
dead-level of inaction" – and, on the other, rumblings of revolution
in their lifetimes.[90] While de Cleyre would not live to see the Russian
Revolution, she witnessed with great enthusiasm the beginnings of
the Mexican Revolution; a mere five months after her death in June
1912, the IWW leader, Eugene Debs, would win nearly a million
votes in his campaign on the Socialist ticket for the US presidency.
At this moment of long waiting and exultant promise, this moment
when it was not yet a foregone conclusion that radical social and
economic change would not take hold across the Americas, de
Cleyre looked to the Commune as a beacon of things to come, as
well as to things as they were unfolding. She thus warned her readers
that "struggle waits – abortive struggle, crushed struggle, mistaken
struggle, long and often. And worse than all this, *Waiting waits*,"
even as she celebrated the revolution rising across the border as
nothing short of the Commune's second coming.[91] As she describes
it in her essay "The Commune is Risen," which ran directly before
the manifesto of the recent Mexican Revolution in the 1912 issue of
Mother Earth:

> In the roar of that fire [in Mexico] we hear the Commune's "earthquake
> tread," and know that out of the graves at Père-la-Chaise, out of the
> trenches of Satory, out of the fever plains of Guiana, out of the barren
> burial sands of Caledonia, the Great Ghost has risen, crying across the
> world, "Vive la Commune!"[92]

Chapter 4

Tasting Space: Sights of the Commune in Henry James's Paris

> Not that an urban vista is quite the same as a loved face, but it isn't
> quite different, either: the despoiled view was suddenly a toothless
> face, say, or suddenly preoccupied, or suddenly dead – to say noth-
> ing, even, of the historical implications surrounding that particular
> change of landscape.
>
> Eve Sedgwick, *Touching Feeling*

What would it mean not to see the remainders of history as they are
writ in space, but rather to *taste* them? To smell buried pasts simmer-
ing below the otherwise glassy surface of a cityscape? And finally, to
possess – and be *possessed* by – pasts that did not, in any real sense,
belong to us?

At least since what Bill Brown has termed its "literary-critical apo-
theosis" in the 1990s,[1] *The American Scene* has been the privileged site
to examine Henry James's fascination with – and affective responses
to – lost landmarks and "instant" ruins, landscapes of loss that have
come, in turn, to stand in for modernity, American-style.[2] While Brown
has suggested that "the most unnerving aspect of *The American Scene*
is the volubility of its buildings,"[3] I would add it is also James's response
to them. For such affecting and untimely absences – in particular, the
"ruthlessly suppressed birth-house" in Washington Square and the
unexpectedly vanished home in Ashburton Place – register for James
as tourist sights quite literally *felt* as much as seen (or, for that matter,
heard).[4] In the section entitled "The Lost Chord," he writes of the dis-
appearance of his Cambridge home, for example:

> I had been present, by the oddest hazard, at the very last moments of
> the victim in whom I was most interested; the act of obliteration had
> been swift, and if I had often seen how swiftly history could be made

I had doubtless never so felt that it could be unmade still faster. It
was as if the bottom had fallen out of one's own biography, and *one
plunged backward into space without meeting anything.*[5]

And as urban historian Nick Yablon has suggested, James "feels
these architectural losses so intensely and personally [that] they linger
on his mental map of the metropolis as absent presences, phantom
limbs representing a history 'amputated' from him."[6] James's uncannily embodied experience of both space and memory – or, rather, his
curiously Jamesian "historic sense" – has thus most often been read
as at once deeply personal and deeply national in scope, provoked by
memory sites bound up simultaneously with James's *own* past and
his reading of America's future.[7]

In this chapter, I turn instead to Henry James's Paris, and, in particular, the sights of and detours around the post-Commune ruins of Paris
in his writings, to chronicle his transformative reading of space and
uncanny connection to more broadly transnational sites of memory.[8]
Examining Strether's encounter with the "irremediable void" left by
the cleared-away ruins of the Tuileries Palace in *The Ambassadors* and
Hyacinth's ghostly tour of the barricades in *Princess Casamassima* in
light of James's curious formulation of the "aftertaste" of ruin in his
1872 letters and early sketches from Paris, I argue that James's visits
to – and meditations on – the "charred sites" and lost landmarks of
Paris should be read not as a return of the picturesque, but rather as
an intimate – indeed, *synesthetic* – indexing of "social space," of space
experienced, in Elizabeth Abel's formulation, as "a sphere of contes-
tation and negotiation through which multiple histories are enacted
and . . . produced."[9] But as we will see, the space of the Commune in
Henry James's Paris at once uncovers and restages another forgotten
transatlantic story: namely, the ways that the now-forgotten ruins of
Paris, and the traces of the Commune they came to stand in for, continued to texture American experience of the City of Light throughout the Gilded Age.[10] In resituating James's own fascination with this
Paris in ruins within the broader mass-cultural archive of American
returns to the scene of the Commune by way of pilgrimages to vanished landmarks and ruined buildings, I simultaneously aim to recover
the way these spatial remainders of the Commune came to function as
unlikely sites of memory in American culture, sustained by an ongoing
visual and discursive industry of memory. These sights – and, at times,
tastes – of Paris were every bit as densely mediated and deeply felt
as the annual Commune celebrations, pageants, and speeches staged
and recirculated in radical print and performance culture that I earlier

explored and which were simultaneously circulating in the US memory mediascape. Yet, as I show, the international feeling brokered by Americans' visceral fixation on Paris's lost landmarks was most often underwritten by an alternate sense of extra-national affiliation, a sensational possessiveness that archives conflicting postbellum memories of Paris as tourist site and revolutionary epicenter – and of what the Commune meant for Americans experiencing which city.

Landscapes of Loss, Terrains of Memory

Before examining James's early writing from Paris in ruins, I want to turn to the broader mass-cultural archive that textures them, for an essential context for understanding James's curiously embodied spatial register – not only in his early travel writings, but also, most particularly, in his later novels – lies in these popular mediums of memory: namely, the photography, periodical remembrances, tourist sketches, and spectacles of Paris in ruins (Fig. 4.1).

As I discussed in my opening chapter, the events of the Commune and its end made front-page headlines in local and national newspapers in the US and garnered significant coverage in the illustrated

Figure 4.1 "The Burning of Paris," July 1, 1871, 596, *Harper's Weekly*, Annex A, Forrestal, Princeton University Library.

weeklies. Paris's newly charred landscape became, in turn, an instant tourist destination. As historian Harvey A. Levenstein explains, "when the conservative troops finally fought their way into the city, [American] tourists followed hard on their heels, sniffing through the ruins."[11] Travel companies began arranging "ruin tours" a mere two weeks after what came to be known as the "Bloody Week." In July of 1871 Charles Dickens was among the tourists that flocked to the ruined Paris, documenting for his *All the Year Round* readers the industry that sprang up to hawk rubble-related memorabilia and maps of Paris "with all the recent burning coloured so as to represent real flames."[12] For those who could not afford to make the trip, illustrated weeklies like *Harper's*, *Frank Leslie's*, and *Every Saturday* provided "bird's-eye" views of the damage, as well as elegiac accounts of the damaged buildings and lost landmarks – thus allowing middle-class American readers to partake in the scene from the remove of their parlors. Foreign correspondents offered eyewitness accounts of the destruction in the newspapers, while French photographers took to the streets, capturing and exporting hundreds of images of "Paris in ruin" before the Third Republic cracked down on the circulation of Commune-related images.[13]

American appetite for experiencing this new Paris first-hand was such that New Yorkers could take "virtual tours" of the city aflame by way of stereopticon shows like "Paris en Feu," which debuted in New York in the autumn of 1871.[14] Ghostly traces of lost landmarks and charred landscape would figure in popular revivals of the panoramic spectacle "Paris by Night," later cyclorama shows that toured the US into the 1880s, and the traveling pyrotechnic spectacular, "Paris, from Empire to Commune," which debuted in Coney Island in 1891.[15] The ruins of Paris thus functioned – and were readily capitalized upon – as instant media sensation, tourist destination, and unlikely place of pilgrimage, a memory site topographically and textually constructed, kept alive in US memory not by commemorative plaques, monuments, or museums but rather by the ongoing circulation of panoramic spectacles, photographic albums, periodical illustrations, and travel sketches in the magazines.

But while middle- and upper-class Americans revisited the spectacle of the Commune's bloody end through the mass circulation of, and discourse on, these images of ruins, in reading about the unprecedented cost of capturing Paris – the thousands of "insurgents" killed in a week in the streets of the city Walter Benjamin would famously later dub the "capital of the nineteenth century" – they most frequently encountered ruined landscapes and editorial elegies to Paris's torn buildings and lost landmarks rather than images of dead or dying Communards in American periodicals,[16] despite the precedent for the photography of bodily ruin sparked in the preceding decade by Matthew Brady's Civil War photography and Gardner's *Sketch Book*.[17] In part, this emphasis of the camera and the press simply testifies to the difficulty of displaying the bodily toll of the "reconquering" of Paris, and the Third Republic's attempts to control the terrain of memory around that event. (Of the nearly 1,750 photographs registered with the Dépôt Légal between June and December 1871, for example, the vast majority concerned the ruins of Paris.[18]) As art historian Alisa Luxenberg evocatively elaborates, "Avoiding the potent and uneasy charge inherent in representations of bodily ruin, French photographers [of both the professional and amateur enthusiast variety] focused on architectural ruins, using the technique of redescription, transferring and transforming the war 'wounds' from bodies to buildings, skin to stone." [19] Such a slippage between building and body is doubly suggestive, I think, imbricating not only the ways in which the image of the Parisian ruins stood in for, and often marked the erasure of, the bodies of the Communards, with the cinders of revolution in turn supplanting the revolution itself in the landscape of French cultural memory, but also the ways in which the "wounds" of the Commune came to be transferred from the sight of bodies to the sites of lost or charred landmarks in mainstream American memory.

Tourists Among the (Uncannily New) Ruins

American foreign correspondents, tourists, and French commentators alike found themselves drawn to Paris's newly minted ruins (Fig. 4.2), and most remarked on the unimaginable *scale* of the damage. An unsigned article in the June 16, 1871, *New York Times* relates, for example:

> I own that before I came here I had expected to find the magnitude of the disaster had been exaggerated in the excitement of the moment. Having seen the ruins, it seems to me that no account I have read as yet has given any adequate idea of the extent to which Paris has suffered from fire.[20]

A year later, Baedeker's guidebook would note that "there is hardly a single public building, or street, or park in Paris which does not bear

PARIS-SPECTACLE — Les étrangers visitant nos ruines.

Figure 4.2 G. Marichal d'après Daniel Vierge, "Paris spectacle – Les Étrangers visitant nos ruines," June 24, 1871, 8, *La Presse illustrée*, Musée d'art et d'histoire Saint-Denis (France). © Tous droits réservés.

numerous traces of the recent devastation, or to which some melancholy story does not attach."[21] But the *sight* these ruins presented often proved oddly illegible, or even deeply uncanny, for visitors. Like the Commune itself, the charred landscape seemed, to many, both out of and ahead of its time – "instant" relics vertiginously poised as at once from the past and the future.[22] The French writer Théophile Gautier, for example, would write of his tour of the city in the immediate aftermath of the fires: "it seems as if *two thousand years* have passed in a night," [as if Paris were] "'a dead city' reduced to 'some scattered debris on the banks of the deserted Seine.'"[23]

Gautier's account is striking not only for the way that it figures Paris as having moved not only 2,000 years into the future – leaving behind only ruins – but also 2,000 years backwards, as well – thus leaving us with a scene more recognizable as antiquity than as either modernity or sci-fi futurity. Five years later, Laura Rees, a young Philadelphian recounting her continental travels in *We Four, Where We Went and What We Saw in Europe*, describes her (by then requisite) visit to the Tuileries ruins with a similar blend of "untimely" nostalgia, insisting that while the palace "received its death-blow in 1871," the ruins left in its stead "were not made by Time!"[24] The poem she includes with her travel sketch echoes Gautier's sense that what made these modern ruins most affecting was precisely their uneasy temporal positioning – a product of a too-recent past but figured as oddly outside of time altogether. Where Gautier, however, in gazing on the smoking ruins, saw *only* a dead city – a city whose near-evaporation stands in for or effaces the way we might see Paris at the moment of his tour not so much as a "dead city" but rather as a city of the dead, with thousands of bodies quite literally still littering its streets – Rees, anticipating James's visit to his vanished house, chooses instead to personify the ruins themselves, mourning their loss as if they, not unlike a person, were gone too soon: "All that was grand was prostrate there/Wrecked in its Glowing Prime."[25]

If Gautier and Rees's respective travel sketches help to recover the ways in which the Parisian ruinscape aroused fascination precisely because they were freshly made and immediately commodified ("Not made by time/Not made by history"), their accounts also bring into relief the way that these ruins were, most notably in American accounts of them, so often in turn imagined as a wounded, victimized body. Such a form of description – I am tempted to say *possession* – signaled an extra-national loss that came to seem (or rather, to feel), for many Americans, strangely *personal*. In my reading, the engraving in Figure 4.2 illustrates – even as it pokes fun at – the tourists' fascination with these newly minted ruins, but also suggests a certain ambivalence towards these "foreigners visiting *our* ruins," an ambivalence that registers a certain anxiety about the threat of dispossession.

In his groundbreaking study, *Untimely Ruins: An Archaeology of Urban Modernity, 1819–1919*, Yablon persuasively argues that America's nineteenth-century fascination with urban ruins – most specifically, *its own* – was rooted in the experience of its uniquely "instant" ruins:

> The actual ruins forged by the great fires that periodically ravaged its cities, by the scorched-earth tactics of General Sherman's rapid advance through the South, or by the equally swift and destructive swings of the capitalist economy, were all *instantaneous* and largely unanticipated, and thus radically different from those formed over time.[26]

Yet it is, I argue, a similarly "untimely" quality that helps make the Commune ruins such an immediate transatlantic sensation and tourist attraction, and in turn such a sight to be conspicuously revisited. While images such as "Ruins in Charleston" no doubt textured the way Americans read the photography of Paris in ruins, scenes from the Great Chicago Fire of 1871 were immediately likened to the "wrecks of Paris" rather than to those of Southern cities, and no explicit connections to America's Civil War ruinscape are drawn in US periodical coverage of the post-Commune ruins. Such symptomatic returns to Paris's broken landscape would seem, then, always to stand in place – and perhaps facilitate the forgetting – of the postbellum US's own war-ravaged cities and landscapes of loss.[27]

Visiting European ruins certainly was, in itself, nothing new, but the sight of Paris *en ruines* presented a far different (and often far more discomfiting) picture for American tourists.[28] Neither a product of "time" nor an already well-trod ruinscape, their fate and their meaning were not immediately reducible to standard Grand Tour narratives of the picturesque. Put simply, the "scars" in the landscape and the body politic were still fresh: images of the pétroleuse and the "savage" Communards needed to be summoned to keep them in check, effectively cordoning off memories of the Commune's suppression and scenes of fraternal urban warfare and replacing them with images of a scarred cityscape.

The ruins of the Tuileries Palace were the only remainders of the Bloody Week left to stand for over a decade in their charred state, and quickly became a pivotal Parisian tourist-pilgrimage sight and emblem of what one American writer would describe as the "gashes and scars" in Paris's landscape.[29] Enshrined in American memory by way of ongoing periodical coverage in the form of commemorative histories of the site and dozens of tourist sketch-pilgrimages that appeared in a variety of high- and lowbrow American periodicals, the Tuileries largely came to stand in for the ruins of Paris; even more importantly, for many observers the Tuileries ruins seemed most acutely to testify to the crimes of the Commune. They thus function as a key site for considering mainstream American memory of – and affective responses to – the post-Commune terrain of Paris. "The pale ghost of the Palace that had died by fire" (as James will describe it in *The Tragic Muse*) will, in other words, become so familiar a sight to Americans that Strether's requisite return to the site in *The Ambassadors* seems highly overdetermined.[30] We will return to this scene more particularly later in the chapter; for now, I want simply to highlight that Strether's return – and more particularly, the historic sense awakened by the sight of the palace that was not there – revisits and crucially reworks a well-trod mass-cultural scene.

With no little emotion, a writer for the *New York Evangelist* thus reports of his 1881 return to Paris after an eighteen-year absence:

Nothing saddens me more than to see the havoc wrought by the wild beasts of the Commune . . . Every day, almost, I pass what were the Tuileries; now, except at the ends, a blackened mass of crumbling ruins; I look across the Seine and there are *the marks of the same fiendish fingers*.[31]

The Philadelphia writer (and good friend of Henry James), Sarah B. Wister, echoes a similar sentiment in *Lippincott's*: "It is not easy to say how long it will be before the deft and diligent hand can heal and hide the gashes and scars of that spring of 1871."[32] While both writers register the physical remainders of revolution as literal wounds, the marks of "fiendish fingers," Wister's figuring of the ruined Paris works at once to conjure the "gashes and scars" of the landscape and to imagine a future moment when such wounds will finally have healed. Yet James's account of the aftertaste of history powerfully suggests that the past will continue to speak, whether or not we see the physical remains of it in front of us.

Certainly, the aim of the French government was to remove any visual remainders of the Commune and the Bloody Week – starting with the Commune's proclamations on city walls,[33] but debates about what to do with the Tuileries ruins curiously raged in France throughout the 1870s, and garnered continuing interest (and copy) in a variety of US periodicals, from architectural digests and general interest journals to children's magazines. An 1883 piece in *Youth's Companion*, reporting on the Tuileries' expected removal, lamented, for example, that

it will not be very long before the last vestige of the ancient palace of the Tuileries, at Paris, will have disappeared . . . Since [it was burned by the Communards] it has stood gaunt and grim, in the midst of the most beautiful quarter of the city, a mass of charred and blackened ruins.[34]

The American humor magazine, *Puck*, adopted a more sanguine take on the matter:

American tourists will be glad to hear that the French Chamber of Deputies has ordered the complete demolition of the ruins of the Tuileries. There will no longer be occasion to flounder about in the endeavor to get within pronouncing distance of the word.[35]

A headline in *The Washington Post* suggested simply "The Tuileries Doomed," its accompanying article emphasizing that clearing away the ruins would leave behind a more gaping problem in the landscape:

> Unquestionably the ruins in their present state are an eye-sore, and recall somewhat too vividly the *année terrible*. But, as M. Haussmann pointed out to his colleagues in the chamber, when the eye-sore is gone, there will remain something yet more unsightly behind.[36]

As the "Tuileries Doomed" article already intimates, the clearing away of the Tuileries ruins in 1883 marks neither their end nor the finale of American fascination with the sight of them. Indeed, American periodicals helped to keep the memory site alive as a visual and discursive landscape, and in turn a "visitable" lost landmark, by way of a number of retrospective features that recounted the history of the now-vanished palace and its savage "death" at the hands of the Communards. "Boston Brahmin" Oliver Wendell Holmes, Sr., noted of his 1884 return to the site where the Tuileries once stood, "The recollection of the sorrow, the shame, and the agony she [that is, the Palace] passed through since I left her picking her way on the arm of the Citizen King . . . rose before me sadly as I looked upon the high board fence [surrounding the remaining ruins]."[37] A decade later, the highbrow *Century* magazine would publish an article, "The Tuileries Under the Second Empire," which not only echoed Holmes's formulation of the "agony" the Tuileries had undergone, but also weirdly figured the actual death of the building for its readers some two decades after its "demise."

In her nostalgic but otherwise anodyne reminiscences of court life at the Tuileries during the Second Empire, Anna Bicknell thus elaborates at length on the final hours of the Tuileries Palace, insistently (and uncannily) describing the building's destruction as a kind of execution:

> But the Tuileries was soon to perish in a catastrophe recalling memories of Nineveh and Babylon. Bergeret, the communist leader, had declared that the Tuileries would be in ashes before he left it, and he kept his word . . . In this dreadful task he was assisted by a butcher named Benot. During the afternoon of that fatal day, omnibuses and carts loaded with gunpowder and petroleum repeatedly crossed the court of the Louvre and the Place du Carrousel . . . When all was ready, with the delight of a madman, Benot set fire to the building. At a few minutes to nine the great clock stopped, under the influence of the fire . . . It was an awful but magnificent spectacle.[38]

Bicknell's sensational account effectively displaces the violence of General MacMahon and the French government troops onto the Communards by emphasizing the "butchery" involved in their burning of the Tuileries. The Communard Benot, in her hyberbolic account, thus gleefully watches his "dreadful task" – and the Tuileries' clock, not unlike a heart, comes to a stop as the flames ravage the building. The horror of the "catastrophe" is put to a happy end in Bicknell's account by MacMahon, who "saves" the Louvre from the hands of the Commune, hands that already "defiled" the Tuileries before they had burned it by having "fetes" inside it. What is most striking about this account of the Tuileries, though, is not simply the way it so vividly literalizes the wounded landscape so many Americans found in Paris, but rather the way it so effectively crystallizes the intensity of the loss many Americans came to associate with Paris's ruined landscape. In that sense it bears out Marx's prescient contention in *The Civil War in France* that "the bourgeoisie of the whole world, which looks complacently upon the wholesale massacre after the battle, is convulsed by horror at the desecration of brick and mortar."[39] For that sensation of loss – and "convulsion by horror" – would, in turn, most often work to bury the memory of that other history of the Bloody Week, the spectacular death toll, and, as James would put it, "the fresh made graves" in Paris.[40]

History's Aftertaste

In "Henry James, Cultural Critic," Pierre A. Walker draws attention to the new accessibility of James's early travel sketches (thanks to the Library of America publication of his *Collected Travel Writings*) and calls on Jamesian criticism to attend to these oft-neglected, harder-to-categorize writings.[41] Yet James Buzard's influential 1993 *PMLA* piece, "A Continent of Pictures: Reflections on the 'Europe' of Nineteenth-Century Tourists," was an early exception to the trend towards privileging *The American Scene* to the exclusion of James's earlier travel writings. In it, Buzard shrewdly suggests the ways in which the young James repeatedly invokes, only to subtly undermine, "the time-honored conventions of picturesqueness" in these early sketches.[42] Deftly drawing our attention to moments of lingering textual tension and ambivalence, Buzard ultimately charts, however, the persistence of what he terms "picturesque politics" – the politics of, in other words, a status quo amenable to the persistence of the picturesque itself – across James's travel writings and into his late novels. Even more importantly, he argues that "in the nearly four dozen essays collected in *Transatlantic Sketches* and *Portraits of Places*, 'Europe' hovers before the young James as a 'poetic' or 'fairy precinct' in which life, properly organized, tends toward a succession of lovely, poignant or sublime pictures."[43]

And yet the young James's sightseeing tour of "the burnt-out ruins and barricades of the Commune" on his first day in Paris in June 1872 would seem a singular interruption in this otherwise fairy precinct.[44] Unlike his French contemporaries, Gautier and Goncourt, who, in Daryl Lee's phrase, see the "open ruins" of the Commune only in terms of "ruinist ideas from earlier in the century,"[45] James finds in Paris a landscape of loss at once more unassimilable and more modern, an already "mediated" space that nevertheless cannot be neatly mapped onto either a charming sketch or sublime picture – indeed, a sight that cannot "speak" and cannot, in turn, generate for James such a sketch. Put simply, while the picturesque ruins of Chester or Rome might allow James to imagine a world where places might become, for the tourist observer, simply pictures, where the ruins themselves always already signify art, his encounter in Paris would seem precisely to interrupt the neatness of this picturesque narrative, for in Paris, James finds a landscape that he does not so much see as *sense*.

In the 1872 sketch he titles "The Parisian Stage," James details his most direct spatial encounter with (and detours around) the Commune:

> I shall never forget a certain evening in early summer when, after a busy, dusty, weary day in the streets, staring at the charred ruins and finding in all things the vague aftertaste of gunpowder, I repaired to the Theatre Français to listen to Molière's "Mariage Forcé" and Alfred de Musset's "Il ne Faut Jurer de Rien." The entertainment seemed to my travel-tired brain what a perfumed bath is to one's weary limbs, and I sat in a sort of languid ecstasy of contemplation and wonder – wonder that the tender flower of poetry and art should bloom again so bravely over blood-stained pavements and fresh made graves.[46]

On the face of it, the passage neatly anticipates readings of the "lesson" Hyacinth Robinson draws in Paris – the consolation, indeed, the triumph of art against (or even born out of) the ruin of history – and James's own languid ecstasy in – or perverse pleasure from – the scenes of devastation before him, but while the theater's ministrations no doubt soothe James's "travel-tired brain," the passage suggests that his tour of the "charred ruins" has not, even in the theater, entirely escaped him. The spectacular visibility of the ruins is, however, synesthetically marked for James not as a sight (or even an afterimage) but rather as a taste – "the vague aftertaste of gunpowder" that shadows the landscape.[47] And James's suggestive evocation of gunpowder, in turn, occasions not a lingering sense of its smell or sound – remainders of a figurative past presence – but rather their aftertaste – as if the city is (and will be) shadowed by its presence, the "aftertaste" of ruin, even after the most outward signs of it – the ruins themselves – have been cleared away. Even more intriguingly, the bodies and bloodshed otherwise occluded by the ruinscape resurface in this moment, for even as the ruins lead James to turn away from "the vague aftertaste of gunpowder," the art James enjoys on the Parisian stage itself is here constituted by – and cannot help but recall, if only so as to cover over – the blood on the Parisian pavements that the theatergoer so readily seeks to forget. The "wounded" landscape thus awakens in James a palpable historical sense, or more precisely a multi-sensory overload. Unlike the tourist-in-ruin who mourns only lost landmarks and butchered buildings, James seems, in this uncanny aftertaste of memory, to actually re-embody (or re-animate) the bloody traces of the past.[48]

The significance of James's brief recollection of the *sensation* of the Commune ruins is perhaps best underscored by their notable absence in his letters home from that same early summer day. In his June 28–9 missive to his parents, for example, James writes of his brief stop in Paris and tour of the city, emphasizing its unchanged quality:

> I find the place very delightful, too; surprisingly, so, for I had expected to receive all sorts of painful impressions and to feel the shadow of Bismarck and the Commune lying on everything. But to the casual eye, *there are no shadows anywhere*, and Paris is still the perfection of brightness and neatness and form and taste.[49]

The letter is curious for what it leaves out, for the way that it so insistently clings to the idea of Paris as "the perfection of brightness and neatness and form and taste" and so assertively claims that nothing, on the surface, has changed in the city, despite the ruins that were everywhere around him and everywhere being written home about. Peter Brooks offers us, in his excellent study of Henry James in the Paris of 1875–6, the prospect of a James on whom something could be lost and it is tempting to read the young James's omission of the visitable and visible past that is right in front of his nose as an instance of curious, even willful, oversight, not unlike Strether's failure in *The Ambassadors* to see what is most plainly staring him in the face. Before we take James to task, however, for seeing only what he wants to see, or worse, for delighting in overlooking the blighted Paris all around him, it seems worth noting that James's disavowal of the scars of history written on the surface of the landscape also oddly anticipates his impressions of the "charred ruins" he claims not to see. The mere anticipation of the sight of Paris in ruins already provokes in him a historic sense marked by sensory overload – a feeling that his body will become the surface upon which the memory will be written – indeed, tasted – the sight imagined to leave a "painful impression"[50] and the spectral presence of the past not registered for James as the very physical sight but rather imagined to be a spectral presence "lying on everything."

This specter of the Commune resurfaces far more pronouncedly in James's September 22 letter to William, but he initially seems to overlook the "gashes and scars" in the landscape all around him. Unlike his fellow tourists, he laments that "Paris continues to be very pleasant, but doesn't become interesting. You get tired of a place which you can call nothing but *charmant*."[51] Yet he goes onto write, "The want of comprehension of the real moral situation of France leaves one unsatisfied, too. Beneath all this neatness and coquetry, you seem to smell the Commune suppressed, but seething."[52] James thus seems to suggest that the history right under his nose is something he smells more than sees, and even more crucially, that everyone else is overlooking what is right in front of them. In other words, in overlooking the ruins and instead "smelling" the Commune's spectral presence below the surface, James not only senses that the revolution is not dead, but also anticipates that, even when the visible "gashes and scars of the spring of 1871" have been cleared away, the revolution will continue to simmer below the surface of the landscape. The past otherwise so completely obliterated, the bodies otherwise so utterly forgotten, the revolution so thoroughly routed nevertheless shadow the landscape, lurking "beneath" the surface but nevertheless almost sensible. However, what sort of subterranean "historic sense" is James invoking here? What sort of refusal to "see," which in turn becomes an injunction to smell what is right in front of you, to feel (or revisit) the impression of a past that refuses to *die*?

The Politics of Detours

To begin to tackle those questions, I turn now to James's invocations of – and even more intriguingly, his detours around – the Commune in *The American* and *Princess Casamassima*, and what they reveal about James's reading of both urban space and spatial memory. At least since the publication of Jonah Raskin's 1965 *American Quarterly* article, "Henry James and the French Revolution," it has been something of a commonplace in Jamesian scholarship that 1789 was the revolution always on Henry's mind, or, rather, "the most important year in history,"[53] for, as Raskin points out, James's fascination with it surfaces again and again throughout his texts.[54] But while 1789 is the revolution about which James no doubt speaks most often and most explicitly, the visitable remainders and strange "aftertaste" of 1871 pointedly circulate through his novels, often shadowing (and being overshadowed by) James's more "speakable" fascination.

Although *The American* was written during his 1875–6 tenure in Paris, and coincides with his dispatches on the French artistic and social scene for the *Herald Tribune*, dispatches that demonstrate a keen awareness of the contemporary political scene, James nevertheless conspicuously avoids the specter of the Commune (and its visitable remainders) by antedating the novel, sending his protagonist, Christopher Newman, to the Paris of the Empire, a Paris as yet unscarred by the Franco-Prussian war and ferocious "fraternal" urban warfare.[55] While this temporal relocation allows James to present Paris *as it was* (or as so many tourists wished it might be), a move not unlike that of the Impressionists who painted over the scars of the Commune by painting Paris *as if it were* (already, once again) *whole*, I wonder if we might read the move not simply as willful forgetting? For its detour provides, as John Carlos Rowe has suggested, insight into precisely the political scene – in particular, the forces of monarchism and republicanism – that will come to a boil in 1871.[56]

Princess Casamassima, written a decade later, seems then, on the face of it, James's most explicit and most spectacular engagement with the memory of the Commune: its history is briefly recounted in the text, its memory is invoked by the novel's radical underground, and its most visible remainder – the Communard refugee, M. Poupin – plays no small a role in its protagonist's life.[57] Yet, even here, the head-on engagement is marked by displacement and disavowal: the revolutionary scene is transplanted to London, and M. Poupin's revolutionary credentials as a Communard are markedly rerouted through 1848.[58] "He was," writes James, "a Republican of the old-fashioned sort, of the note of 1848, humanitarian and idealistic, infinitely addicted to fraternity and equality, and inexhaustibly surprised and exasperated at finding so little enthusiasm for them in the land of his exile": the Commune's entrance into the text is thus dressed, as it were, in the now safer garb of an earlier revolution.[59] Even more pointedly, it is also the text that would seem most assiduously to efface 1871 from the landscape of Paris during Hyacinth Robinson's pleasure tour of the city.

Not unlike James himself in 1872, Hyacinth travels to Paris in the early 1880s, and finds no scars in the built world, no painful impressions or reminders of either the Commune or the terrible reprisals that followed it – despite the earlier evocation of them in the novel and their ongoing presence in mass-cultural memory. James's protagonist–tourist is dazzled instead by the crowds, the cafés, the shops, and "the general magnificence of Paris on a perfect evening in June"[60]: "he recognized, he greeted, with a thousand palpitations, the seat of his maternal ancestors – was proud to be associated with so much of the superb, so many proofs of a civilization that had *no visible rough spots.*"[61] And though Poupin provides him with contact information for fellow Communards still alive in Paris, the "radical" bookbinder notably fails to pay them a visit. Hyacinth, by this point in the novel, has begun to show a change of heart, a falling away from revolutionary principles, and sees no reason to "pretend that he cared for what they cared for in the same way as they cared for it."[62]

In short, Hyacinth goes to Paris and finds it simply "splendid,"[63] but what interests me about this visit is not the way that falling in love with Paris seems so coterminous with falling away from radical politics, but rather what Hyacinth's walks suggest about James's reading of history written in space. While Mark Seltzer persuasively argues that *The Princess Casamassima* is "a novel about spectatorship, about seeing and being seen," it is also a novel about what lies beneath and beyond the visible.[64] Hyacinth is, for example, notably accompanied on his sightseeing tours of the city by "that vague yet vivid personage," his ghostly grandfather, a fallen '48er: "the pair had now roamed together through all the museums and gardens, through the principal churches (the republican martyr was very good-natured about all of this), through the passages and arcades, up and down the great avenues."[65] The "republican martyr" consents to the new Paris "good-naturedly"; there is no hint of "the ecstasy of the barricade" still lingering around him.[66] But while this might seem simply a further detour away from politics, Hyacinth's refusal to see the scars of

1871 – to see anything but a "splendid Paris" – makes his visit to the site that is not there – the (no longer visible) barricades of 1848 – all the more remarkable: "Wondering, repeatedly, where the barricade on which his grandfather fell had been erected, he at last satisfied himself (but I am unable to trace the process of the induction) that it had bristled across the Rue Saint-Honoré, very near to the church of Saint-Roch."[67] While the barricade that is not there functions here as a kind of tourist site, part of the list that Hyacinth seems to cross off as he tours Paris, it also points, however fleetingly, to the possibility that two contents can occupy one space, a site where space – not unlike the barricade that bristles – can be *felt* as much as found.[68] And Hyacinth's trip to the barricades anticipates Strether's visit to the palace that is not there in *The Ambassadors*, even as it draws our attention to the "irremediable voids" in the landscape and the layers that lie beneath them, the spaces in which more than one history – or, rather, more than one Paris – spectacularly collide.

Landmarks and Marked Absences

Cynthia Ozick's artful 2010 reworking of *The Ambassadors* is acclaimed for, among other things, its deft act of relocation, retaining its Parisian setting but offering us an altogether changed place. As Matthew Shaer puts it in his review for *Book Forum*, "*Foreign Bodies* . . . can be read as a kind of corrective, written with the benefit of hindsight: This is what war did to the Eden of *The Ambassadors*. Behold the shattered city."[69] While I do not want to equate the Gilded Age fixation with "Paris in ruin" with the lingering "fumes of the death camps" that Ozick recaptures in her portrait of Europe circa 1953, the prelapsarian image of Paris that Shaer invokes in relation to *The Ambassadors* altogether forgets the aftertaste of ruin – and uncanny sites of memory – haunting both James's Paris and his 1903 novel. The most salient reminder of that ruined Paris lay on the grounds of the Tuileries, the only remainders of 1871 left to stand for over a decade in their charred state. As we have seen, while these remains had been cleared away long before Strether's return to Paris in *The Ambassadors*, pilgrimages to this lost landmark and remembrances of the vanished palace continued to garner copy in a variety of American magazines into the 1890s.

Not unlike James himself, Strether arrives at a moment when that turbulent history literally speaks to him from Paris's scars and empty spaces, from ancient streets razed to create its *grands boulevards* and no less so from its missing palaces. If it is a voice that haunts Strether throughout the novel – a vague disquiet that, like the relationship between Chad and Mme. de Vionnet, cannot be directly articulated – it is nonetheless a voice that speaks of a past that has played upon the streets even as it has been erased – one might say literally – from the very geography of the city. Much as it does in Balzac, Paris opens up to Strether on foot; as Edwin Sill Fussell rightly notes, "[our hero] seldom takes cabs and the Métro never."[70] In his walks, James's flâneur stumbles upon, and sometimes would even appear to pass by, this history that seems at once scrawled upon the streets and echoing from them. Such topographical lacunae are, however, suggestive, resurfacing in provocative and provocatively unspeakable ways. In the course of nearly 500 pages, then, not a single mention of the Commune surfaces in James's text, yet, as Fussell points out in respect of the novel more generally, "*The Ambassadors* is the world's great testimony to the art of leaving things out (as of course also to the art of putting things in, without which inclusion the leaving out would have no relevance)."[71] And so it is with its treatment of the Commune: what is left out only makes what is left in all the more striking.

James stations Strether a mere minute's walk from the Tuileries gardens, the rue de Rivoli, and the Pococks' hotel. Although the text does not care to name his hotel, it is nevertheless one located along a touristic side-street that is exactly mapped out for us; as Strether reflects on the figure on Chad's balcony, the "sole attenuation of his excluded state was his vision of the small, admittedly secondary hotel in the by-street from the Rue de la Paix, in which [Maria Gostrey's] solicitude for his purse had placed him."[72] Although the text specifies that he makes at least one trip to the Tuileries, and several to Sarah Pocock's hotel, from whose balcony the garden can be seen, it falls silent on one particular point: the unavoidable landmark standing between Strether and the rue de Rivoli, for the rue de la Paix curves off the avenue de l'Opéra in one steadfast spoke directed firmly at the Tuileries, and in the middle of this chic commercial street is the Vendôme Column, elevated – at 142 ft. – to such a height that it literally dominates all progress between the rue de Rivoli and the bustle of the Opéra. None too surprisingly, the column found its way onto the itinerary of travel bibles like *Baedeker's*; *Paris in a Week*, a guide put out as a "detailed programme" for British and American tourists and published shortly after Strether's trip, noting the Vendôme's "imposing appearance," begins its tour of the city by way of that very spot.[73] (James himself claims it as the site of his first memory of Paris, glimpsed in his second year from the vantage point of a pram.)[74]

This somewhat begs the question of just how Strether might have missed it in passing, yet to overlook the column, or even simply failing to mention it altogether, seems itself an intricate oversight. For such a silence gestures back to the landmark's highly politicized past. Although it was rebuilt in 1874, well before Strether's return, its unmarked presence in the topography of the text summons the specter of the 1871 destruction of the monument, the moment when, amidst much celebration, the Communards – reading the column as a sign intimately bound up in imperial ambition and authoritarian rule – toppled it to the ground. This staged erasure of the Vendôme – condensing within in it the fall of the Second Empire – was regarded by one particularly fierce critic of the Commune as nothing short of an attack on history itself, but the fall of the Column was not so much a destruction of history as a spatial marker for the crossroads of it; in Ross's suggestive formulation, "An awareness of social space, as the example of the Vendôme column makes clear, always entails an encounter with history – or better, a choice of histories."[75] If an encounter with the Colonne Vendôme is a confrontation with such a choice of histories, its re-entry into the landscape marked a none-too-subtle erasure of the Commune and the choice it implied for the city, but not to see the Column – to forget or even to fall silent in the face of it – is no less an encounter with social space. Indeed, the lacuna marks Strether's first encounter with history as it plays out in space, even as the landmark's non-appearance in the novel opens a textual gap that will be filled in by yet another encounter with history as it is written on the landscape. This silent, unremarked-upon landmark will be, in other words, coupled with a none-too-silent marked absence in Paris's terrain, and what opens up to him by its remarked-upon absence is a shadowy signifier that will not – indeed, cannot – be named.

Strether encounters the Tuileries Palace, or rather, the empty site where it once stood, on his second day in Paris while strolling with an "accidental air" through the city, a bout of flânerie that forestalls a meeting with the first batch of letters from "his chief correspondent."[76] His trip to the Tuileries is similarly underscored by its own deferment, with the text leading us first "across the Tuileries and the River, [where he] indulged more than once . . . in a sudden pause before the book-stalls of the quay," before seamlessly returning Strether back to the gardens.[77] In proceeding analeptically past it before folding back into it, then, the narrative delays his moment of arrest before the space that was the palace, much as Strether determinedly delays the pause that will bring him face to face with the letters.

Yet that initial suspension of Strether's visit to the Tuileries seems particularly unwarranted, for in the gardens, all would seem to be sweetness and light – the scene itself picturesque to the point of its becoming almost paradigmatic, its figures themselves predictable as the hands of a finely wound clock. Strether, no doubt occupying the role of tourist, looks, then, for Paris and finds it in a multitude of senses, in the sound of a morning that, like a well-tuned clock, strikes its "cheerful notes," in the smell that is so redolent of the morning that is said to be sprinkled before being inhaled, and finally in the sight of French life that is not simply well ordered but itself a kind of testimony to order under the ensign of the military and the church – with the milder steps of the "straightpacing priest" meeting "the sharp ones of a . . . soldier."[78] The staging of this scene of well-ordered Frenchness – everything in its place, as it were – is likened by Strether not only to a clock but also to a kind of open-air restaurant: "the air had a taste as of something mixed with art, something that presented nature as a white-capped master-chef."[79]

Critics such as Roxana Pana-Oltean have found in this moment proof that Strether-as-tourist never encounters a Paris beyond that of the picturesque,[80] yet the artful Paris that Strether initially finds in the gardens is ultimately shattered by his encounter – through the experience of the missing palace – with Paris as social space, with sightseeing recast as rereading the lost landmark as a charged site of historical memory. All, in other words, is not in its place, finely tuned and finely wrought, and in a turn away from the picturesque, a turn away from Strether-as-tourist, it is the nothing that is palpably not there that painfully arrests his attention:

> The palace was gone, Strether remembered the palace; and when he gazed into the irremediable void of its site the historic sense in him might have been freely at play – the play under which in Paris indeed it so often winces like a touched nerve. He filled out the scene with dim symbols and scenes.[81]

The palace is gone, and while Strether clearly remembers it, with characteristic narrative opacity, we are told nothing of where it went or how it got there. A tourist in ruins – but in ruins that are now no longer visible, Strether is transfixed by the "irremediable void," forced to fill in the gap of the burned-down palace with "dim symbols and scenes" of what was. To do so relies not only on his own past – his own memories of seeing it as a sightseer – but also on that of the palace, a past that the text can dimly gesture to but wills not to explain.[82] That the landmark's absence is in turn marked by a wound that can never be alleviated is, however, pronounced – as is the way in which the memory – "the historic sense" – set in motion by the void is suggested to be itself a kind of violence; whereas the narrative is reluctant to speak affirmatively of what exactly Strether feels in the face of it, resorting to the hypothetical – "the historic sense in him *might* have been freely at play" – it nevertheless concludes that such a play of memory is palpable, as if the memory itself plays out directly on the body, "winc[ing] like a touched nerve" in the face of such a sight. As Strether fills in the gap opened by the palace that is both present-in-memory and absent-in-fact, those "dim symbols and scenes" with which he does so leave everything unsaid – namely, the history Strether confronts in the scene of the palace – while the very onslaught of such scenes nonetheless summons that very history that remains otherwise opaque and unspoken. As Hazel Hutchison points out, "*The Ambassadors* is all about vision, but it is the ability of vision to suggest or reveal something beyond the visible that is its strongest theme."[83]

Strether's first tumble into this curiously visceral reading of Paris's past is a particularly suggestive one, for the burned palace is a remarkably densely coded site of historical memory. Its remarked-upon absence in the text cannot but recall the fires that leveled it, yet it is simultaneously these fires that come, metaleptically, to stand in for the Commune itself in transnational memory – revolution subsumed into its fiery aftermath. Indeed, as we have seen, representations of the palace's destruction would be repeatedly used to illustrate the "crimes of the Commune," and in the politics of memory, the summary executions of Communards in the Tuileries would be buried beneath the weight of this lost landmark, the palace that is not there becoming the most salient of spatial signifiers.

The fires that are at once evident – etched in, as it were, by the missing palace – and yet left unremarked upon in the gardens thus find another entry into the text, erupting from an otherwise innocuous nighttime view of the City of Light. During Strether's last night vigil – his long waiting up for Chad – Paris spreads out before him, from the interior of Chad's rooms, no longer as an iridescent jewel but rather most markedly as a well-lit landscape: "The night was hot and heavy and the single lamp sufficient; the great flare of the lighted city, rising high, spending itself afar, played up from the Boulevard and, through the vague vista of the successive rooms, brought objects into view."[84] No doubt the city is here most immediately lit up by the gas lamps for which it was most famous, but the description of the city evokes the specter of a landscape devoured by light, with "its great flare . . . rising high, spending itself afar" – a Paris, in other words, consumed in one vast flame. Pana-Oltean thus argues that "Strether . . . sees [in the great flare] an already painted 'city in flames' or 'urbs incensa' composition, and his vista too is a *trompe l'oeil*."[85] Yet for all that she might wish simply to re-inscribe – or, perhaps, re-inter – the scene as silent landscape, confining it to the rubric of the picturesque, her reading falls curiously short. To gesture, in other words, even in general terms to the genre of "city in flames" without striking some memory of the Commune seems an oddly glaring oversight, falling silent, as it does, on the way in which such paintings would directly recall Paris and those May days when, very literally, the city was awash in flame – and, moreover, the way in which those days came to be represented on canvas. (A famous example of such a representation, Numa fils's *Paris Incendié* (1871), is itself a kind of trompe l'œil; originally a photogravure, it was retouched and recolored to dramatically highlight the conflagration of Paris. Yet the moment it arrests is nevertheless a sweeping horizon of the cityscape, whose flare, as in Strether's view of it, "spends itself afar.")

The historical nerve that winces under an "assault of images" in Gloriani's garden and which trails him even into the deepest recesses of Parisian interiors is one that is, again, given to us as "easily so struck in Paris,"[86] and this is brought into further relief by Strether's own increasing sense of the cost of stops – of sightseeing – in the city:

> Poor Strether had at this very moment to recognize that wherever one paused in Paris the imagination reacted before one could stop it. This perpetual reaction put a price, if one would, on pauses; but it piled up consequences until there was scarce room to pick one's steps among them.[87]

Indeed, this touched nerve is keenly felt for Strether, for he reacts to Paris much as he reacts to the Tuileries and the home of Gloriani – sensually – and is thereby often overwhelmed. He does not, in fact, so much see Paris as experience it, taking in the "charged iridescent air" of the Louvre even as he seems able quite literally to taste it: "The Paris evening in short was, for Strether, in the very taste of the soup . . . in the pleasant coarse texture of the napkin, and the crunch of the thick crusted bread."[88]

But if Paris is consumable, it is in turn all-consuming, its landscape insinuating itself on his body. Like his visit to the Tuileries, Strether's walks are textured by multi-sensory overload, the constant hum of something that Strether can displace, if not formally acknowledge:

> It was the evening hour, but daylight was long now and Paris more than ever penetrating. The scent of flowers was in the streets, he had the whiff of violets perpetually in his nose, and he had attached himself to sounds and suggestions, vibrations of the air . . . a far off hum . . . a voice calling, replying, somewhere and as full of tone as an actor's in a play.[89]

The crowd, the past, the hum overtake him as readily as the smell of the violets that penetrates his nostrils, eventually putting such a premium on pauses that he is compelled to keep walking: "all voices had grown thicker and meant more things, they crowded in on him as he moved about – it was the way they sounded that wouldn't let him be still."[90]

The hum of the city comes, however, to be transposed from the terrain of the city onto the body of Sarah Pocock, with the effect she strikes on Strether intensifying and embodying that of Paris's own. The disquiet awakened in the garden is thereby displaced, occulting not only the ghosts of the past but also the relationship between Chad and Mme. de Vionnet that Strether is increasingly unwilling to comprehend. At Chad's grand final soirée, Strether is so struck by her presence that he confides to Little Bilham that "the sound of Mrs. Pocock's respiration drowns for me, I assure you, every other. *It's literally all I hear.*"[91] The hum is thus isolated, in other words, from the rumble of the city and the vague murmur of its streets, and revaluated as the sound of Sarah's breathing. Even as her breathing swallows him, drowning out everything else, her presence plagues him so much that Strether in turn is assaulted by the sight of her, much as he has earlier been assaulted by images, memories, and dull rumblings. Such a sight becomes then itself a kind of violent site of memory, with the landscape of her body given as "dressed in a splendour of crimson which affect[s] Strether as the sound of a fall through a skylight."[92] Under the hallucinatory effect of her fiery dress, then, Strether experiences full-blown synesthesia, with the sight of it curiously likened not to an image at all, but rather to an intense sensation of sound, and the sound is itself a violent kind of rupture, one portending death or the onslaught of a dizzying, terrifying fall that, once set in motion, cannot be checked.

That, under the sway of Paris, sight for Strether becomes very literally experienced as *sound* – the crimson dress registered as the crash of a dizzying fall – is underscored – indeed, culminates – in Strether's final encounter with Mme. de Vionnet. She is perhaps the ultimate example of the unmarked landmark of the text, and Hannah Nesher-Wirth goes so far as to argue that "she is Paris . . . becom[ing] the city's most compelling landmark."[93] Her home provides Strether with a sense of access to "the ancient Paris that he was always looking for," and from "the cold chambers of the past" the something that has haunted him throughout the novel finally crystallizes from a sight to a name:

> From beyond the court, beyond the *corps logis* forming the front – came, as if excited and exciting, the vague voice of Paris. Strether had all along been subject to sudden gusts of fancy in connexion with such matters as these – odd starts of the historic sense, suppositions and divinations with no warrant but their intensity. Thus and so, on the eve of the great recorded dates, the days and nights of revolution, the sounds had come in, the omens, the beginnings had broken out. They were the smell of revolution – the smell of the public temper – or perhaps simply the smell of blood.[94]

Behind the tranquil "plash of the fountain" lurk the omen of revolution and the "vague voice of Paris," and what Strether hears echoing up from the court becomes in turn most readily figured as what he smells – the sound of thunder registering as the smell of blood, with the sight of blood itself displaced, free-floating, like the crimson of Sarah's dress. Here, in other words, the intimation of blood does not take on the contours of a sound, with the color figured instead by its smell and by the very whiteness of Mme. de Vionnet's blouse – a whiteness that summons for Strether, albeit metonymically, the specter of Mme. Roland: "His hostess was dressed . . . in the simplest coolest white, of a character so old-fashioned . . . that Madame Roland must on the scaffold have worn something like it."[95]

The text initially tries somewhat to contain the vague voice that here finds Strether – the historic sense awakened in his final fateful meeting with Mme. de Vionnet – by ascribing such "suppositions and divinations with no warrant but their intensity" to "the effect of thunder in the air, which had hung about all day without release."[96] The effect of thunder is pronounced, however, for the blouse of Mme. de Vionnet is itself said to be the attire of "thunderous times,"[97] and it is her presence that speaks back to what the text has fallen most silent upon, her presence that summons most articulately the dim scenes and symbols that afflict Strether from the irremediable wound of the landscape.

Fussell writes energetically of the scene, "the habitat of Marie de Vionnet . . . is French history according to Henry James, and American revenant abroad, French history consisting almost entirely of the Revolution and the First Empire."[98] Yet the thunderous times that she portends, while it reaches back to Mme. Roland, no doubt marshals the specter of revolution more generally, and while her interior of sphinxes' heads and the far-off roar of cannons might audibly invoke for Strether the space of the First Empire, the reference is nevertheless layered and bound up with the sign of that world's spatial destruction in the toppling of the Vendôme Column. What is awakened for Strether in the Tuileries is not 1789 but 1871, and the sensation of those thunderous times finds him here.

Perhaps it is not strange to find, in a novel itself marked by all it does not wish to say about its primary narrative coup, that the Commune, while present, is never spoken of and indeed finds a name only in "the vague voice of Paris." That it does so only after the relationship between Chad and Mme. de Vionnet has been glimpsed by Strether seems only to underscore the way in which the weight – or rather, the sense – of the city always shadows that plot. E. M. Forster famously argues of *The Ambassadors* that

> Paris irradiates the book from end to end. It is an actor, though always disembodied . . . and when we have finished the novel and allowed its incidents to blur that we may see the pattern plainer, it is Paris that gleams at the centre of the hour-glass shape.[99]

To which we might add: the Paris that gleams back at us is one whose vague voice erupts from lost landmarks and speaks of blood in the streets as certainly as it murmurs the splendid hum of the boulevard. In the next chapter, we turn from James's visceral spatial memory to a series of radical texts that return to and reclaim precisely this "other" Paris in James's fiction – and with it, the horror of its history – for the Popular Front.

Chapter 5

Restaging Horror: Insurgent Memories of the Commune in the 1930s

The Paris lying so superficially quiet beneath its warm blanket of July days and nights was like a volcano about to vomit up the future.

Herbert Gorman, *Jonathan Bishop*

Utopia's deepest subject, and the source of all that is most vibrantly political about it, is precisely our inability to conceive it, our incapacity to produce it as a vision, our failure to project the Other of what is, a failure that, as fireworks dissolving in a night sky, must once again leave us alone with *this* history.

Fredric Jameson, *Ideologies of Theory*

On March 15, 1925, the Worker's Party of America, together with the Young Communist League, staged a lavish celebration at Madison Square Garden to commemorate the fifty-fourth anniversary of the Paris Commune. The *Boston Globe* estimated that some 13,000 people attended the event, while *The New York Times* noted that "from the cover of the program to the draperies of the platform, women's blouses and men's boutonnieres, the color scheme in the historic Garden was red."[1] The festivities were opened by Julia Stuart Poyntz, longtime labor advocate and founding member of the Communist Party of the United States (CPUSA), who quipped that "We are now going to overthrow the United States government, so be prepared for the worst," presumably for the benefit of the many policemen waiting in the wings to disband the gala.[2] But the highlight of the evening was Alexander Arkatov's *The Paris Commune*, a pageant that represented various scenes from the 1871 uprising and featured a cast of several hundred. Two days later, the *Times* acidly observed of the dancing that followed: "Apparently, the 'proletariat' of New York City has not been reduced to the hapless condition where it is incapable of response to the appeal of a good jazz band."[3] But as the dancing and the size of the cast help to highlight, Arkatov's worker theater production aimed both to retell the story of the Commune and to find a new theatrical mode for doing so – incorporating humor, jazz, and outsized scale into its revolutionary repertoire. And the spectacle was hailed by *The Daily Worker* as "the first time in the history of the revolutionary movement [that] a fitting memorial has been arranged for the Paris Commune."[4]

Even as the Commune was being remembered, then, it was also being made anew in New York City, in both the show and its audience, cries of "Long Live the Commune!" merging with "Long Live the Soviet Republics!" as Moissaye Olgin, a founding member of the Worker's Party, assured the crowd that "The new Commune stands firm as a rock."[5] It seemed 1871 was alive and kicking, in other words, but it was now being relived through 1917, for in the aftermath of the Russian Revolution, which loudly proclaimed itself to be the direct successor of the Parisian uprising, the Commune's revolutionary legacy was newly energized through ongoing coverage in left-wing US periodicals like *The Daily Worker*, *The Labor Defender*, and the *New Masses*, even as its history was increasingly revisited through John Reed Club-sponsored pamphlets such as *Paris on the Barricades* (1929), as well as in yearly commemorative pageants and worker theater plays held across the country.[6] While the crowds at Madison Square Garden and elsewhere commemorated the event, however, they were remembering its legacy and limitations with a blend of retrospective revolutionary memory and amnesia. For the evening's mix of pageantry and dancing capitalized on the spectacular role that the Commune had long played in American radical culture, in particular the yearly postbellum celebrations sponsored by anarchists, the Socialist Labor Party, and the Wobblies, as discussed in Chapter 3, while simultaneously overlaying and supplanting that radical tradition.

In *The American 1930s*, Peter Conn has suggested that radical writers were prone in the decade to utter conventionality: "The future might be 'undreamed of' . . . but its utterance was inscribed in strictly familiar vocabularies and forms."[7] In this chapter, I turn to a series of radical fictions that, in reclaiming the Commune for the American proletariat, and repurposing pulp to do so, tell a different story. Resituating Guy Endore's sensational 1933 bestseller, *The Werewolf of Paris*, alongside agitprop like William Siegel's

The Paris Commune: A Story in Pictures (1932) and George Spiro's *Paris on the Barricades* (1929), I show how horror became the unlikely conduit for insurgent memory in the 1930s. Turning to Herbert Gorman's recently rediscovered 1933 novel, *Jonathan Bishop*, I reconsider the work of gothic tropes in highbrow historical fiction, arguing that Gorman's return to the Commune, and its plot of counter-conversion, crucially sheds light on the way in which Endore's monster novel transforms and profoundly unsettles the work of writing the history of the Commune, even as it draws into further relief the extra-national threat and promise the Commune most seemed to hold in this moment.

Pulp Fictions, Radical Memories

Pound's famous injunction to "make it new" became the battle cry of modernism, yet the aesthetic and political stakes involved in doing so were of equal concern for Marx. As Russ Castronovo has reminded us, *The Eighteenth Brumaire* is a meditation marked in "technicolour writing" with the question of how exactly to make such a radical break with the past, how to translate tradition in a new language – how, in other words, to make a revolution "new."[8] William Siegel's *The Paris Commune: A Story in Pictures* (1932) was sponsored by the John Reed Club, and joined the ranks of pamphlets like Grace Burnham's *Social Insurance* and Harry Gannes's *Yankee Colonies*.[9] Yet in his introduction to Siegel's pictorial retelling of the Commune, Alexander Trachtenberg emphasizes the innovation of the pamphlet's graphics:

> In the following pages the reader will find the story of the Paris Commune told in pictures. This is a medium in which little working class literature has previously been done. It is graphic, dramatic, and simple and should give the reader the story.[10]

Moissaye Olgin, in his introduction to George Spiro's 1929 Little Red Library pamphlet, *Paris on the Barricades*, similarly underscores the newness of Spiro's revolutionary method. Although Spiro would later go onto write *The Road: A Romance of the Revolution*, a text that Walter B. Rideout would dub an "unrepresentative anachronism,"[11] Olgin suggests that Spiro's short fiction of the Commune, anchored in the conceit of an aging Communard, Émile Ducasse, recounting his memories to a group of spellbound American workers who long to hear an eyewitness account of those days, should not be understood as a throwback to older forms of historical fiction. Instead, he insists, it should be read as a new form of radical history in the vein of "post-November Russian writers dealing with the Revolution."[12] The unremarked-upon ingredients that both pamphlets draw onto "make it new" are, however, gothic horror and pulp fiction, but Olgin is quick to invoke the *realism* underlying the narrative's most sensational turns: "As [Spiro] proceeds to visualize the butchery, horror is piled upon horror until the burden is crushing" but he "records events in their *actual proportions*."[13]

While Spiro's story offers glimpses of life during the Commune – in particular, the jubilation of its proclamation day – and a sense of a new Paris unfolding around the narrator, it focuses its central narrative energies on the unmitigated horror or, as its narrator, Ducasse, puts it, "the gory nightmare" of the Commune's repression.[14] To convey that story, Spiro repeatedly offers the reader sensational scenes of violence and gothic moments of fright. (Our narrator's hair repeatedly stands up on his head, and – despite his young age during the Commune – it eventually turns gray overnight from sheer terror.)[15] Describing the street-by-street fighting, Ducasse relates, for example, that "my eyes fell upon the soldiers of our 'brothers.' Like ferocious, wild beasts they prowled through the barricade, dispatching the wounded"; when these "wild beasts" catch a boy Communard on the barricades, "they pounded him with their heavy boots and smashed his head into a mass of brains and blood. I raved in a fit of madness and fled aghast from this scene of horror."[16] Such scenes are everywhere. Diving into a cellar to hide from the Versaillist onslaught, Ducasse discovers "fifteen bodies of dead Communards, which accounted largely for the presence of these swarms of vermin. The slime that I had slipped on when I crept into that burial place was a pool of clotted blood,"[17] and wherever he turns, "as far as the eye could reach, were enormous piles of corpses white with chloride of lime."[18] Yet the goriness of the scene is perhaps best crystallized in Ducasse's image of the Parisian sky: "A strange sight! A rain of blood was descending upon Paris. Large red drops out of a lead-colored sky were falling into the street, and, forming streamlets and rivulets, were running into sewers."[19] This "strange sight" is, in turn, made sensationally palpable for the reader: while the front cover of Spiro's pamphlet depicts a scene of heroic fighting and a red flag waving, its back cover, echoing the visuals of a pulp magazine, depicts blood dripping from the book itself (Fig. 5.1). Michael Denning argues in his groundbreaking volume, *The Cultural Front: The Laboring*

Figure 5.1 Back cover, George Spiro, *Paris on the Barricades* (New York: Workers Library Publishing, 1929). Author's collection.

Figure 5.1a Front cover, George Spiro, *Paris on the Barricades* (New York: Workers Library Publishing, 1929). Author's collection.

of American Culture in the Twentieth Century, that "the impact of the Cultural Front was not simply the product of individual political commitment" but instead "the result of the encounter between a powerful democratic social movement – the Popular Front – and the modern cultural apparatuses of mass entertainment and education."[20] However, these pamphlets signal, I argue, not only how central that encounter was to the movement, but how thoroughly radical writers appropriated mass culture for their own ends.[21]

Siegel's text similarly dwells most on the horror of the Commune's final hours, its captions highlighting scenes of bayoneting as the "Commune [being] drowned in its own blood" (Fig. 5.2), "huge mounds of corpses and those not yet dead," and the "ghastly parade" of Commune prisoners.[22] The starkness of his black-and-white images – their fierce angularity – would seem the antithesis of Spiro's sensational "realism" and yet here they seem precisely to heighten the shock of Siegel's story.

tured. Thousands were killed where they stood; other thousands—
children, the old and sick—were herded to open places to be shot.
Each detachment of the maddened Versailles troops was an execu-
tioner's gang, summarily killing every suspected sympathizer. The
Commune was being drowned in its own blood.

22

Figure 5.2 William Siegel, *The Paris Commune: A Story in Pictures*
(New York: International Pamphlets: 1932), 22. Author's collection.

The effect, however, of such ghastly sights and sensible horror is,
the pamphlets suggest, neither titillation nor stupefaction. Instead,
they argue, much as de Cleyre earlier did, that the vividness of these
scenes serves to immerse the reader in the story and enlist us in the
action: "As the drama unfolds before our fascinated mind, we, ourselves, are swallowed up by the torrent of revolutionary action; we
become part of those masses; we defend the Commune against the
onrushing enemy."[23] The horror invites the reader to remember that,
as Siegel puts it, "The Commune was the first step,"[24] and Spiro's
narrative explicitly suggests that its work is an injunction to pass on
the baton of memory (and indignation): "You, comrades, children of
the working class, remember the Paris Commune."[25] This brand of
radical memory does not, in other words, shrink from returning to

atrocities or "gory nightmares" and does not rest at mourning them. Dominic LaCapra, in discussing "scenes marked by the compulsive return of a traumatic past," suggests we find therein "the future is blocked or fatalistically caught up in a melancholic feedback loop."[26] Yet these pamphlets, in their returns to the Commune's end, demonstrate anything but what Peter Starr, apropos of LaCapra, terms a "melancholic fixity on the past."[27] Instead, they rework horror to their own ends, redeploying horror itself as a form of protest, as a kind of memory that can spark a revolution and re-animate the future – a medium of what I want to call insurgent memory.

In mobilizing this insurgent memory, both pamphlets explicitly invoke alternative itineraries of memory and an "other" Paris for Americans. *The Paris Commune: A Story in Pictures*, for example, reminds readers that the wall in Père-Lachaise stands "at once a challenge to capitalist rule and a monument to the martyrs of the Commune."[28] *Paris on the Barricades* takes this move a step further, enjoining reader–comrades who visit Paris to experience a specifically alternative scene, and with it, an alternative memory of the city:

> Thousands of American tourists, sons of the rich, go to Paris yearly. They live a gay life there. They visit theaters, restaurants de luxe, cabarets, houses of ill repute. You, comrades, if you ever happen to be in Paris, visit the cemetery of Pere-la-Chaise. Visit the cemetery. Bare your heads before the wall, and think of the men, the women, and the children on whose blood and bones the French bourgeoisie has built its prosperity and happiness. Think of the martyrs of the Commune!"[29]

Spiro's injunction to avoid expatriate Paris and visit "Pere-la-Chaise" instead would seem, in other words, to open up for working-class Americans in Paris two simultaneous cities within a city. Jonathan Crary writes apropos of the Surrealist Manifesto, it was a case of

> turning the spectacle of the city inside out through counter-memory and counter-itineraries. These would reveal the potency of outmoded objects excluded from slick surfaces, and of derelict spaces off its main routes of circulation. The strategy incarnated a refusal of the imposed present . . . implicitly figuring an alternative future.[30]

In the case of *Paris on the Barricades*, Spiro similarly stages a counter-itinerary aimed at a revolutionary future.

As Trachtenberg makes clear, from the outset, the story these pamphlets relay is a familiar one: "again and again," he writes, "the story has been told."[31] Yet he lays claim to that story – or, rather, memory – for the present moment:

> Wherever workers will gather to hear the story of this heroic struggle – a story that has long since become a treasure of proletarian lore – they will honor the memory of the martyrs of 1871. But they will also remember the martyrs of the class struggle today who have either been slaughtered or still smart in the dungeons of capitalist and colonial countries.[32]

Looking back, in other words, is figured here as also looking forward. In particular, remembering the Commune after 1917 requires remembering the Soviet Union as at once the continuation *and* the successor of the Commune, for even as the final pages of the pamphlet depict Lenin under the caption, "The Commune lives again!,"[33] Trachtenberg argues that the Soviet Union represents "the society of which the Paris Commune was a 'glorious harbinger.'"[34] Commemoration must, in other words, be kept in check: in recounting the "lessons" of the Commune, radical readers are exhorted to remember that "*The absence of a disciplined, well-knit revolutionary leadership both prior to and after the establishment of the Commune spelled disaster at the outset*"[35] – a subject that Endore will explicitly revisit in *The Werewolf of Paris*. Much as it had for postbellum radicals, the Commune in the late 1920s and 1930s served as touchstone for the left, but this alternative past and future now needed to be redirected: what was symptomatically to be remembered was, on some level, that the revolution of 1871 had not succeeded. (Terry Eagleton, writing some fifty years after Trachtenberg, would make a similar claim: "There are those who overlook one of the most significant points about the Paris Commune, the fact that it failed."[36])

Olgin similarly wrestles with the temporality of the Commune – the way in which it continues to inhabit the present, and yet should be remembered as simultaneously superseded by the Russian Revolution brought to life by it: "A romantic halo surrounds the Paris Commune of 1871, yet the event is strangely vibrant with life. There is the ring of legend to the narratives of those heroic days, yet history clothes them with ever new flesh and blood."[37] Even more pointedly, *Paris on the Barricades* suggests that the Commune's memory matters more than ever to Americans: "Now, after eleven years of Soviet rule, the Paris Commune is more alive and more meaningful to the working class than it was fifteen years ago."[38] Concern over precisely that threat – and the "pointed modern implications" of a leftist internationalism born out of that ongoing return to the Commune – everywhere marks the novel to which we now turn.

Looking Backwards

In his critical re-evaluation of the 1930s, Conn singles out Herbert Gorman as a "first-rate but undervalued writer" too long overshadowed by modernism and more than deserving of renewed critical attention.[39] In particular, Conn cites *Jonathan Bishop* as an "eloquent defense of established orders, a counter-statement to the revolutionary texts of the 1930s that preached the need for fundamental and even violent change."[40] But that impulse was never deeply veiled in Gorman's work. Indeed, *Jonathan Bishop* was, from the start, heralded and marketed as a novel set during the events of the Commune but aimed at its *own* historical moment. His publisher, Farrar & Rinehart, suggested in its advertisements that Gorman's text drew on "the romantic and violent events of the past to illuminate problems of today," while a *New York Times* review headlined the novel's "pointed modern implications."[41] And an acerbic reviewer slammed the book for precisely these reasons in the pages of the left-wing *Partisan Review*, dubbing the novel "a dilettante's sermon on how a young American becomes disillusioned with revolution."[42]

Jonathan Bishop, not unlike the Commune romances of the 1890s discussed in my second chapter, sends its eponymous protagonist, a young Bostonian and recent Harvard graduate, to Paris to find himself, but unlike his fin-de-siècle predecessors, Jonathan goes to Paris to be neither a painter nor a tourist. Instead, he leaves home expressly in search of revolution, or more precisely, in pursuit of a radical revolutionary, Gautier Saint-Just, "the Man from Hyde Park," whose radical sentiments had altogether captivated him during a chance encounter in London several years before. His search for Saint-Just conveniently positions him to observe the political clubs of the Paris Commune first-hand, and to encounter a number of Communards up close, but his time in Paris pointedly wipes out any incipient radicalism he might have brought with him. Our "Yankee spectator," as *Time Magazine* described him, divides his time between the American colony – and more to the point, the world of wealthy Americans cozying up to the collapsing Empire and the court of Napoleon III – and the rough clubs of Belleville and Montmartre that the novel calls "the powder-magazine of Paris."[43] While Bishop's first impressions of the Paris of the Empire are unsavory – not unlike Marx, he sees it as altogether illusory – he eventually falls for (and loses) a lovely *cocodette*, the mysterious Mme. Zinh, gets mixed up in the Battle of Sedan, and, together with the real-life character, American dentist Dr. Evans, lends no small a hand in helping the Empress Eugénie escape from Paris as the Empire falls. In turn, this brush with imperial greatness ushers in a radical change of heart in our Yankee protagonist. While he continues to seek out Saint-Just, he comes to claim he does so only to find out what had come over him in the first place: "It was curious, now that he thought of it, that he still desired so violently to see his mysterious acquaintance while he no longer believed implicitly in the cause for which that acquaintance stood."[44]

As Rideout first pointed out in his seminal early study of the American radical novel, the "conversion" plot, wherein a middle-class protagonist is won over to the cause of class struggle after participating in a strike or radical demonstration at which his "middle-class faith in capitalist justice is shattered," was a central developmental arc of proletarian fiction.[45] Gorman's historical fiction seems aimed, then, to be its exact antithesis, a counter-conversion narrative, for Bishop's *Bildung* in Paris is precisely to *lose* all faith in revolution and utopian futures. Bishop thus confronts Saint-Just, and comes to see this fictional string-puller as the "organizational" core of the Commune.[46] Unlike his predecessors in the works of King and Savidge, Bishop does not, however, establish his fortune, solidify his marriage prospects, and eventually leave home to spread the gospel of "Americanism." Rather, by book's end, he has literally swapped places with a Frenchman, mistakenly shot while trying to surrender to the oncoming Versaillist soldiers. The book, rather than the hero, is thus left to stand as the proselytizing tract.

But if its lesson from Paris had been learned again and again in US Commune romances of the 1890s, Gorman's brand of counter-conversion differs from its antecedents in several crucial respects. *Jonathan Bishop* does not, in other words, simply rehash that earlier terrain; instead, it imagines a native-born, Anglo-American who might be likely to fall for the Commune – a threat that, as we saw in Chapter 2, no American novel of the 1890s would be willing to entertain. Moreover, the novel underscores Bishop's abolitionist pedigree, the radical Bostonian milieu in which he grew up, and his nagging sense that the revolution to come – the *liberté, égalité, fraternité* for which he has such mixed feelings – is connected to his own nation's republican past: "Liberty should be the star that all men followed. But he was doubtful about fraternity and he was quite sure he did not believe in equality. Yet his own country was based on these ideals."[47] And while the novel shows him conscripted to build barricades against his will – and thus lending a hand for the Commune only by force, a staple of the earlier romances – it nevertheless betrays deep doubts over and anxiety towards (less savvy) Americans falling for the Commune. As Bishop is watching, with no little disgust, the festivities surrounding the Commune's felling of the Vendôme Column, for example, he overhears in the lull between speeches the strains of "Hail, Columbia" (the unofficial anthem of the US, replaced by the "Star-Spangled Banner" only two years before the novel went to press) from a nearby hotel and stands transfixed as "a girl came out on the balcony [of the Mirabeau Hotel] and waved a small American flag."[48] That an American might be swept up by the possibilities of the Commune is historically accurate – certainly, some contemporary visitors were – but this flag-waver seems a stand-in for Americans who held out faith in the 1930s both in revolution and CPUSA-sponsored international solidarity. For the novel glimpses her so as to savage her misguided enthusiasm: "The young man felt a wave of disgust flow through him as he saw his young compatriot lean over and cheer the red-sashed orator. Poor foolish girl, with her delusions of liberty, her superficial knowledge of what was actually transpiring."[49]

To further ward off such misplaced affiliations, Gorman's novel explicitly positions the Commune as an unprecedented eruption of the future into the present: "The Paris lying so superficially quiet beneath its warm blanket of early July days and nights was like a volcano *about to vomit up the future*."[50] And in this contest between the future and the past, its hero solidly sides with the latter, but in doing so, the Bostonian slowly begins to revise his views on American history and his own prior radical commitments. In a move that anticipates the backward glance of the runaway 1930s bestseller, *Gone with the Wind*, but this time from a pronouncedly "Yankee" perspective, the novel thus re-imagines the defeat of the South during the Civil War as a defeat of "civilization" itself, much as postbellum periodical coverage of the Commune portrayed it as a similar affront to global order. While Bishop initially disdains those Americans he meets early in the novel who spend their days currying favor with the Emperor and likely sympathized with the Southern cause during the Civil War, by book's end he explains – in a heated dialogue with none other than the female firebrand, Louise Michel:

We had a Revolution which succeeded in isolating us from all the finest civilization in the world . . . then we had the Civil War which destroyed the half of the Republic that was most richly steeped in tradition and the ease of living.[51]

In this sense, Gorman's novelistic return to the Commune echoes the broader racial politics of rightward writing in the 1930s – what Lawrence J. Oliver has diagnosed as the now less well-remembered "virulent racism and right-wing Americanism that pervaded the 'Red Decade.'"[52] The novel, in allowing Saint-Just to briefly state his case, has him take specific aim at America's racial past and the hypocrisy of Bishop's previous reformism: "You, being a Northerner, believed in the emancipation of the negroes but you would not marry your sister to one"; in turn, Saint-Just rhapsodizes that "The day must come when the priest is cast down from his altar, when patriotism is an obsolete word, when national demarcation lines will be a memory, when all men will be joined in a vast international federation of equality."[53] In thus accessing the Commune's revolutionary non-national designs, the novel is quick to quash Saint-Just's revolutionary platform: "[Jonathan] realized that it was the tones and not the words that thrilled him so."[54] But the novel thus sheds light on the anxiety that the Commune, rerouted through as well as amplified by 1917, seemed most to summon for the 1930s: in particular, the specter of internationalism, radical racial equality, and the mesmeric sway of revolutionary ideas – or, as Gorman puts it, "of hocus pocus and mumbo jumbo."[55] While the banner of the Commune was always international, the novel repeatedly emphasizes its threat to nationalism, formulating the most potent threat of the Commune for the present not as savages with rings through their noses overtaking Paris, but rather as internationalism and racial equality overrunning the nation-state.

To contain these threats, the novel emphasizes the "horror" of the Commune's reign in Paris, a generic switch that erupts from its ostensibly historical narrative, but this switch helps to highlight the gothic tropes always already embedded in earlier accounts of the Commune, whether in the form of sensational histories, anodyne magazine remembrances, or bestselling historical adventure stories. Gorman thus suggests of the street-by-street retaking of the city that "the Commune was snarling and fighting like a cornered wolf," even as he figures the fires in Paris as a kind of murder, with "blood-red bubbles" engulfing the city's grand edifices."[56] By book's end, Gorman literalizes the monstrous metaphor further, offering readers a glimpse of the Commune as an explicitly monstrous body: "a blood-drunken, floundering, defeated and wounded monster called the Commune was staggering backwards from MacMahon's ferocious blows and leaving destruction and death in the wake of his maniacal retreat."[57]

This metaphorical footwork takes our eyes off the French government troops and their, as Preston calls it, "wolfish work" in the city, but the narrative employs another sleight of hand to contain the violence of the reconquering of Paris and the brutality of the violence that ultimately sweeps up Bishop himself. Although Conn reads Bishop's death as meant to be simply meaningless – "[He] has simply disappeared into the reigning chaos. His inadvertent and pointless death, and the accidental name under which he is buried, comprise a grimly appropriate emblem for a world emptied of significance"[58] – the moment performs, in my reading, far more ideological and mnemonic work in the text. Let us turn, then, to Bishop's grim final moments:

> He held his hands high above his head as he walked so that they might know that he was unarmed and surrendering . . . He had walked but a few paces when suddenly an invisible fist reached out of the smoke and struck him violently in the shoulder . . . It was difficult to see; the smoke appeared to grow more and more thick, like a sort of grey blanket from which the light on the opposite side was being removed . . . And then the blanket seemed to tear apart and he was struck a terrible blow between the eyes . . . He turned up his hands in a helpless gesture and fell heavily upon his face.[59]

Bishop is here caught up in the Versaillist juggernaut, the "ferocious blows of MacMahon" that the novel otherwise fails to see, but as we experience this death from Bishop's own perspective – the disorienting smoke covering his line of sight "like a sort of grey blanket" – we never actually observe who was responsible for his death or what is transpiring around him. His confusion over what is in front of him becomes, in other words, our own, and as the novel makes clear, Bishop's corpse is the only dead body that merits our attention as, in the novel's closing, "the forces of law and order pass onto victory"[60] – a victory that Bishop himself championed and foretold throughout the novel. If Gorman's text thus offers us a glimpse of the human cost of suppressing the revolution, his narrative everywhere obscures it. Guy Endore will, however, turn precisely to this scene in his weird fiction of the Commune, redeploying the genre of horror to bring that memory into spectacular relief.

Monstrous Histories

Alan Wald opens his study of misfit leftist writers, *Exiles From a Future Time*, with the case of Endore, popular novelist, committed Communist, and Oscar-nominated, later blacklisted, Hollywood screenwriter, whose literary output – ranging from pamphlets for the Scottsboro Boys to mystery novels and a bestselling biography of Joan of Arc – exemplifies Wald's argument about mid-century radical writers in America: namely, that their cultural production bears "scant resemblance" to what we might imagine "proletarian fiction" would look like.[61] However, while he notes, in passing, that *The Werewolf of Paris* was Endore's "masterpiece of the Paris Commune," Wald gives it no further attention in his book.[62] Barbara Foley, in her magisterial study of the proletarian novel, similarly sidesteps Endore's pulp classic to offer an extended reading of *Babouk*, his remarkable 1934 novel of the Haitian revolution – a text less frequently read but more legibly political and more categorically *radical*.[63] And to look, for example, at the 1951 Avon paperback edition of *Werewolf*, with its pulpy cover displaying a swooning blonde bombshell and menacing werewolf beneath a headline that sums up this radically experimental text as "A weird novel about a monster–wolf in human form," it is perhaps not surprising that even those critics aimed at recovering radical writing from the 1930s have so often glossed over or altogether neglected this text (Fig. 5.3).

Endore's monster novel has not proved more legible for fantasy and horror critics, either, and not simply because werewolves have so far garnered less scholarly attention than vampires and other gothic monsters.[64] To date, the novel's only extended critical treatments have appeared in the journal *Studies in Weird Fiction*, and for horror critics the novel presents almost as much of a conundrum. The frustration is perhaps best expressed by horror critic Jerry Ball, who concedes that *The Werewolf of Paris*, by virtue of its early critical acclaim, success in the marketplace, and continued cult status, holds the title of the "definitive" werewolf novel. As he goes onto argue, however, that title is troubled by "the novel's rather annoying tendency to de-emphasize the werewolf" – its tendency, in other words, to "provide digressions (mainly historical) at nearly every opportunity."[65] That an early reviewer of the book praised it precisely for these historical meanderings – "the part of the book dealing with the Commune is by far the most interesting – *a real contribution to fiction*" – is, for these literary critics, only a further a strike against it.[66] What to make, then, of this "weird" novel?

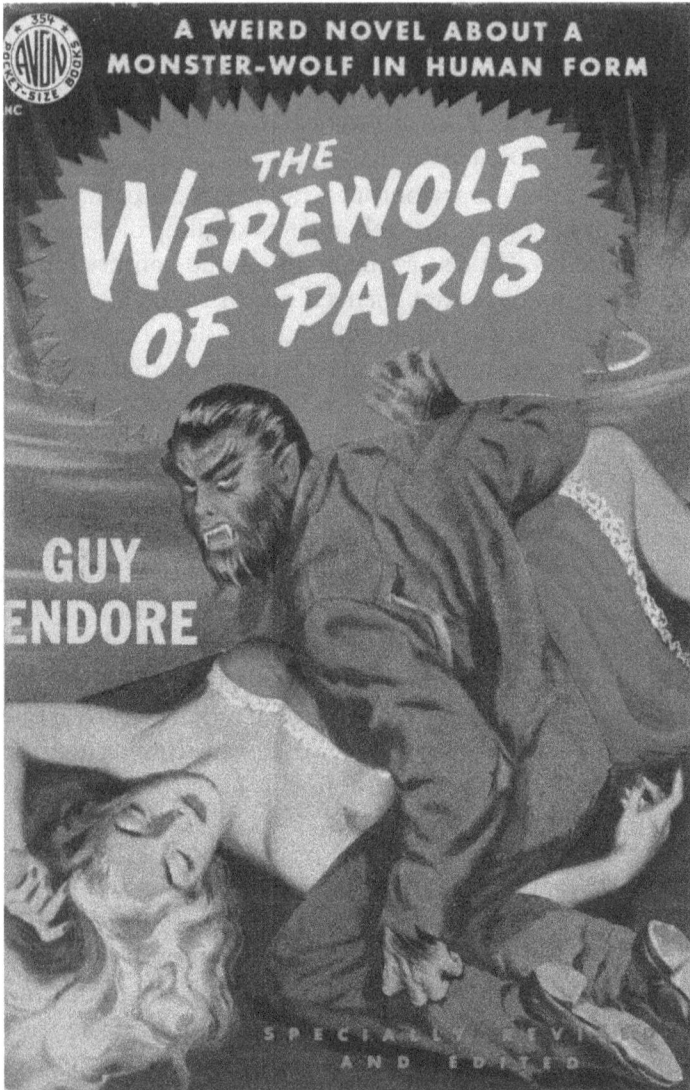

Figure 5.3 Cover, Guy Endore, *The Werewolf of Paris* (New York: Avon, 1951). Reprinted by permission of HarperCollins.

In her piece on "Hit-Man Modernism" for the 2006 volume *Bad Modernisms*, Lisa Fluet aptly describes pulp fiction as "badly behaved and hard to pin down," and suggests that what Paula Rabinowitz's work on "pulp modernism" most helped to remind us of is that "pulp is in fact one of modernism's ways of wandering beyond historical, categorical, and institutional boundaries and showing up, unannounced, where we least expect it."[67] If modernist pulp, however, is figured here as likely to show up almost anywhere, it has, as Leif Sorensen has pointed, most often been read as synonymous with the realm of hardboiled noir. This synecdoche "crucially misses the broad range of pulp writing" – in particular, the horror and sci-fi fiction published between the wars in journals like *Weird Tales*.[68] Reading Endore as repurposing exactly this kind of pulp to his own radical ends, but also trading in sensational forms to rewrite history is, I want to argue, to begin to grasp this text.[69]

Judith Halberstam points out in the opening of *Skin Shows* that gothic horror is not simply marked by its monsters or its ability to generate a certain affective response in the reader. Instead, Halberstam argues, it is a matter of form as much as content: "The Gothic topos is the monstrous body à la Frankenstein, Dracula, Dorian Gray, Jekyll/Hyde; in its generic form, Gothic is the disruption of realism and of all generic purity."[70] Her formulation of the monstrous generic excess of horror, of the "story buried within the story buried within the story,"[71] is a particularly apt description of Endore's experimental proletarian horror novel (or modernist gothic historical fiction). The opening frame of its narrative is set in modernist Paris, where our never-named American expatriate narrator is researching his dissertation on an unnamed topic. His quiet life of the mind and general distaste for "Americans who have just come over" are interrupted by the unexpected arrival of Eliane, an acquaintance from back home.[72] Through their evening outing – an already clichéd circuit of celebrated cafés and well-trod Parisian places – our narrator stumbles on the monster story at the heart of the novel in the form of a manuscript pulled from a trash heap. Penned by Aymar Galliez, an aging '48er, for the 1871 court-martial of Bertrand Challiet, the eponymous protagonist of Endore's novel, these "thirty-four sheets of closely written French" serve as the foundation – and authenticating historical document – for the rest of Endore's werewolf novel. What follows is, then, ostensibly the report on the werewolf of Paris as recounted by his uncle Aymar, an eyewitness, but filtered and filled in by our narrator:

> I had thought at first of publishing the resume as it stood and providing this curiosity with the necessary notes to help the reader to an understanding of the case. But on second thought, I determined to recast the whole material into a more vivid form, incorporating all the results of my own investigations.[73]

If, for Prufrock, the overwhelming question was "how shall I begin?," for Endore's American expatriate narrator it is always "where shall I begin?"[74] The refrain explicitly opens the narrative and is echoed in the "where shall I end my tale?" that returns to close it,[75] but the question also functions to structure much of the vertiginously nested plot of the novel. Like the ongoing narrative gesture of interruption at work here, the narrator's question immediately problematizes the writing of the text and its narrative unfolding. The novel further underscores the difficulty of beginning by suggesting where the story "might" commence: "I might, for example, begin with Eliane . . . She has nothing to do with the story, except that she happened to start it off."[76] While the text thus asserts that it has a singular story to tell, it simultaneously signals that to choose a beginning for the history of the werewolf is always already to begin to designate for your reader which characters – and more to the point, which pasts – merit our attention. As Alex Woloch has shown in his influential study of the space of the minor character in realist fiction, "narrative meaning takes shape in the dynamic flux of attention and neglect toward various characters who are locked within the same story but have radically different positions within the narrative."[77] But *Werewolf* radically destabilizes the relationship between the protagonist and minor characters, even as it swerves between its ostensibly major and minor plots. That it does so is not, however, simply to foreground the difficulty of writing monstrous histories. In "The Moment of Deep Time," Bruce Robbins invites us to consider the way in which the narrative device of analeptic prolepsis, in interrupting the central narrative in order to flash forward into a future one, acts to inject suspense about a minor character – even one who enters the narrative only fleetingly – and thus to unsettle – if only for a moment – whose story really matters.[78] In my reading, Endore's narrative excess and gesture of interruption similarly work always to question whose stories – and even more crucially, whose histories – matter.

The novel thus begins in 1920s Paris, plunging backward to 1871 and further backward into the mists of time, into another possible beginning to the story. Turning to a bloody medieval feud between the rival houses of the Pitavals and the Pitamonts, the narrator admits "the incident herein noted would seem at first glance to have nothing to do with the case."[79] But while this detour does not explicitly untangle for the reader the genesis of werewolfism as an inheritable trait, the backward glance insists that Bertrand's story, or, rather, his case, begins well before he is born. The novel then turns to the more immediate back story of Bertrand's life – his young mother,

Josephine's, arrival in Paris to be a serving girl to the Didier-Galliez family, and her rape by the monstrous priest, Father Pitamont; but the narrative also turns its attentions to Aymar Galliez, the author of the manuscript, relating how he fought and was injured on the barricades in 1848 and now lives as a struggling writer–pamphleteer in the bourgeois home of his widowed aunt, Mme. Didier. As the novel proceeds, the narrator intersperses sections about Bertrand's boyhood – and later crimes – with sections on Aymar: his slow turn away from radical politics, his long wrestle with what to do with Bertrand, and his dawning recognition that the preternaturally sweet-natured boy in his care is slowly becoming a nocturnal monster. The narrator continues to make his presence felt, however, intruding into the narrative and speaking through the various authenticating footnotes – a multiplying archive of other texts – inter-threading the narrative (one of which even directs the reader to "see copy in the Forty-second Street Library, New York").[80]

Bertrand's werewolfism dawns on Aymar long before Bertrand himself realizes what or who he is. Unexplained animal mutilations begin to crop up in their small village, but Bertrand has no memory of his nocturnal doings. Despite his uncle's misgivings, the young man is primed to pursue his studies in Paris in the fall of 1870, and it is en route there that he begins to come to terms with what he is becoming. Having fallen asleep on the road to Paris, he wakes to find that

> the ravaged face of his friend, Jacques Bramond, appeared plain before him. "Will these nightmares never stop?" he complained . . . But there was no stepping down to the floor from this bed. This was reality. In the thinning darkness he saw the mutilated corpse. His own mouth was sticky with clotted blood.[81]

In Paris, the young man is free to indulge his monstrous appetites, and eventually joins the National Guard because, as our narrator points out, during the siege that fall "the workshops were empty, there wasn't a job to be had."[82] The meek National Guardsman by day/werewolf by night eventually falls in love with Sophie Blumenberg, a young woman of means and morals otherwise betrothed to the aristocratic Captain Barral de Montfort. Bertrand's love affair with Sophie in turn interrupts the romantic subplot begun between Sophie and Montfort, and eventually launches Montfort into plotting the fall of the Commune. (As the narrator puts it, "The task of spying for the Versailles government was a delicate one. He found in its intricacies the necessary antidote to his misery."[83]) In turn, Bertrand and Sophie's increasingly sado-masochistic relationship seems to "cure" Bertrand's werewolfism, and he assures his uncle as much when Aymar finally tracks him down in Paris some months later. It eventually becomes clear to Bertrand, however, that his nightly cravings are returning, and to save Sophie from himself he rushes out into the streets in search of another prey. This final plot twist lands him in prison, facing court-martial by the Commune for having attacked a fellow guardsman, a trial at which Aymar presents his summation of the case.

Alexander Woolcott observed in his glowing 1933 review in the *New Yorker* that

> [Endore] has artfully fabricated a sinister and subtly insidious yarn calculated to evoke in susceptible bosoms that nightmare shiver for which our own language has no name ... More specifically, Mr. Endore has boldly gone out after the overrated scalps of "Dracula" and Huysman's "Là-bas" and, to my notion, come back with those ensanguined trophies dangling from his belt.[84]

But for all that Endore's hybrid text indulges Bertrand's sanguinary appetites and its own horror plot – proffering readers opportunities to partake of disarrayed, disinterred corpses, gashed-open bodies, and a man's bloody forearm kept under the bed as a late-night snack – it also takes equal pains to interrupt that plot to show the reverberations of Bertrand's monstrous feeding. Turning its attentions to the lives lost in never being able to shake the guilt that was not theirs, the novel turns our attention – and its airtime – to these minor characters, and confronts Bertrand with the aftershocks of his deeds even before his formal trial by military court. When Aymar finally tracks down his nephew, he pointedly elaborates the stories to which the reader has already been made been privy:

> In the matter of digging up the miser, Vaubois, it never occurred to you that the shepherd, Crotez, would be accused of the job. Or in the matter of General Darimon's daughter that a poor *croque-mort*, the coachman, Jean Robert, would go to jail for it, and his family become destitute? How many others have suffered through you I cannot say.[85]

But even as *Werewolf* draws on and disrupts the expectations of horror fiction, it further adapts conventions of the historical novel by conveniently placing its eponymous monster at the time of the Commune so that this other history unfolds in the background of Bertrand's story. That Bertrand's real-life counterpart, Sergeant

François Bertrand, was court-martialed in 1849 for disinterring and rending corpses and other crimes whose "details were," in the words of one nineteenth-century report, "too revolting for reproduction,"[86] Endore's relocation of the story to 1871 seems all the more telling. Yet what is most remarkable about Endore's use of – and experiments with – the historical novel within the body of what purports to be horror fiction is the way that the narrative does *not* use its hero's temporal position to give us insight into – or the slightest perspective on – the historical backdrop to which he is privy. As *Jonathan Bishop* so well illustrates, the historical novel asks us to care as much for the protagonist and his doings as for the world in which he finds himself – he remains, in other words, our center of readerly attention and our entryway into the events unfolding around him. By contrast, Endore's novel interrupts its presumably major plot – namely, Bertrand's own story – precisely to shift our readerly attention fully onto the history ostensibly in the *arrière-plan* of the novel. To underscore that Bertrand is no longer the center of readerly attention, the character who matters, he is in jail – and, thus, "offstage" – through this section of the novel, and our narrator details that it is he – rather than the original manuscript – that has brought this history into such relief:

> Writing as he did, when the cataclysms through which Paris were passing were at their height and fresh in everybody's mind, Galliez makes little attempt to fill in the historical events of the moment. I have been at some pains to remedy this omission, for our day has forgotten these matters.[87]

The novel thus enlists our unnamed American in Paris to excavate and reconstruct that otherwise buried history for a specifically mainstream American audience.

In retelling that history, the novel, like *Paris on the Barricades* and other agitprop pamphlets of the period, focuses on recapturing the horror of the Commune's end and the methodically ferocious fighting that retook Paris. Of the Versaillist entry into the city, our narrator observes,

> They were beginning to encircle the remainder of the city still in the hands of the Commune, and wherever their assaults carried a barricade, they set up at once their temporary booths of methodic, pitiless, thorough repression: court-martial, summary execution. And their revenge was 50 to 1.[88]

Moreover, the narrative's account of the judicially sanctioned executions – "No witnesses, no defense. A couple questions and off went another group of wretches to a convenient wall" – is highlighted not as a filling-out of Aymar's manuscript, but rather as a filling-in of the historical record,[89] for, the narrator relates, in becoming the victors, the Versaillists "became the legitimists" and the cruelty of their siege was in turn "lightly passed over by historians."[90] In turn, *Werewolf* begins to shift our perspective on the horror plot we have so far encountered, leveraging that very plot against the historical one now in front of us. Aymar, in looking out at "streets of cadavers," comes to see, in other words, our eponymous werewolf as "but a mild case."[91] As he puts it, "What was a werewolf who had killed a couple of prostitutes, who had dug up a few corpses, compared with these bands of tigers slashing at each other with daily increasing ferocity!"[92] In that sense, the novel would seem to suggest that horror is the proper genre not only for marshaling radical memory but also for telling certain otherwise forgotten histories.

The novel goes on, however, to pose a question not usually brokered by horror fiction: namely, whose deaths really matter? After describing the thousands of Communards transferred to Versailles and awaiting trial, the "scores . . . condemned to death, hundreds [who] were to be sentenced to imprisonment for life, thousands [who] were to be deported to tropical islands," the narrator interrupts to suggest the novel could stop there: "Why should you want to know of the death of the werewolf rather than another? Consult your mortuary registers. Were these not men and women?"[93] Although the chapter ultimately indulges the reader by recounting the death of Sophie and Bertrand's ultimate admission to an "enlightened" asylum, it nevertheless presses us on why it must do so, why the whereabouts of major characters matter more than the fate of those masses in Paris.

Yet even as it fills in the gaps left by historians, Endore's novel obsessively authenticates the history it relates by directing us to a series of other histories of the Commune in its footnotes, but it at once draws on and unsettles the authority of these texts, particularly in their treatment of the day-to-day doings of the Commune itself. Even as it offers us an unflattering portrait of Citoyen Gois, the Communard in charge of administering Bertrand's trial who was rumored to be speculating in garlic, among other illicit things, the narrator interrupts himself to cast doubt on his sources: "Or are these tales mere anti-Communard inventions?"[94] That he does so further opens up the gaps in the historical record, and recalls

San Francisco journalist and future founder of the literary journal *Argonaut*, Frank Pixley's, 1871 assertion that "The history of the Commune is written by its enemies. Like all lost causes, it will be misrepresented. What there was of good in it will be suppressed. What there was of bad will be exaggerated."[95]

As we have seen, horror critics tend to de-emphasize – or be utterly bewildered by – Endore's historical machinations, while those literary critics invested in recovering proletarian fiction who have taken any note of the novel at all simply hail it as a "masterpiece of the Paris Commune." This might stem from the fact that though the novel is unequivocal in its condemnation of the Commune's suppression, its descriptions of the Commune itself are often equivocal. So much so, in fact, that Greil Marcus insists, in his sonic archeology of the twentieth century, *Lipstick Traces*, that "the most convincing rejection of the Commune remains Guy Endore's 1933 horror potboiler, *The Werewolf of Paris*."[96] That reading sidesteps the degree to which Endore unsettles his sources and foregrounds the difficulty of piecing together the Commune's history from the paper trail of anti-Communard materials, but it nevertheless merits attention, for the most damning critique of the Commune in its pages would seem to come not from conservative histories but rather from leftist recuperations of the event post 1917:

> The Russians have made a national holiday of March 18, when the Commune was formed. But they are worshipping a legend, though it is true that the Commune was a mistake from which a new generation of revolutionaries was to learn a lot. The Commune was a proletarian government, yes, but so is a hobo camp.[97]

Where *Jonathan Bishop* saw in the Commune a nightmare of organization – a revolution orchestrated by a single, mesmeric string-puller, Saint-Just – Endore's novel sees in it the hapless assemblage of a "hobo camp" in need of just such organization. That it does so has, I argue, everything to do with the cultural politics of what the Commune meant for the Left in the 1930s for, as both the pamphlets and the Madison Square Garden gala attest, radical memory of the Commune most emphasized the lessons the Commune taught later revolutionaries, and in particular, the way in which the Bolshevik state was authorized by the Commune and also always already supplanting its vision of revolutionary association and bricolage. Yet, for all the narrator's vitriol, the narrative's return to this moment, and consistent challenge to conventional histories of it, opens up the possibility that insurgent memory might re-activate not simply the legend of March 18, but rather that other potential vision of revolution – and with it, the free-for-all of the hobo camp. As I take up the epilogue that follows, it is this vision that resonates most with student radicals of the 1960s, as they reclaim the Commune and relive the future via that once again not-so-distant past.

Barricades Revisited – the Commune on Campus from FSM to SDS

> It's hard to see what's possible. It's hard to see the future. It's easy to look in hindsight. I think our problem is that when we look in hindsight, we tend to focus on the failures and losses and the intransigence of power. If our expectation is that you can challenge power and create space for new possibilities, then we have millions of examples of that.
>
> Robin D. G. Kelley[1]

In January 1965, embattled University of California President Clark Kerr gave an interview with the *Los Angeles Times* about what he termed the "uprising" on Berkeley's campus, an uprising that would come to be known as the Free Speech Movement (FSM).[2] A month previously, over 800 Cal students had been arrested at a sit-in on Sproul Plaza, protesting the banning of political agitation on campus; three days later, the young face of the movement – Mario Savio – had been dragged from the platform of the Greek Theater, where 15,000 students had assembled to hear him, by police there to arrest him. Kerr warned the paper and, by extension, the American public that "a new student generation, very much different than those that preceded it, is now with us."[3] But if he claimed these young activists represented a threat unlike any seen previously, he also cordoned them off from the rest of the country – and, by extension, other university campuses – by suggesting that they were uniquely the product of a bit of Berkeley that was itself cut off from the rest of the nation: "If anything in the United States could be said to resemble the Paris of the left bank, it is the area around Telegraph avenue just off campus."[4] These new radicals were, in Kerr's estimation, forged by a "disorganized, 'left-bank' crowd" that had sprung up alongside the cafés and bookstores that lined a single street bordering the campus, a street that Kerr notably did not read as a spillover of the intellectual and political life of the university and could not make sense of as American. If, however, he turned to an image of Paris in the early 1960s – a Left Bank of left-wing thinking and existentialist café philosophers enshrined in American films such as *Funny Face* (1957), as well as more recent newspaper coverage of escalating demonstrations against the Algerian War – to understand and internationalize the "uprising" at his door, the new radicals on his campus reached for an earlier moment of radical Paris to articulate both their movement and its horizon of demands.

In "Berkeley, A Follow-Up," a report on the burgeoning FSM movement that appeared in *Solidarity*, a 1965 pamphlet published by a Socialist group in London, FSM student leader Marvin Garson offered a distillation of the excitement and the creative chaos around him:

> FSM is not bureaucratic, nor democratic; it's meta-bureaucratic, a unique combination of anarchy and bureaucracy that is hard to describe. It generates a tremendous energy, but wastes a lot of the energy it generates. Volunteers work feverishly all night on their own, then discover some other group has already finished the task ... I'm sure the Paris Commune was like this.

He adds, though, pointedly, "that doesn't mean it is good."[5] While Garson's assessment of the "feverish" collective action around him by way of 1871 echoes the message that CPUSA-sponsored Commune celebrations of an earlier era had done much to hammer into their audiences – namely, that the message to be taken from its memory was always ultimately that it had *failed* – Savio found in its name an altogether different legacy for the movement unfolding on campus. In a speech he gave at a thirty-six-hour "teach-in" against the Vietnam War in May 1965, he began by relating, "This is going to be a very different style speech from the speeches which we've been listening to, because I don't have a very set idea just how history's going to turn out," before turning his attentions to a revolutionary history that spoke to the set of questions he wanted to pose for their struggle. As Savio puts it,

> I remember last semester at one point some of us were trying to decide, "Should we have the sit-in in Sproul Hall or in the Student Union?" since the latter would be more in the spirit of the Paris Commune – we don't want anything you own, we want *our* things.[6]

In so doing, Savio equates the Commune with a set of demands that allowed students to re-imagine the spaces that should be – or were already – theirs. This formulation of the Commune is striking not just for the way in which it makes the uprising not a symbol of the FSM's fight but, in fact, the spirit behind its tactics, for though Kerr was insistent that the trouble on campus originated from a "leftbank" crowd of outside agitation, Savio intimated that day that he had come to his reading of the Commune by way of studying European history. (James Simon Kunen, who participated in the Columbia occupation in 1968, would similarly point out in a letter home that "one of the dangers of going to college is that you learn things, and that my present actions are much influenced by my Contemporary Civilization readings."[7])

Six years later, Hal Draper, a key figure in the FSM movement now better known for mentoring Savio and authoring a detailed defense and history of the movement, *Berkeley: The New Student Revolt*, edited a collection of Marx's published and unpublished writings on the Commune. It aimed to be the most comprehensive account of Marx's thought on the 1871 uprising, and expanded beyond the scope of *The Civil War in France*, Marx's official address on it, for reasons that echoed Draper's earlier rationale for writing about the new student radicals. As he writes in his Foreword,

> One of the background facts is that, while Marx and Engels had been discussing the prospect of a new French revolution for most of the year before, the "bourgeois mind" was unable to see what had happened even after it took place.[8]

Yet this radical preoccupation with Paris did not, as Kerr insisted, find roots only in Berkeley.

In the summer of 1966, future Students for a Democratic Society (SDS) activist and Weather Underground founder, Mark Rudd, capped off the end of his freshman year with a trip to Paris. As he describes it, "My first stop as a tourist was Père Lachaise Cemetery to pay my respects to the Communards. My impression of them was quite romantic."[9] In so doing, Rudd unwittingly enacted exactly the Parisian pilgrimage that CPUSA pamphlets had urged upon radicals of a previous generation:

> You, comrades, if you ever happen to be in Paris, visit the cemetery of Pere-la-Chaise. Bare your heads before the wall, and think of the men, the women, and the children on whose blood and bones the French bourgeoisie has built its prosperity and happiness. Think of the martyrs of the Commune![10]

Yet that memory would be re-animated at Columbia two years later, as students affiliated with SDS occupied five buildings on campus to protest the university's decision to open a gymnasium in Morningside Park, a public space previously open to the largely African American surrounding community, and its ongoing links with the US Defense Department.

The name the occupiers chose for themselves – Communards – was, as Rudd explains in his memoirs, "joyously seized upon, both as a historical reference to the short-lived Paris Commune of 1871 and even more so as a symbol of a new, collective future."[11]But if the term summoned the past and the future, it also mediated the way occupiers experienced their present situation, speaking directly to their day-to-day organizational tactics. As Tom Hayden describes it,

> The next five days were an experience resembling the Paris Commune of the nineteenth century . . . The theory of democratic participation held firmly in the occupied buildings, requiring that the thousand or more strikers be given a voice in the fateful decisions ahead, not to mention immediate ones like the obtaining of food and basic supplies.[12]

The Commune was not, then, simply a static, nostalgic site to be revisited in Paris in the 1960s. As Garson and Savio's reflections on the FSM movement by way of 1871 and Draper's revisionist historiography of that touchstone uprising reveal, and its resurfacing in Columbia in 1968 would later further solidify, the Commune was newly visible in this moment as US student radicalism made it at once newly visitable on campus and newly vital for the New Left. But its re-appearance had neither the organizational apparatus of commemoration of the CPUSA nor the earlier, motlier annual cycle of postbellum celebrations to keep it in circulation. For McCarthyism had helped to rupture its place in the radical calendar even as it had helped to erase our memory of that lived practice of internationalist feeling, though it had not fissured the resilience of its re-occupation and resurfacing by radicals with no affiliations per se to any party.

These 1960s invocations suggest that the legacy of the Commune reached not only into the earlier twentieth century and the politics of the Cultural Front but also into the later twentieth. It survived the reign of the McCarthy era – and with it, the decimation of the radical print and performance culture that had done so much to sustain leftist memory in the US – because it offered radicals at once a vital international touchstone and a viral alternate future, a detour away from both 1917 and capitalism as they had known it. Echoing Endore's likening of the uprising to "a free-for-all," lacking the top-down organization of a party, prone to spring up anywhere unannounced, the story of the Commune that survived the 1950s, by way of university classrooms as well as sit-ins, offered 1960s radicals not so much a program as a promise – a memory of a revolutionary future that might be "vomited up" at any moment.

As I write this, students across the US have once again begun to occupy public spaces on university campuses. They have successfully demanded the resignation of the president of the University of Missouri system, protested police brutality off campus and ongoing structural racism on campus, called on universities to remove Confederate flags and related monuments from campus, and powerfully coalesced around a chant and a social media hashtag that have increasingly become symbols of a highly energized movement: #Black Lives Matter.[13] At Princeton, a place where I spent many years as a graduate student, and rarely known for being a hotbed of activism, members of the Black Justice League staged a sit-in in Nassau Hall, occupying the President's office and calling on the university to remove honorific murals and monuments to Woodrow Wilson because of his staunch segregationist stance both during his time as president of the university and later as president of the United States. Despite these early successes and a recent articulation of common core demands, students have largely been taken to task by commentators, who write off the anger they have vocalized at micro- and macro-level racial aggression as, in short, collective *whining*. As one college president recently put it in an open letter that has gained attention in an array of mass media, as well as social media, outlets, "This is not a day care. It's a university."[14] (A similarly dismissive refrain can be found in coverage of student protests during the now high-water-mark era of US campus activism: *Newsweek*'s piece on the occupation of Columbia in 1968 was titled "Columbia at Bay: When Students Revolt the Target can be Cafeteria Food – or Society Itself."[15])

That this new student movement faces critique from right-wing commentators, as well as from frustrated campus administrators, and, if op-eds in *The Chronicle of Higher Education* and *The Times Higher Education* are any indication, a range of baffled/disgruntled professors should not, I think, be taken as a sign that we are reliving, in a more densely mediated way, the culture wars of the 1980s and 1990s. Instead, I think it is symptomatic of a larger story of radical activism both within and outside the borders of the US: namely, that movements provoke reaction precisely insofar as they unsettle the terms of the lived and the possible, and tracking the range of hyperbolic responses to them can help us index the way in which radical movements created "spaces for new possibilities," as Robin D. G. Kelley describes them in my epigraph to this chapter, rather than simply testify to the "intransigence of power" against which they wrestled. While these most recent occupations and articulations of demand cannot yet be measured with the benefit of hindsight or by the longevity of their afterlives, they do ask us fundamentally to rethink the terms and the space of the university, as well the world outside it. As Tav Nyong'o writes in a recent blogpost on the movement entitled "The Student Demand,"

> The new black student movement is teaching me that it is not enough to protest wrongful death, or to chant each other's names (as we must) when another one of us is murdered. We must also challenge the terms of our living as well as our dying; we need an actual say in how we live and thrive, and how we learn and grow.[16]

What this new student movement has given us, in other words, is a new nomenclature for at once articulating and making visible oppression, as well as a new horizon for imagining everyday life otherwise. That we have been slow to see this is not because the movement has not come to us sufficiently packaged with the battle slogans and costumes of earlier eras but instead because we are too often slow to see what is right in front of us.

To put this a little differently, the question is not now, nor should it ever really have been, "Why no Left in America?,"[17] for as this book has argued, we too often do not remember the vibrant leftist imagination we have had in this country; we are also too quick to discredit radical activism in our own moment (much the same argument could be made of Occupy Wall Street as Black Lives Matter) precisely because movements most often gain recognition and, more to the point, validation as more than moments only when they are safely ensconced in the past. It bears underscoring that this declension narrative is not new: much as Leslie Fiedler looked on the New Radicals of the 1960s as pale analogues of the Popular Front in "The Two Memories," a piece he wrote for the 1968 collection, *Proletarian Writers of the 1930s*, Henry James dramatizes the way postbellum suffragists like Verena Tarrant and Olive Chancellor looked backwards to the days of abolition as the high-water mark of American activism, by then already passed, in his 1886 novel *The Bostonians*.[18]

Of course, another argument this book has made is that radical pasts rarely stay put: they possess us and we, in turn, re-occupy them. As the "viral" recirculation of the Commune across a variety of print forms, media technologies, and performance cultures in the long nineteenth century has shown, radical memories unmoored from nation-based infrastructures of memory – official museums, archives, and national histories – work to a variety of affective and material ends precisely by allowing us to experience memory as at once an act of sensation and affiliation, a modality of feeling that resurfaces at key moments to re-order the horizon of the present, as well as remap what Rancière has elsewhere described as the "distribution of the sensible."[19]

Notes

Introduction

1. On the Commune as "the dictatorship of the proletariat," see Engels's 1891 "Preface" to *The Civil War in France*, 22.
2. See Harvey, *Rebel Cities: From the Right to the City to the Urban Revolution*; Panero, "Commune Plus One"; Grim and Sacks, "Corporate Citizenship"; Rebecca Solnit, "Victories Come in All Sizes." Sep. 15, 2013 <tomdispatch.com> (last accessed May 1, 2015); Ross Douthout, "The Decadent Left." *New York Times Sunday Review* Dec. 3, 2011; Justina, "Anti-Capitalist Meet-up: Karl Marx on the Paris Commune and Occupy Wall Street." *Daily Kos* May 30, 2012; "The Paris Commune and Its Legacy." May 5, 2012 <http://occupyeverything.org/2012/the-paris-commune-and-its-legacy/> (last accessed May 1, 2015); Rebecca Solnit, "The Occupy Movement: Drumbeats of Change." *Los Angeles Times* Sep. 15, 2013; Barry Treb, "The Paris Commune" <http://www.occupypoetry.net/the_paris_commune> (last accessed May 1, 2015); Nicholas Mirzoeff, "The Spirit of Commune Past: A Picture Essay," in his blog "Occupy 2012," a "daily observation on Occupy," <http://www.nicholasmirzoeff.com/O2012/sample-page/> (last accessed May 1, 2015); Rebecca Rothbaum, "A Slow Motion Drama About the Occupiers of 1871." *Wall Street Journal* Mar. 30, 2012; Thai Jones, "As Occupy Wall Street Fades, Powerful Ideas May Live On" <http://www.bloombergview.com/articles/2012-09-21/as-occupy-wall-street-fades-powerful-ideas-may-live-on> (last accessed May 1, 2015); Saswat Pattanayak, "Occupy Wall Street: Challenges, Privileges, and Futures" in the blog "Radical Notes" Oct. 26, 2011; Paul Mason, "Preoccupying." *The Occupied Times* May 8, 2012; Paul Mason, "Global Unrest: How the Revolution Went Viral," *The Guardian* Jan. 3, 2012.
3. Ross, *Communal Luxury*, 2.
4. Zoe Beloff, "History of the Commune," <DaysoftheCommune.com> (last accessed September 30, 2013).

5. Brantley, "'Paris Commune' From the Civilians at BAM Next Wave Festival." *The New York Times* Oct. 4, 2012, <NYTimes.com> (last accessed Aug. 26, 2015).

6. In his monumental volume on the rise and mobilization of (selective) memory in American culture from the Gilded Age to the 1990s, Michael Kammen sums up the commonplace of American amnesia by turning to a 1965 *Esquire* cartoon: "Mexican troops," writes Kammen, "are storming the Alamo and an American soldier responds, 'Oh, stop worrying. The public has a short memory.'" See *The Mystic Chords of Memory*, 9.

7. Quoted in Katz, *From Appomattox to Montmartre*, 171.

8. See Rogin, *Subversive Genealogy*, and Reynolds, *European Revolutions and the American Literary Renaissance*. On the political reverberations of 1848, see Roberts, *Distant Revolutions*. On the Haitian Revolution and American literary and cultural history, see Brickhouse, *Transamerican Literary Relations and the Nineteenth-Century Public Sphere*; Dillon and Drexler, *The Haitian Revolution and the Early United States*; White, *Encountering Revolution*; and Clavin, *Toussaint Louverture and the American Civil War*.

9. See, for example, Blight, *Race and Reunion*; Cloyd, *Haunted by Atrocity*; Shackel, *Memory in Black and White*; Romano and Raiford, *The Civil Rights Movement in American Memory*; Peterson, *Lincoln in American Memory*; Bodnar, *The "Good War" in American Memory*; Sturken, *Tangled Memories* and *Tourists of History*; Doss, *Memorial Mania*; Flores, *Remembering the Alamo*; and Kropp, *California Vieja*.

10. Andreas Huyssen argues that "historical memory is not what it used to be" because of the ways that "untold recent and not so recent pasts impinge on the present" through new media technologies – and thus "the past has become part of the present in ways simply unimaginable in earlier centuries." See *Present Pasts*, 1.

11. A number of historians of urban culture and labor history (Christine Stansell, Frank Donner, Gerald Grob, Samuel Bernstein, and Heather Cox Richardson, among them) have detailed the ways in which the Commune's specter closely shadowed American urban reform movements, repeatedly resurfacing in postbellum discourses on crime, strike-breaking, Red-baiting, and Reconstruction. In these accounts, however, the Commune's continuing cultural reverberations are consistently figured as a synonym and cipher for only the very real anxieties about Gilded Age urbanization and labor agitation, and are most often linked to the unprecedented upheaval of the Great Strike of 1877. As Nell Irvin Painter emphasizes, "the Commune, with its scenes of violent confrontation, served as the prevailing image for Americans faced with labor unrest." See *Standing at Armageddon*, 18.

12. Katz, *From Appomattox to Montmartre*, 187 and 186.

13. See Streeby, *Radical Sensations*.
14. See, for example, Pizer, *American Expatriate Writing and the Paris Moment*, and Kennedy, *Imagining Paris*. Méral's *Paris in American Literature* traces a longer genealogy of the ways the city is figured in and shapes American writing, but offers only a passing mention of the Commune's treatment in American novels and generally dismisses the idea that American writers ever registered the pressing socio-political dimensions of the city around them. McCullough's *The Greater Journey* similarly demonstrates the key role that Paris played in shaping a generation of nineteenth-century American doctors, artists, and writers, but pays scant attention to the moment of the Commune. While Alice Kaplan's *Dreaming in French* focuses on a much more contemporary moment, my work shares Kaplan's interest in the ways that French political and social realities fundamentally shaped American writers and thinkers.
15. Tamarkin, *Anglophilia*, 1 and xix.
16. Ibid., 1.
17. "internationalism, n." *OED Online*. Oxford University Press, <http://www.oed.com/view/Entry/98074> (last accessed Aug. 2015).
18. Much recent scholarship has focused on the way US consumerism was mobilized at home and exported abroad as "soft power" during the Cold War. See, for example, Colomina et al., *Cold War Hothouses*; Castillo, *Cold War on the Home Front*; and Oldenziel and Zachmann, *Cold War Kitchen*.
19. Robbins, *Feeling Global*, 42.
20. Giles, *The Global Remapping of American Literature*, 12.
21. See Edwards, *The Practice of Diaspora*; Kelley, *Freedom Dreams*; Robinson, *Black Marxism*; Baldwin, *Beyond the Color Line and the Iron Curtain*; and Makalani, *In the Cause of Freedom*.
22. Ross, *Communal Luxury*, 11.
23. "Would Hang Capitalists: Declaration Made at a Socialist Rally." *Los Angeles Times* Mar. 17, 1902: 9.
24. Merriman's recent study of the Commune argues that the most lasting legacy of the uprising's bloody suppression has been state-backed massacres and our willingness to broker them. See *Massacre*.
25. "The Commune and Liberty." *The New York Times* May 31, 1871: 4.
26. Castronovo, *Beautiful Democracy*, 89.
27. Bernstein, "The Impact of the Paris Commune in the United States," 60.
28. Throughout, in theorizing sensation and the sensational mode, I draw on Streeby's elaboration of the sentimental and the sensational, in particular her suggestion that these "modalities . . . exist on a continuum rather than as opposites." See *Radical Sensations*, 2. On the affective registers of the sensation novel, see Cvetkovich, *Mixed Feelings*. On the radical work that the "aesthetics of astonishment" might do, particularly in modernist experimentation, see Entin, *Sensational Modernism*.

29. My reading of the Commune's circulation in US media culture draws on Rigney's recent work on Sir Walter Scott and "memory on the move," as well as Bolter and Grusin's earlier work on the ways in which new digital media recycle and respond to previous visual and media forms – though I am concerned with earlier instances of this "remediation" phenomenon. See Rigney, *The Afterlives of Walter Scott*, and Bolter and Grusin, *Remediation*. My exploration of the Commune's "virality" in late nineteenth- and early twentieth-century US print culture is indebted to McGill's work on the antebellum "culture of reprinting," as well as Ryan Cordell's more recent work on anonymous "viral" content in antebellum newspapers. See McGill, *American Literature and the Culture of Reprinting*, and Cordell, "Reprinting, Recirculation, and the Network Author in Antebellum Newspapers."

30. Robert Tombs, "A Time for Cherries." *Times Literary Supplement* Jun. 17, 2015: 8.

31. Théophile Gautier quoted in Ross, *The Emergence of Social Space*, 149. Also discussed in Merriman, *Massacre*, 207.

32. Rydell, *All the World's a Fair*, 10.

33. In the 1870s and 1880s the static circular panorama was dubbed a "cyclorama." Miller argues that the popularity of Philippoteaux's "Siege of Paris" near-singlehandedly sparked the so-called Panorama Revival of the late nineteenth century. See "The Panorama, the Cinema, and the Emergence of the Spectacular," 54.

34. From the Boston Center for the Arts (housed in the former Boston Cyclorama Building) website. Its historical page on the "Siege of Paris" suggests that the cyclorama left Boston in 1879 for a run in San Francisco ("The Boston Cyclorama"). My research has unearthed "Siege of Paris" descriptive booklets for later runs in Chicago, San Francisco, and Los Angeles as well.

35. As Hyde explains, "An American on a pleasure tour in Europe, a descriptive book tells us, visited [the original 'Siege of Paris'] in the Champs-Elysées in 1874. So vivid an impression did the panorama make on him that he resolved to exhibit it two years later during the celebrations of the one hundredth anniversary of the Declaration of Independence." See *Panoramania*, 170.

36. Foner, "French Trade Union Delegation to the Philadelphia Centennial Exposition, 1876," 240.

37. Quoted in ibid., 241.

38. Quoted in ibid., 264; emphasis mine.

39. Ibid., 277.

40. On the sense of heightened embodiment and uncannily "immersive spectatorship" experienced by panorama-goers, see Miller, "The Panorama, the Cinema, and the Emergence of the Spectacular," 55, and Griffiths,

Shivers Down Your Spine, 42. It bears remarking that the great irony – and archival challenge – of writing about these larger-than-life, spectacularly visual forms – spreading out in 360 degrees across, at times, more than 20,000 square feet of canvas and reaching such vast audiences of men, women, and children in nineteenth-century America – is their paradoxical *spectrality*: few examples of the panoramic form are now extant, and only a few contemporary images of them remain. My reading of panoramic memory and the Commune has been necessarily confined to ephemera archived from the Centennial Exposition – catalogues, guidebooks, letters, and newspaper reports advertising or documenting visits to "Paris By Night" and "The Siege of Paris."

41. Landsberg, *Prosthetic Memory*, 2.
42. Miller, "The Panorama, the Cinema, and the Emergence of the Spectacular," 47.
43. Hyde, *Panoramania*, 7.
44. *Colosseum Hand Book*, 5.
45. Brooks, *Bodies in Dissent*, 78.
46. *Colosseum Hand Book*, 3 and 8.
47. See Boime, *Art and the French Commune*, 94.
48. "The Siege of Paris" circular remarks on this subsidization in detail, and Hyde further adds that "the French government gave encouragement and support, supplying the [corps of artists] with military data and remitting half the freight and export charges." See *Panoramania*, 170.
49. "Cyclorama of the Siege of Paris: Opinions of the Press" advertisement, Philadelphia, 1876. Rare Books and Special Collections, Princeton University.
50. The Franco-Prussian war began in July 1870; by September 4, the Emperor Napoleon III, along with 100,000 French troops, had been captured at Sedan and a republican coalition voted to overthrow the Second Empire and inaugurate a new Government of National Defense (a government that would eventually become the Third Republic). Following a four-month Prussian siege that encircled Paris and cut it off from all lines of communication with (and food supplies from) the provinces, a disastrous peace accord was signed on January 28, 1871. In February, Adolphe Thiers, a royalist with only the vaguest of republican sympathies, was elected *chef du pouvoir exécutif* of the new republic. His decision not only to allow the victorious Prussian army to parade through Paris, but also to dissolve the National Guard, end the war-time moratorium on rent and debts in Paris, and attempt to seize the National Guard's munitions in Paris would help to spark the popular uprising on March 18 that led to the election of the Commune.
51. Guidebook for *The Siege of Paris* cyclorama (Boston, 1877), 8. Theater Collection, New York Public Library.
52. Hyde, *Panoramania*, 169.

53. Oettermann, *The Panorama*, 342.
54. A reviewer in *Forney's Morning Press* (a local Philadelphia newspaper) notes,

> We saw the same idea in Paris symbolized from the inside or French view of the siege . . . the present diorama, by the same artists, is from the German attack on the French capital . . . Schools with their teachers, and families with their parents, and citizens and strangers, should see and study this fine work; and, as they leave, let them gaze upon the touching, descriptive tragedy of the massacre of the Archbishop of Paris by the Commune in 1871.

Quoted in "Cyclorama of the Siege of Paris: Opinions of the Press."
55. Ibid.
56. Griffiths, *Shivers Down Your Spine*, 63.
57. Ibid., 4.
58. By 1872, images of the Commune had been banned in France, and no doubt such a spectacular invocation of the event would have been deemed too sensational for French audiences. I find it all the more telling that the painting, partly funded by the French government, was crafted for an American audience primed for yet another representation of the Commune.
59. Quoted in "Cyclorama of the Siege of Paris: Opinions of the Press."
60. See Constantine, *Letters of Eugene V. Debs*. Vol. 1, 11.
61. I am riffing here on Derrida's reading of revolutionary time by way of his reading of *Hamlet* in *Specters of Marx* but drawing as well on an emerging body of scholarship on queer temporalities and their centrifugal effects on the cultural and literary histories that literary texts and literary scholars might tell, in particular Freeman's *Time Binds*, and Pratt's important work on the multiple temporalities of American modernity in *Archives of American Time*.
62. See Stein, "American Literary History and Queer Temporalities," 863.

Chapter 1

1. James, *The Bostonians*, 433. While James's novel was published in 1886, it is set in the Boston of the 1870s.
2. "The Week." *The Nation* May 25, 1871: 351.
3. Tax, *The Rising of the Women*, 42. Painter explains, for example, that newspaper accounts of the Great Strike, noting the "singular" involvement of wives and mothers of the strikers, "often described these unshrinking, uninhibited working-class women as 'pétroleuses.'" See Painter, *Standing at Armageddon*, 18. On the connections drawn

between women involved in the Great Strike and the unsexed women of the Commune, see Bellesiles, *1877*; Brown, *Beyond the Lines*; and Katz, *From Appomattox to Montmartre.*

4. Short stories such as "Une Petroleuse: A Souvenir of Versailles" and "A Petroleuse" garnered copy in periodicals like *Every Saturday, Peterson's Magazine,* and *Youth's Companion* throughout the 1870s, and Aaron Burr Joyce's poetic return to the figure, "La Petroleuse: May 1871," ran in *Belford's Monthly and Democratic Review* in 1892. Articles on the petroleuses, either as a historical or a contemporary phenomenon, continued to circulate in US newspapers into the early 1900s. (A search on Newspapers.com and Cengage's 19th Century US Newspapers, for example, locates nearly 400 hits for "petroleuse" in regional newspapers from more than thirty US states, including *The Atlanta Daily Sun, The Milwaukee Sentinel,* and *The Daily Cleveland Herald.*)

5. "A New Order of Amazons." *Frank Leslie's Illustrated Newspaper* Mar. 16, 1872: cover.

6. Ibid.

7. Quoted in Gullickson, *Unruly Women of Paris*, 4. See also Alexandre Dumas, fils, *Une Lettre sur les choses du jour*, 16–17.

8. Gullickson, "La Pétroleuse: Representing Revolution," 248. See also her discussion in *Unruly Women of Paris.*

9. "Bloodshed in Paris." *Harper's Weekly* Jul. 8, 1871: 629; emphasis mine.

10. Dror Wahrman situates the rise of "gender panic" in late eighteenth-century England, and identifies it as "a pattern of change that decisively reversed, over a relatively short period of time, a variety of interconnected cultural forms through which eighteenth-century Britons signaled their recognition of the potential limitations of gender categories." See *The Making of the Modern Self*, 34. I would argue that the gender panic we see in the 1870s is part of this larger transatlantic trend, and is similarly constituted by a hardening of gender categories in the wake of the increasing gender mobility and fluidity experienced during the Civil War: for example, women's cross-dressing to participate in it. On narratives of American women's gender-bending during the Civil War, see Young, *Disarming the Nation*; Blanton and Cook, *They Fought Like Demons*; and Ginsburg, *Passing and the Fictions of Identity.*

11. My reading of the "viral" circulation of these late nineteenth-century texts is indebted to Meredith McGill's formulation of the "culture of reprinting" in antebellum America, as well as Ryan Cordell's important recent work on anonymous "widely reprinted snippets" in antebellum newspapers. See McGill, *American Literature and the Culture of Reprinting, 1834–1853,* and Cordell, "Reprinting, Circulation, and the Network Author in Antebellum Newspapers." On the literary circuits and cultural repercussions of newspaper recirculation, see Garvey, *Writing with Scissors,* and Langer Cohen, *The Fabrication of American Literature.*

12. Balliet, "Let them Study as Men and Work as Women."

13. See, for example, the cut "Vive la Ligne" which appeared in the July 15, 1871 edition of *Harper's Weekly*.

14. Brown, *Beyond the Lines*, 5.

15. While Brown most often focuses on the way in which the visual codes of an image work in concert with the text around them, he does note that the images of the Great Strike in *Frank Leslie's* "contradict[ed] the visual typing suggested by its words" and thereby "reformulated the meaning of the Great Uprising." See *Beyond the Lines*, 162. He is, however, less interested in what that means for how we might read the images in concert with the news than in what these images suggest about the changing representational face of the Gilded Age.

16. Ibid., 72.

17. "Women of Paris." *Harper's Weekly* May 27, 1871: 485.

18. Ibid., emphasis mine. The "Red" analogy cut both ways, at once condemning Communards for their savageness and the Native Americans for their threatening "Communistic" tendencies. On this pervasive equation, see Paul C. Rosier's "'They Are Ancestral Homelands,'" 131–6.

19. Ibid., emphasis mine.

20. "Women of Montmartre." *Harper's Weekly* Jul. 8, 1871: 620.

21. Ibid.

22. Ibid.

23. Ibid. The Boule Noire was an infamous Montmartre nightclub turned political club during the Commune. Women's clubs met there regularly to discuss wages and "free unions"; under the direction of Sophie Poirier, the "Boule Noire Women's Club" organized a women's "vigilance committee" for the defense of the 18th arrondissement. For a further discussion of the club's activities, see Carolyn J. Eichner, *Surmounting the Barricades*, 111.

24. By this I mean that the scenes posed a spectacular challenge both to American periodicals' ability to represent the scenes and to Americans to digest or make sense of them. I am drawing here on Trouillot's formulation of the "thinkable" event (the Haitian revolution was not, in his reading, "thinkable" for Europeans) in *Silencing the Past* and also on Ross's work on the "representable" event in *May 68 and Its Afterlives*.

25. Gullickson, *Unruly Women of Paris*, 187.

26. Ibid.

27. "La Pétroleuse." *Harper's Weekly* Jul. 8, 1871: 628.

28. Ibid.

29. Quoted in Gullickson, *Unruly Women of Paris*, 177; "La Pétroleuse." *Harper's Weekly*, 628.

30. "La Pétroleuse." *Harper's Weekly*, 628.

31. Ibid.

32. In 1871 King was an up-and-coming foreign correspondent who covered the Commune for the *Boston Journal*. He would go onto author *The Great South* (1875), a record of his journey through the Reconstruction South, along with a number of influential works on the political and social situation in Europe, several volumes of poetry, and an 1895 boys' book on the Commune, *Under the Red Flag*, that I discuss at length in the following chapter.

33. Katz, *From Appomattox to Montmartre*, 78.

34. The poem ran, for example, on the cover of the Little Rock *Morning Republican* (Aug. 24, 1871), the *Georgia Weekly Telegraph* (Sep. 5, 1871), the *Junction City [Kansas] Weekly Union* (Sep. 2, 1871), and the *Osage County Chronicle* (Sep. 14, 1871), as well as in the Boston suffragist paper *Woman's Journal* (Sep. 2, 1871) and *Albion: A Journal Of News, Politics and Literature* (Oct. 21, 1871). It was later reprinted on the cover of the *Philadelphia North American and United States Gazette* (Feb. 4, 1881).

35. "Books of the Week." *The Nation* Jul. 8, 1880: 35–6.

36. Streeby, *Radical Sensations*, 2.

37. Edward King, "A Woman's Execution (Paris, 1871)." *Scribner's Monthly* 2 (Sep. 1871): 500, 1–4.

38. Nearly two decades later, King would return to the story of "a woman's execution" in his volume of journalistic reminiscences: "On Thursday a very beautiful young girl . . . was marched down the Rue de la Paix to the Place Vendôme for execution." See *Europe in Calm and Storm*, 488. It bears remarking that central details of the poem remain intact here: the remarkable beauty of the long-haired girl about to be shot, her resolution in the face of death, and the transposition of the violence of the execution scene to the "snarling women" in the crowd rather than the soldiers carrying out the summary execution – details that strikingly echo the image "The End of the Commune – Execution of a Pétroleuse" that ran in *Harper's Weekly*.

39. King, "A Woman's Execution," 10; 12–14.

40. "Women of Montmartre," 620; "Women of Paris," 485.

41. King, "A Woman's Execution", 1; 17–18; 2.

42. Ibid., 3.

43. Ibid., 21–2.

44. Ibid., 28. On the ongoing role of melodrama in sentimental culture, see Berlant, *The Female Complaint*, and Anker, *Orgies of Feeling*.

45. King, "A Woman's Execution", 32; 25–6.

46. Ibid., 14.

47. Ibid., 1.

48. Ibid., 6; 7; 8.

49. Ibid., 7; quoted in Beaumont, *Utopia Ltd.*, 163.

50. Giordano, "'A lesson from' the Magazines," 24.

51. Bennett, *Poets in the Public Sphere*, 5.

52. Ibid., 136. Giordano writes, for example:

> In light of the magazine's support of both her work and of
> poetry in general, it is wholly appropriate that it was in the
> *Independent* that she placed "The Palace-Burner," a poem
> that, by expressly referencing items from a magazine, reaf-
> firms how pointedly Piatt was enmeshed in her periodical
> milieu. And given that the poem is built on an intertextual
> allusion to *Harper's*, a competitor of the *Independent*, it indi-
> cates Piatt's self-conscious awareness of, and preoccupation
> with, her cultural role as periodical poet.

See "'A lesson from' the Magazines," 25.
53. "The End of the Commune." Editorial. *The Independent* Jun. 1, 1871: 6.
54. Ibid.
55. Wearn, "Subjection and Subversion in Sarah Piatt's Maternal Poetics,"
    168; see also her discussion in *Negotiating Motherhood in Nineteenth-
    Century Literature*, 105–34.
56. Such identification is not, I want to argue, sentimental identification
    (that is, identification *as* introjection). It relies on sympathetic reading,
    and yet the desire it incites is not imagined martyrdom but rather active
    emulation – "acting like" rather than "feeling the pain of" another.
57. Sarah M. B. Piatt, "The Palace-Burner: A Picture in a Newspaper." *The
    Independent* Nov. 1872, 9–12.
58. On "A Child's Party," see Gray, *Race and Time*, 103–26.
59. Piatt, "The Palace-Burner," 37.
60. "Bloodshed in Paris." *Harper's Weekly*, 629; emphasis mine.
61. Piatt, "The Palace-Burner," 11–12.
62. These poems notably rework the anecdote of the "boy with the
    pocket watch," which originally ran in *Le Figaro* on June 3, 1871,
    was first circulated in the US in the "Home and Foreign Gossip" sec-
    tion of *Harper's Weekly* (Jul. 15, 1871: 651), and was reprinted in
    Appleton's Journal (Aug. 19, 1871: 223), remaining vital and viral for
    at least three decades, and resurfacing in a variety of cultural forms
    – from wildly popular histories of the Commune to widely antholo-
    gized poetry and bestselling historical romances. In my reading, the
    story of the boy Communard who was spared comes to play a pivotal
    role in helping Americans negotiate the Commune's violent suppres-
    sion and, quite often, in creating a counter-memory of that event. For
    a further discussion of the wide reprinting of this anecdote, see Katz,
    From Appomattox to Montmartre, 78–9. For some historians of the
    Commune the anecdote curiously becomes an occasion to forget
    (or at the very least, highly delimit) the role children played in fighting
    and dying for the Commune. See, for example, Edwards, *The Paris
    Commune of 1871*, 175.

63. Born in Philadelphia to an academic family that moved to Virginia but remained staunchly pro-Union, Margaret Junkin Preston married a Southerner and counted Stonewall Jackson as her brother-in-law. Opting to remain in Lexington while her father and sister returned home to Pennsylvania when war broke out, she eventually made a name for herself as the most famous "Southern" woman writer of the period. Although her poems were regularly published in prominent American periodicals in the late nineteenth century, and widely anthologized into the twentieth, she has received scant recent critical attention. A few notable exceptions: Paula Bennett includes a Preston poem in her groundbreaking anthology, *Nineteenth Century American Women Poets*; and Preston receives a brief mention in Alice Fahs's volume, *The Imagined Civil War*. See also Stacy Jean Klein's 2006 biography, *Margaret Junkin Preston, Poet of the Confederacy: A Literary Life*.
64. Margaret Junkin Preston, "The Hero of the Commune." *Scribner's Monthly* Apr. 1872: 660–1, 4; 10–15.
65. Ibid., 2.
66. "Home and Foreign Gossip." *Harper's Weekly* Jul. 15, 1871: 651.
67. Preston, "The Hero of the Commune," 5–6.
68. Ibid., 19–20; 37–8.
69. Quoted in Harvey, *Paris, Capital of Modernity*, 329.
70. Preston, "The Hero of the Commune," 51.
71. Although now most remembered for his role as Secretary of State under McKinley and Roosevelt, Hay was, in 1872, a promising young editorial writer for the *New York Tribune* and his work regularly appeared in highbrow literary journals like *Harper's Weekly*, *Scribner's Monthly*, and *The Atlantic Monthly*. Recently returned from diplomatic stints in Paris, Vienna, and Madrid, he garnered significant acclaim with the publication of his volume of "western dialect" ballads, *Pike County Ballads and Other Pieces* (1871).
72. Kirkpatrick, *Reference Guide to American Literature*, 220. The poem was anthologized in, for example, Stedman's anthology. In addition, it circulated in several early twentieth-century textbooks and was reprinted as a poem for workers by the Amalgamated Woodworkers' International Union of America in 1907.
73. John Hay, "A Triumph of Order," *The Atlantic Monthly* Apr. 1872: 219; 4.
74. Preston, "The Hero of the Commune," 7; Hay, "A Triumph of Order," 5–8.
75. Hay, "A Triumph of Order," 12; 11.
76. Ibid., 13.
77. Ibid., 37–40.
78. William Dean Howells, "Mr. John Hay's Volume of Poetry." Editor's Study. *The Atlantic Monthly* Sep. 1890: 638; emphasis mine.
79. Thayer, *The Life and Letters of John Hay*, 377.

80. Piatt, "The Palace-Burner," 34; 22–3; 35.
81. Ibid., 9.
82. Hendler, *Public Sentiments*, 197.
83. Zimmerman, *Panic!*, 57.
84. Havelock Ellis, *Man and Woman: A Study of Secondary and Tertiary Sexual Characters*, 310.
85. Piatt, "The Palace-Burner," 33, 36; 32.
86. Ibid., 32.
87. "The 'New Woman' Denounced; Bishop Doane of Albany in Closing the St. Agnes's School Gives His Views on Female Suffrage." *The New York Times* Jun. 7, 1895: 11. Doane's address was reprinted as a pamphlet by the Albany Anti-Suffrage Association in *Extracts from the Addresses of the Rt. Rev. William Croswell Doane* (Albany, NY: 1895).
88. "The 'New Woman' Denounced," 11.
89. See, for example, "Badly Advised: The Unemployed Step Onto Anarchist Ground." *New-Yorker Staats-Zeitung* Aug. 22, 1893; "A Family Affair." *The Galveston Daily News* Sep. 19, 1886: 2; "Gather Them In." *The Scranton Republican* May 24, 1906: 4; and Vivian Gornick, *Emma Goldman*, 39. For a further discussion of Goldman as "the reincarnation, for most Americans around the turn of the century, of the pétroleuse," see Zimmerman, *Panic!*, 39–80.

Chapter 2

1. See, for example, Brooke Allen's "G. A. Henty and the Vision of Empire"; Mark Oppenheimer, "What They're Reading at the Kitchen Table"; and Margaret Talbot's "A Mighty Fortress."
2. Beneath an emblem of a boy in coonskin cap, book in hand, bow and arrows over his shoulder, and dog at his side, the now-defunct Vision Forum Ministries website cites its "All-American Boy's Adventure Catalogue" as "one step on th[e] journey" to reclaiming "courageous boyhood." See Vision Forum.com: All-American Boy's Adventure Catalogue (last accessed Feb. 15, 2009); now accessible at <https://web.archive.org/web/20090320183141/http://www.visionforum.com/boysadventure> (last accessed Mar. 15, 2016). This evangelical ministry, known for promoting homeschooling and a culture of "biblical patriarchy," closed in the wake of a 2013 sex scandal involving its founder, Doug Phillips.
3. See Martin Cothran, "G. A. Henty and the Tradition of Adventure Writing for Boys." *Memoria Press*, n.d. <www.memoriapress.com/articles/henty.html > (last accessed Feb. 3, 2009). Although Henty was by trade a reporter, several American publishers have repackaged him as a "historian" because of his own claims to historical authority in his fictions. In an article that ran posthumously in the *Boy's Own Paper*,

for example, Henty insists that "I have never permitted myself to deviate in the slightest degree from the historical facts, except when the boy hero is, so to speak, on the loose." Quoted in Butts, "Exploiting a Formula," 13.

4. Although a broad body of scholarship exists on Henty as a writer of empire – Seth Lerer, for example, dubs him "the most prolific of the [Victorian] imperial boys' writers" – virtually no work has been done on Henty's popularity in the US with readers at the turn of the twentieth *and* twenty-first centuries. Lerer, *Children's Literature*, 162.

5. Marsh, "A History of the Commune," 84.

6. Quoted in Holmes, *The Autocrat*, 125; quoted in Paul Shorey, "The Paris Commune." *The Dial* Mar. 16, 1896: 167.

7. *The Century Illustrated Magazine*, for example, ran three extensive features on the Paris Commune between 1892 and 1901: a front-page, two-part series by celebrated British war correspondent Archibald Forbes (whom *The New York Times* called, in 1899, "the most notable war correspondent now living"), an explicit rejoinder to Forbes's 1892 piece published nearly a decade later by William Trant, a British–Canadian economist who, like Forbes, had covered the Commune first-hand, and an account of "What an American Girl Saw of the Commune" (C. W. T.). The latter is noteworthy for offering readers a lengthy but extremely limited account of the events it claims to resurrect for display. Yet the piece was printed in a highly respected American magazine with some 200,000 subscribers, and warranted specific notice in both the *Review of Reviews* and the *Century*'s own advertisements. That it did so suggests that highbrow American readers in the 1890s might be hooked by its title alone.

8. Kaplan argues that American imperialists like Senator Albert Jeremiah Beveridge "saw imperial warfare as an opportunity for the American man to rescue himself from the threatening forces of industrialization and feminization at home." See *The Anarchy of Empire in the Making of U.S. Culture*, 92–3. Bederman similarly details the way in which anxieties about American masculinity and racial superiority were twinned in America's fears about the declining frontier. See *Manliness and Civilization*, 22. In my reading of American Commune romances, the Communards are primitivized and racialized so as to more easily demonstrate their unsuitability for self-governance in the logic of these novels.

9. The Great Fade Out of the Commune in American memory is, for historian Philip Katz, a product of it being "too firmly linked to what can be called the age of democratic civil wars." It is his contention, then, that precisely because the Commune became a focal point in America's changing view of popular uprisings abroad, which shifted "from the romantic traditions of rebellion towards the new traditions of social revolution and terrorism; [a shift] inspired by fears of

domestic unrest," it eventually faded from view. This contention does not account, though, for the literary resurgence of the Commune in the 1890s, and largely glosses over the fact that the struggle for what would constitute a democratic revolution was far from settled in 1877. See Katz, *From Appomattox to Montmartre*, 191–2.

10. Renan, "What is a Nation?," 11.
11. Quoted in Wilson, *Paris and the Commune*, 1.
12. Several lithographs of the Mur des Fédérés in the Musée d'Art et d'Histoire in St. Denis bear Hugo's phrase, "Le cadavre est à terre mais l'idée est debout" ("The body is buried but the idea is still standing" (translation mine).) The idea circulates implicitly in his collection of poems on the Franco-Prussian war and the Commune, *L'Année terrible*.
13. As McGill has reminded us, US readers, particularly before the International Copyright Act of 1891, read British books extensively. See *American Literature and the Culture of Reprinting*. Henty's tremendously popular boys' books were read in both authorized and pirated editions. They were also regularly advertised in *The Dial* and received notice in, for example, *The Bookman*, the *American Monthly Review of Reviews*, and *The Literary World*. *A Woman of the Commune* was published in both London and New York editions in 1895 under the title *A Girl of the Commune*.
14. King, *Under the Red Flag*, 548.
15. Mailloux, *Rhetorical Power*, 104.
16. Kidd, *Making American Boys*, 55; Mailloux, *Rhetorical Power*; and Jacobson, *Being a Boy Again*.
17. Cohoon, *Serialized Citizenships*, xiv.
18. Ibid., 154.
19. Bristow, *Empire Boys*, 147.
20. Hunt, "G. A. Henty," 71.
21. Quoted in Wheeler and Crane, "General Gossip of Authors and Writers," *Current Literature: A Magazine of Contemporary Record* Jan. 1903: 111.
22. Bristow, *Empire Boys*, 1.
23. Quoted in ibid., 147.
24. Conservative critic Brooke Allen criticizes Henty's new-found popularity in the American homeschooling community on the grounds that homeschoolers mistake Henty for literature when, quite properly, his books – of the adventure or empire variety – can only be read as history. See "G. A. Henty and the Vision of Empire," 21.
25. Clark, "Imperial Stereotypes," 44.
26. Ibid., 47.
27. Cutting across boys' adventure fiction and the genre of historical romance, not to mention highbrow and middlebrow fiction, the motif draws on Henri Murger's *The Bohemians of the Latin Quarter* (1851) and surfaces in such canonical figures as Chad Newsome in *The*

Ambassadors. It is a commonplace, in other words, that an American or British man might go to Paris in search of a bohemian lifestyle, seeking culture and corruption in the city Benjamin dubbed the "capital of the nineteenth century." I am less interested, then, in the conventional trope that gets these characters to Paris than in these novels' reworking of that plot – with Paris figured as the site of potential political contamination or conversion for these men rather than as a site of sexual or high cultural "awakening."

28. Henty, *A Woman of the Commune*, 108; emphasis mine.
29. Kaplan, "Nation, Region, Empire," 259.
30. In her suggestive reading, Kaplan posits that historical romances represent and render invisible the politics of empire-building. See "Romancing the Empire," 667.
31. Although King's writing for adults – particularly his 1875 volume on his travels during Reconstruction, *The Great South* – has received continuing scholarly attention (see, for example, Jennifer Rae Greeson's 2006 *ALH* piece, "Expropriating the Great South and Exporting 'Local Color,'"), no previous critical work has been done on his writing for children.
32. King, *Under the Red Flag*, 18.
33. Frank's unlikely friendship with the General parallels Archibald Forbes's time with Dombrowski in "What I Saw of the Commune," which ran as a cover story in *The Century* in October and November of 1892.
34. King, *Under the Red Flag*, 335.
35. Ibid., 420.
36. Pratt, *Archives of American Time*, 22.
37. King, *Under the Red Flag*, 159.
38. Ibid., 503. Admittedly, the novel's forgetting of the Civil War is, in itself, not surprising, as many novels of the period attempt to gloss over, or reconcile the divisions between, North and South. The text's attempts to forestall any parallels between "the Civil War in France" and the American Civil War are symptomatic, however, of its larger work to obscure any broader identification between the Commune and the US.
39. En route to their hotel near the place Vendôme, Grandpa Drubal and his grandchildren encounter a line of Communard National Guardsmen, who let them pass after one Communard in the ranks cries out: "Citizens, I ask you to allow this son of liberty from free America, with his protégés, to pass through the lines to regain his hotel. In the name of liberty the Commune must accord all favor to the land of freedom!" See *Under the Red Flag*, 13. Though the scene is layered in a certain irony, it nevertheless echoes Frank M. Pixley's reports in the *San Francisco Chronicle* that "Americans had a universal pass in the city" during the Commune. Quoted in Friedman, *State-Making and Social Movements*, 87–8.

40. King, *Under the Red Flag*, 62.

41. Ibid., 63.

42. Henty, *A Woman of the Commune*, 259.

43. Henty hints that Dampierre's complexion reveals mulatto blood and Hartington later links his friend's radical political sentiments to time spent on his father's plantation. On the connections made between "unruly" Communards and African Americans during Reconstruction, see Richardson, *The Death of Reconstruction*, 96–7. On anti-Communard rhetoric mobilized against African Americans involved in cross-racial organizing or simply seeking racial and economic uplift in this period, see Schechter, *Ida B. Wells-Barnett and American Reform*, 74, and Charles Chesnutt's short story, "The Web of Circumstance," in his 1899 collection, *The Wife of His Youth*. Chesnutt will later flip this rhetoric on its head by slyly suggesting that unruly white lynch mobs are would-be Communards in his 1901 novel, *The Marrow of Tradition*.

44. As if to underscore the relation to Michel, albeit in a slightly domesticated and eventually conveniently killed-off version, Minette is described as "one of the priestesses of the Commune [who] rides about on horseback with a red flag and sash." See Henty, *A Woman of the Commune*, 242. At her death, she is marked as the worst of her lot, shooting from every barricade, rallying troops at every turn.

45. Ibid., 260.

46. Ibid., 243.

47. Ibid., 74.

48. Quoted in Boime, *Art and the French Commune*, 201.

49. King, *Under the Red Flag*, 268.

50. Ross elaborates a strategic use of space and time to avoid "the metaleptic 'it couldn't have been otherwise' dead end" style of analysis. See *The Emergence of Social Space*, 11. While this move is directed most explicitly against new historicist analysis, it also characterizes much of the analysis of the Commune, and not simply from its vitriolic critics.

51. Gullickson, *Unruly Women of Paris*, 124.

52. Quoted in ibid., 169.

53. Henty, *A Woman of the Commune*, 278.

54. The novel's revisioning assiduously forgets that the National Guardsmen were rarely given a chance to fight. As Clayson points out, "'Combat as its absence' could title so many National Guardsmen in Paris during the fall and winter of 1870–71." See *Paris in Despair*, 97.

55. Henty, *A Woman of the Commune*, 282.

56. Ibid., 278.

57. Translation mine. "Tout le peuple de Montmartre est là. Qui dans le peuple? Bien sûr, il y a des gens avec des fusils . . . mais il y a surtout des femmes. Elles arrivent de partout . . . [et] crient: 'Vive les soldats! Vive l'armée!' Elles leur tendent des bouteilles de vin . . . N'ont-ils pas marché toute la nuit sans rien à manger, sans rien à boire . . . Et tout

à coup se produit cette chose extraordinaire: en une heure ou deux, l'armée disparaît; elle fond comme sucre dans l'eau." See Lefebvre, "La Commune," 42.

58. Henty, *A Woman of the Commune*, 285.
59. King, *Under the Red Flag*, 390.
60. Henty, *A Woman of the Commune*, 289.
61. Much as King avoids or glosses over the specter of the Civil War, Henty's novel takes pains to put to rest the question of women in politics. We see Mary engaged early in the novel with the cause of women's suffrage but the novel never allows its readers to glimpse the political clubs where women were meeting daily during the Commune, and Mary renounces politics altogether at the moment she succumbs to Henty's hero.
62. Henty, *A Woman of the Commune*, 289.
63. Ibid., 292. For a rich reading of the way Frederic Isham's 1904 novel, *Black Friday*, similarly links feminist agitation with the Commune and the need to contain threats to both American capitalism and "domestic anarchy," see Zimmerman, *Panic!*, 39–80.
64. Henty, *A Woman of the Commune*, 388.
65. King, *Under the Red Flag*, 305.
66. Ibid., 550.
67. Ibid., 358.
68. Katz finds in this passage a striking attempt on King's part to draw attention to the parallels between the Commune and the American Civil War. See *From Appomattox to Montmartre*, 191. I would argue, however, that while the passage makes explicit a tension that permeates the novel, it is overshadowed by the way in which the text can only make this parallel in retrospect.
69. Harvey, *Paris*, 323.
70. Ibid., 356; 236.
71. King, *Under the Red Flag*, 158.
72. Kaplan, "Romancing the Empire," 681; 689.
73. Henty, *A Woman of the Commune*, 108.
74. Ibid., 290.
75. Chambers, *The Red Republic*, 1. *The Bookman: A Literary Journal* quips in its March–August 1897 edition that

> the adjective "red" seems to have a peculiar attraction for novelists lately, judging from the frequency with which it appears on the title-page of recent fiction. It would seem too that it is a lucky word to use, for strangely enough, nearly all the "red" books [including *The Red Republic* and Francis Gribble's novel of the Commune, *The Red Spell*] have been *more than usually successful*. (emphasis mine)

See "Bookmart," 87.

76. "Recent Fiction." *The Dial* 1 Jun. 1896: 335.

77. See "Robert W. Chambers," *The New American Supplement to the Encyclopedia Britannica*, 741, and "Recent Fiction," 335; emphasis mine. Ann Rigney offers a rich analysis of the hybrid nature of nineteenth-century fiction in the work of Sir Walter Scott but also in the genre more generally, and suggests that it actually "calls into question any easy separation of fictional narrative and historical fact." See *Imperfect Histories*, 16.

78. In laying claim to this "eyewitness"-style credibility, these novels are also cashing in on larger US publishing trends. As Matthew Schneirov persuasively suggests, the Magazine Revolution of the 1890s – the birth of the popular magazine – had everything to do with the turn to immediacy in the form of eyewitness accounts of both the muckraking and the quotidian varieties. See *The Dream of a New Social Order*.

79. Savidge, *The American in Paris*, Preface.

80. "Recent American Fiction." *The Dial* 16 Dec. 1895: 384.

81. "Recent Fiction." *The Atlantic Monthly* Sep. 1896: 426. Castronovo argues that "clashes between strikers and soldiers often seemed like grand spectacles" in this period, and points out that "the American characters in Chambers' *The Red Republic* repeatedly look down on the barricades and battles as though such sights were bits of street theater." See *Beautiful Democracy*, 86.

82. On the relationship between incest and the domestic novel, see Connolly, *Domestic Intimacies*; Barnes, *States of Sympathy*; and VanDette, *Sibling Romance in American Fiction, 1835–1900*.

83. Chambers, *The Red Republic*, 366.

84. Amy Kaplan notes that, "in contrast to the domestic novels of the 1850s, heroines of the 1890s romances escape from the home to participate in imperial adventures." See *The Anarchy of Empire*, 95.

85. The move here to "primitivize" the Communards is not a new one. Contemporary French commentators on the Commune likened it to "savages with rings through their noses ruling the city" (quoted in Ross, *The Emergence of Social Space*, 149). It is rather its recurrence at this moment that interests me here – particularly in Henty and Chambers, but also in, for example, Molly Elliot Seawell's movement to liken the pétroleuses to uncivilized "cannibals in Africa." See "The Commune of Paris," 707.

86. Chambers, *The Red Republic*, 3.

87. As we have seen in *Under the Red Flag*, Grandpa Drubal encounters Communards, such as Jules Raisin, who claim a fraternity between the two republics, despite the fact the novel quickly forestalls this identification, while in *A Woman of the Commune*, Minette's love for the American Dampierre concretizes this possible affinity. It bears remarking again that the American boys' book can only imagine Communards – rather than Americans – indulging this sentiment.

88. Katz does not, for example, focus on any American Communard except Cluseret.

89. In my reading, the novel "domesticates" the Commune – exporting its threat home – while working, through the figure of the "native-born" Landes, to contain that very threat. It also archives the presence of Communard refugees in New York and the early visibility of Commune supporters in that city, a topic I take up at greater length in the next chapter.

90. Chambers, *The Red Republic*, 314.

91. Ibid., 302.

92. Savidge, *The American in Paris*, 18.

93. Ibid., 11.

94. Ibid., 266–7.

95. Ibid., 254.

96. Ibid., 267.

97. Ibid., 260.

98. Quoted in Kaplan, *The Anarchy of Empire*, 92.

Chapter 3

1. Advertisements for "Paris, from Empire to Commune" ran in various New York papers. See, for example, *The Evening World* Jul. 3, 1891: 3 and *The Sun* Jul. 3, 1891: 10. For more on Pain, "self-proclaimed 'pyrotechnist of her Majesty the Queen,'" who spent twenty-five years staging elaborate pyrotechnic spectacles centered on historical cataclysms such as "The Defeat of the Spanish Armada," "The Destruction of Pompeii," and "The Bombardment of Alexandria" at Coney Island, see Immerso, *Coney Island*, 34. For a further discussion of the visual technics of Pain's pyrodramas in the context of the emergence of the cinema, as well as a reading of Pain's "Last Days of Pompeii," see Yablon, "'A Picture Painted in Fire'."

2. "Paris." *The Ohio Democrat* Jul. 8, 1893: 1.

3. See "Fireworks Draw Well." *Rocky Mountain News* Jun. 28, 1894: 5. For a further discussion of the Coney Island debut of "Paris, From Empire to Commune," see, for example, "Fireworks at Manhattan Beach." *The Sun* Jun. 26, 1891: 2; "Our Theaters Next Week." *The New York Evening World* Jul. 4, 1891: 2; and "Fireworks at Manhattan." *The New York Times* Sep. 8, 1891: 5.

4. See *Brooklyn Daily Eagle* Aug. 21, 1891: 2 and "News of the Theater." *The Sun* Aug. 2, 1891: 15.

5. "Paris." *The Ohio Democrat*: 1.

6. Of the Versaillais troops' entry into Paris, the anonymous author writes, for example: "I cannot say I saw very much, for I was not the first at the

window, but I do not believe my youngest brother saw anything." See C. W. T., "What an American Girl Saw of the Commune," 61–3.

7. "Paris, From Empire to Commune" advertisement in *The Times* Oct. 13, 1892: 2.

8. "The Night Crowd." *The Times* Oct. 22, 1892: 5.

9. "Paris." *The Ohio Democrat* Jul. 8, 1893: 1.

10. Ibid., 1.

11. Although the term "radical" emerged in this period to describe the "Radical Republicans" who approved the strongest measures against the South following the Civil War, the term circulated in media coverage of anarchists and labor activity, although these figures were more often than not labeled "agitators" or "agitatresses" by newspapers in the pre-Popular Front era. I follow scholars such as Shelley Streeby, Mary Jo Buhle, Paul Buhle, and Timothy Messer-Kruse in using the term in relation to nineteenth-century activists and agitators, and like cultural historian Marcella Bencivenni, I employ it to gesture to what she identifies as "the whole range of class-based ideologies associated with the European Left: anarchism, socialism, syndicalism, and communism," as well as the more motley crew of postbellum leftist reformers that historian Timothy Messer-Kruse has dubbed the "Yankee International." See Bencivenni, *Italian Immigrant Radical Culture*, 2.

12. See Streeby, *Radical Sensations*, 253; Kelley, *Freedom Dreams*, 41; and Avrich, *An American Anarchist*, 94.

13. See, for example, "Badly Advised: The Unemployed Step Onto Anarchist Ground." *New-Yorker Staats-Zeitung* Aug. 22, 1893; "A Family Affair." *The Galveston Daily News* Sep. 19, 1886: 2; "Gather Them In." *The Scranton Republican* May 24, 1906: 4; and Vivian Gornick, *Emma Goldman*, 39.

14. My reading of nineteenth- and early twentieth-century radicals' reclamation and rethinking of defeat is indebted to contemporary theorizations of failure that have emerged out of queer studies in the past decade: in particular, Halberstam's formulation of failure "as a way of refusing to acquiesce to dominant logics of power and discipline as a form of critique. As a practice, failure recognizes that alternatives are embedded already in the dominant and that power is never total or consistent." See *The Queer Art of Failure*, 88. For a rich discussion of revolution and the poetics of failure – and moving beyond it – in African American studies, particularly vis-à-vis formulations of Afro-pessimism and "optimism," see Moten, "Black Op," and Wilderson, *Red, White and Black*.

15. Clymer argues that the changing mediascape of the late nineteenth-century US allowed Haymarket to become "one of the earliest sites where citizens are convened as a public body around mass-mediated repetitions of an intentional atrocity" and that the media's portrayal of the condemned anarchists drowned out counter-narratives by the men

themselves. See *America's Culture of Terrorism*, 38. For a rich analysis of the elegies that emerged to commemorate the executed anarchists in a variety of labor, socialist, and alternative newspapers, see Boudreau, "Elegies for the Haymarket Anarchists," 319–47. On the ongoing role of Haymarket in radical world movements and global radical memory, see Streeby, *Radical Sensations*.

16. See Brooks, *Bodies in Dissent*, 9, and Rusert, "The Science of Freedom," 291.

17. *From Appomattox to Montmartre*, 186. Seminal studies of the US left, such as Paul Buhle's *Marxism in the United States*, make no mention of the Commune's ongoing role in the consolidation of leftist memory and identity, and recent studies on Haymarket in a global context do not situate the international feeling it provoked within the wider memory culture of the Commune of which it was part, despite the fact contemporary anarchists such as Peter Kropotkin suggested at the time that Haymarket had "*almost* acquired the same importance as the Paris Commune." See Kropotkin, "Before the Storm," in Roediger and Rosemont, *Haymarket Scrapbook*, 140 (emphasis mine). On the importance of the Commune's memory in the Chicago anarchist community and movement culture, see Roediger and Rosemont, *Haymarket Scrapbook*; Avrich, *The Haymarket Tragedy*; Green, *Death in the Haymarket*; and Litwicki, *America's Public Holidays*.

18. As Gutman and Bell, in their study of late nineteenth- and early twentieth-century Italian–American radicals, point out, "Socialists and anarchists tended to create a radical world within a conservative one, replacing orthodox ceremonies with their own." See *The New England Working Class and the New Labor History*, 277. For a further discussion of Italian–American "rich oppositional" culture, see Bencivenni's *Italian Immigrant Radical Culture*. On subversive balls in Yiddish memory culture, see Michels, *A Fire In Their Hearts*; on Jacobin culture and Commune festivals within Chicago's German anarchist community, see Schneirov, *Labor and Urban Politics*, and Keil et al., *German Workers in Chicago*.

19. "Multiple News Items." *The North American* (Philadelphia), Mar. 25, 1884.

20. *Rocky Mountain News* Mar. 18, 1887: 4.

21. Quoted in Peter Glassgold, *Anarchy!*, xxxvii.

22. "Resisting Left Melancholy," 26. Anker adopts a similar stance towards left-wing nostalgia in her recent book, *Orgies of Feeling*. In her analysis of what she terms "left melodrama," she argues in particular that "while [it] intends to galvanize radical social change, its conventions and attachments limit its capacity to depict the distinct challenges and specific conditions of political life." See *Orgies of Feeling*, 204.

23. Brown, "Resisting Left Melancholy," 20.

24. Muñoz, *Cruising Utopia*, 106.

25. Funchion, *Novel Nostalgias*, 191–2 and 194.
26. Herron, *From Revolution to Revolution*, 13.
27. "Would Hang Capitalists," 9.
28. Goyens, *Beer and Revolution*, 48–9.
29. "'Red' Emma Makes Anarchistic Speech in Milwaukee to Curious Listeners." *Los Angeles Times* Mar. 23, 1908: 13.
30. Kropotkin, "Commune of Paris." *Mother Earth* 7.3 (May 1912): 79.
31. Ross, *Communal Luxury*, 11.
32. Ibid., 29.
33. Messer-Kruse cites the parade as a prime example of the "interracial cooperation" at the heart of the motley crew of New York socialists that he terms the "Yankee International" and points out that the event had especial purchase for African Americans because the IWA had asked prominent abolitionist Wendell Phillips to speak that day on behalf of the Commune. See *The Yankee International*, 195–7. Scriabine, Sullivan, and Buhle identify the parade as "one of the largest in New York City's history." See *Voices of the Left: 1870–1960*, 2. Although Katz dismisses the organizers of the parade as "easy to ridicule, easy to ignore," he offers a brief discussion of the parade. See *From Appomattox to Montmartre*, 164–6. On Victoria Woodhull's involvement in the event, see Gabriel, *Notorious Victoria*, 151–4. For contemporary coverage, see, for example, "Parade of the Internationals." *Milwaukee Weekly Sentinel* Dec. 19, 1871: 1 and "Rule or Ruin: Communist Parade in New York." *Pittsburgh Daily Post* Dec. 18, 1871: 1.
34. "The Parade of the Internationals." *Frank Leslie's Illustrated Newspaper* Jan. 6, 1872: 263; "The Internationals Parade." *Lawrence Daily Journal* Dec. 19, 1871: 2.
35. "The Internationals." *Vermont Chronicle* Dec. 23, 1871: 2.
36. Quoted in Rumble, *The Swifts*, 81.
37. "Recalling the Paris Commune: An Assemblage Where Every Shade of Red Could Be Seen." *New York Times* Mar. 24, 1884: 5. Coverage of the previous year's festival similarly fixated on the provocation of the color scheme; see, for example, "Domestic Dispatches." *The Galveston Daily News* Mar. 20, 1883: 4.
38. "The Communist Anniversary." *New York Times* Mar. 17, 1884: 2.
39. At times, these annual festivities even elicited international coverage: in 1906, the *Winnipeg Tribune* ran an article entitled "Socialists in U.S. Cities Celebrate Anniversary," which detailed the celebrations, complete with "living pictures, singing, instrumental music and several stirring addresses" by prominent anarchist and socialist leaders, held that year in Chicago, Milwaukee, and Paterson, New Jersey, in honor of the Commune's thirty-fifth anniversary. See "Paris Commune: Socialists of U.S. Cities Celebrate Anniversary." *Winnipeg Tribune* Mar. 19, 1906: 3.
40. See Kelley, *Freedom Dreams*, 41, and Ashbaugh, *Lucy Parsons*, 253. Over the last decade, Streeby has near single-handedly revived Lucy

Parsons's place in the canon of American literary studies: see her chapter on Parsons in *Radical Sensations*; "Doing Justice to the Archive Beyond Literature"; and "Labor, Memory, and the Boundaries of Print Culture." For a further brief biography of Parsons, see Avrich, *The Haymarket Tragedy*.

41. Davis, *Women, Race, and Class*, 152.
42. Streeby, "Labor, Memory, and the Boundaries of Print Culture," 414.
43. Streeby, "Doing Justice to the Archive Beyond Literature," *Unsettled States*, 104.
44. For a rich analysis of the ways in which later forms of surveillance, in particular by the Federal Bureau of Investigation (FBI), impinged upon and crucially shaped twentieth-century African American literature, see William J. Maxwell's recent book, *F.B. Eyes*, and Douglas Field's new biography of James Baldwin, *All Those Strangers*.
45. "A Parsons Family Affair." *Galveston Daily News* Sep. 19, 1886: 2.
46. Luciano and Wilson identify their important recent collection as "written by scholars working in the 'minor' fields of critical race and ethnic studies, feminist and gender studies, labor studies, and queer/sexuality studies" who "share what we might describe as a diffusely minoritarian orientation." They also productively "unsettle" our assumptions of both minor fields and "minority" or marginalized subjects. See *Unsettled States*, 6. This chapter's excavation of Parsons as a "viral" postbellum media sensation builds on McGill's work on the antebellum literary market, as well as Cordell's more recent study of the wide reprinting of anonymous snippet content in antebellum newspapers, an early occasion of "viral" circulation he argues is newly visible to us because of recent developments in digitization and the digital humanities. While Cordell is most concerned with what these print networks reveal about communal forms of authorship, I am interested in how such mass reprintings continue in postbellum periodical culture and critically shape American memory as well as literary history. See McGill, *American Literature and the Culture of Reprinting, 1834–1853*, and Cordell, "Reprinting, Circulation, and the Network Author in Antebellum Newspapers," 417–45.
47. Coverage included "The Dusky Anarchist Delivers Tirade." *Los Angeles Times* Mar. 25, 1889: 4; "Chicago Anarchists." *Poughkeepsie Daily Eagle* Mar. 25, 1889: 1; "Chicago Anarchists Talking Again." *The Milwaukee Sentinel* Mar. 25, 1889: 3; "The Anarchists Still Shouting." *Detroit Free Press* Mar. 25, 1889; "Lucy Parsons At It Again." *Garnett Journal* (Kansas) Mar. 29, 1889: 1; "Anarchist Ravings." *Morning Oregonian* Mar. 25, 1889: 1; "Lucy Wants a Revolution." *Pittsburgh Dispatch* Mar. 25, 1889: 5; "Lucy Wants a Revolution." *Pittsburgh Daily Post* Mar. 25, 1889: 1; "Lucy Parsons At It Again." *The Bronson Pilot* (Kansas) Mar. 29, 1889: 1; "The Female Anarchist Shrieker." *The McCook Tribune* (Nebraska) Apr. 5, 1889: 3; "Mrs. Parsons Wants

A Revolution." *The Galveston Daily News* Mar. 25, 1889: 4; "Loud-Mouthed Lucy." *The Tennessean* Mar. 25, 1889: 1; "Thirsting for Blood: Mrs. Parsons Trying to Inflame the Chicago Anarchists." *San Francisco Chronicle* Mar. 25, 1889: 1; and "Honoring the Red Flag: Anarchists Celebrate the Anniversary of the Paris Commune." *Chicago Daily Tribune* Mar. 24, 1889: 9.

48. "Honoring the Red Flag: Anarchists Celebrate the Anniversary of the Paris Commune." *Chicago Daily Tribune* Mar. 24, 1889: 9.

49. "The Woman Anarchist" ran in North Dakota's *The Bismarck Weekly Tribune* Nov. 12, 1886: 3. This report by wire from a special correspondent was reprinted in, for example, *The Decatur Weekly Republican* Nov. 4, 1886: 4; *The Topeka Daily Capital* Nov. 7, 1886: 4; *The Marion Star* (Ohio) Nov. 9, 1886: 2; and *The Lawrence Gazette* Nov. 4, 1886: 6.

50. "Honoring the Red Flag." *Chicago Daily Tribune* Mar. 24, 1889: 9.

51. "The Dangerous Classes." *Buchanan's Journal of Man* 1.3 (April 1887; Project Gutenberg, 2008, <http://www.gutenberg.org/files/25890/25890-h/25890-h.htm> (last accessed Oct. 1, 2015). This staging was a staple visual trope of such celebrations; coverage of the 1891 Chicago celebration in *The Atchison Champion* and Raleigh (North Carolina) *News and Observer* similarly emphasized the red flag and the busts of Spies and Ling standing in place of the American flag and American heroes.

52. "The Commune Celebration." *The Cincinnati Enquirer* Mar. 5, 1887: 4.

53. "Mrs. Parsons in New York." *The Milwaukee Sentinel* Oct. 18, 1886: 2.

54. "Honoring the Red Flag," 9.

55. Ibid., 9.

56. Ibid., 9. See earlier note on the cross-country coverage of this event.

57. Quoted in Parsons, *Life of Albert R. Parsons*, 231.

58. See Garvey, "Nineteenth-Century Abolitionists and the Databases They Created."

59. Lucy explicitly signals, for example, that the version of the famous "Haymarket speech," which her husband redelivered during his trial and which she in turn reprints in *Life of Albert Parsons*, is taken from the account of it that ran in the *Chicago Times*. See *Life of Albert Parsons*, 117. Similarly, she explains that the 1885 Labor Day address she includes in the volume was "eloquent and of some length, but only a portion of it has been preserved" and specifies the portion that follows is "quoted from a daily paper of the 8th of September." Ibid., 70. While Clymer argues the media onslaught ultimately drowned out the counter-narratives of the event circulated by the Haymarket anarchists and their defenders, I would argue, as Streeby does, that the vast dissemination of scenes from the trial and execution actually made it a "battle-ground of competing meanings and memories." See Streeby, *Radical Sensations*, 44. I would add that Parsons works to make it an avenue for radical political transformations.

60. Parsons, *Life of Albert Parsons*, 229.
61. Influential labor historian Richard Schneirov describes Greunhut as "Bohemian-born, German-speaking, and American-bred" and "part of the new line of class conscious labor thinkers who had come of age during the 1870s depression and helped bridge the gap between German socialists, American labor reformers, and trade unionists." See *Labor and Urban Politics,* 147.
62. Parsons, *Life of Albert Parsons*, ixx.
63. Keil et al., *German Workers in Chicago*, 264.
64. Parsons, *Life of Albert Parsons*, ixx.
65. Quoted in Ashbaugh, *Lucy Parsons*, 29.
66. See "Anarchists Celebrate." *The Atchison Champion* Mar. 17, 1891; and "Festivities at Chicago." *The News and Observer* Mar. 17, 1891.
67. Although concentrating on a later moment, Burwood's work on "heartland socialism" and the internationally focused Midwestern newspapers and lecture circuits associated with the Socialist Party of America between 1901 and its fissuring in 1919 makes a similar case for studying US Socialism from an international perspective – though, as he points out, "few historians of any bent have looked at the SPA in other than purely national terms." See Burwood, "Debsian Socialism Through a Transnational Lens," 259.
68. Parsons, *Life of Albert Parsons*, 19.
69. Ibid., 70–1.
70. Ibid., 73 and 77.
71. Ibid., 121.
72. De Cleyre, "The Commune is Risen." *Mother Earth* Mar. 1912: 10.
73. Havel, "Biographical Sketch," in Berkman, *Selected Works of Voltairine de Cleyre*, 13.
74. DeLamotte, "Refashioning the Mind," 154.
75. Quoted in DeLamotte, "Refashioning the Mind," 154.
76. Avrich, *An American Anarchist*, 94.
77. See Avrich, *An American Anarchist*; DeLamotte, *Gates of Freedom*; and Presley and Sartwell, *Exquisite Rebel*.
78. See Berkman, *Selected Works of Voltairine de Cleyre*. We know, for example, that de Cleyre spoke at a 1906 Paris Commune celebration in Philadelphia at the Radical Library, along with George Brown, Frank Stephens, Chaim Weinberg, and several prominent French and Italian radicals. See Falk et al., *Emma Goldman*, 459.
79. On the unfinished translation, see Havel's "Biographical Sketch," in Berkman, *Selected Works of Voltairine de Cleyre*, 13. Louise Michel's memoirs were eventually edited and translated in 1981 through funding from a National Endowment for the Humanities grant. See Lowry and Gunter, *The Red Virgin*.
80. Herron, *From Revolution to Revolution*, 4.

81. "The Paris Commune," in Glassgold, *Anarchy!*, 64. De Cleyre's essay was originally published in the March 1914 issue of *Mother Earth*.
82. "The Paris Commune," in Berkman, *Selected Works of Voltairine de Cleyre*, 243.
83. Ibid., 244.
84. Ibid., 245.
85. De Cleyre, "The Commune is Risen," 12.
86. "The Paris Commune," in Glassgold, *Anarchy!*, 64.
87. Ibid.
88. Ibid., 66.
89. Ibid., 64.
90. "The Paris Commune," in Berkman, *Selected Works of Voltairine de Cleyre*, 251.
91. Ibid.
92. De Cleyre, "The Commune is Risen," 12.

Chapter 4

1. See Brown, *A Sense of Things*, 178.
2. See, for example, Graham, "Notes of a Native Son"; Brown, *A Sense of Things*, 177–88; and Yablon, *Untimely Ruins*, 258–63. Most recently, Shari Goldberg has offered a fascinating reading of the way buildings "testify" in James. See Goldberg, *Quiet Testimony*, 120–48.
3. Brown, *A Sense of Things*, 177.
4. James, *The American Scene*, 91.
5. Ibid., 229; emphasis mine.
6. Yablon, *Untimely Ruins*, 260.
7. For example, James's celebrated biographer, Leon Edel, insists

    > *The American Scene* contains an exuberance of observation, a depth of historical feeling, and a personal involvement not to be found in his other travel writings. The others had been written mainly to bring home to Americans – then still distant from Europe – a sense of the picturesque, the quaint, the beautiful, in foreign lands.

    See Edel, "Introduction," viii.
8. I am borrowing here but also departing from Nora's formulation of "lieux de mémoire," most particularly his notion of the memory site as purely self-referential – cut off from history – and his implicit sense of the national boundaries that structure collective memory and sites of memory – memory culture organized by archives, monuments, and orchestrated celebrations of a "shared" national past. See Nora, "Between Memory and History."

9. Abel, *Signs of the Time*, 17. See also Ross's influential formulation of the concept in *The Emergence of Social Space* and Merrifield's helpful discussion in *Metromarxism*.

10. In his 2008 biography of the James family, Paul Fisher points out that Henry "avidly monitored the Prussian occupation of Paris during the autumn of 1870 by means of telegraphed reports in newspapers *as if he himself* were a cane-wielding bourgeois Parisian on the boulevard." See Fisher, *House of Wits*, 275; emphasis mine. While James's fascination with the Franco-Prussian war and the Commune that followed on its heels was actually far from exemplary – many Americans shared it – what interests me is Fisher's notion that James followed the events in Paris *as if he were* French. That unlikely feeling of possession nicely points to the way the sensational (ostensibly international) news from Paris comes to seem deeply personal.

11. Levenstein, *Seductive Journey*, 140. He also points out that tour companies had already been organizing tours while the bombardment itself was still ongoing for those interested in catching glimpses of it from the hills outside the city.

12. Dickens, "How Paris Mourns," 152.

13. Art historian Jeannene Przyblyski notes that

> the widespread demand for photographs quickly became a part of the hyped-up haze of notoriety and fascination through which mass journalism participated in the process of mythologizing and commodifying the Commune. In July, Jules Moinaux reported in *Le Charivari* that an English businessman had purchased fifty thousand images of the toppled Vendôme column for sale abroad . . . Disderi took out a paid advertisement in the same publication for his *Ruins of Paris and the Surrounding Areas*, billed as a complete itinerary to aid the diligent tourist in visiting each site.

See Przyblyski, "Moving Pictures," 265.

14. Katz, *From Appomattox to Montmartre*, 81–2.

15. My introduction offers a further discussion of "Paris by Night"; for more on the Coney Island pyrodrama, "Paris, from Empire to Commune," see Chapter 3.

16. Despite the fact that few photographs of the Commune dead were officially circulated in US print culture, a market for them seems nevertheless to have existed. *Anthony's Photographic Bulletin* warns readers, for example, that the demand for such images was so high that, in a curious case of body-swapping, negatives of Confederate dead were being reprinted in Paris and shipped back to the US as "[authentic] pictures of the killed about the Paris fortifications." See Viator, "From Across the Water." *Anthony's Photographic Bulletin* (Dec. 1871): 397.

17. On Civil War corpse photography, see Finseth, "The Civil War Dead: Realism and the Problem of Anonymity"; Sweet, *Traces of War*; Trachtenberg, *Reading American Photographs*; and Lee and Young, *On Alexander Gardner's Photographic Sketch Book of the Civil War*. Sweet, in particular, argues that "During and after the Civil War, photographic representation of corpses in the landscape was an important mechanism of the *legitimation* by appropriation" and that conventions of landscape portraiture in the photographs allowed the photographer to capture "traces of violence [that were] transformed into signs legitimating the Union." See *Traces of War*, 85.

18. Fournier, "Les Photographies des ruines de Paris en 1871 ou les faux-semblants de l'image," 137.

19. Luxenberg, "Creating *Désastres*," 117. For a rich reading of the Tuileries ruins as "mutilated body," see Wilson, *Paris and the Commune, 1871–78* and "Memory and the Politics of Forgetting: Paris, the Commune, and the 1878 Exposition Universelle"; for further analysis of the photography of Paris in ruins, see Fournier, *Paris en ruines*; Tillier, *La Commune de Paris, révolution sans images?*; and Przyblyski, "Moving Pictures."

20. "The Ruins of Paris." *New York Times* Jun. 16, 1871: 2.

21. Baedeker, *Paris and Northern France*, vii. For a further discussion of post-Commune Paris, see guidebooks such as Spark, *The Stranger's Vade Mecum* and Baedeker, *Paris et ses environs*.

22. I am thinking here of Communards who lamented that "the only crime of the Commune was to have *anticipated* the future," while their critics complained, instead, that the revolution portended or instantiated a turn to the (primitive) past. Quoted in Beaumont, *Utopia Ltd.*, 480.

23. Quoted in Blix, *From Paris to Pompeii*, 2.

24. Rees, *We Four, Where We Went and What We Saw in Europe*, 81.

25. Ibid., 81.

26. Yablon, *Untimely Ruins*, 10; emphasis mine.

27. Sweet argues that images such as "Ruins in Charleston" demonstrate "the restorative but evasive pastoralism" that allowed Northern viewers to re-appropriate the Southern landscape. See *Traces of War*, 163. On the connections between the Paris Commune and the Chicago Fire in US visual and political culture, see Katz, *From Appomattox to Montmartre*, 124–6, and Smith, *Urban Disorder and the Shape of Belief*, 49–50 and 301. For a rich analysis of the fragmented nature of Civil War ruins in US memory, see Nelson, *Ruin Nation*.

28. On the perverse thrill occasioned by observing the curious perfection of a building in decay, see Macauley's discussion of "ruin-pleasure" in *The Pleasure of Ruins*, 348.

29. Wister, "Why Do We Like Paris?" *Lippincott's Magazine of Popular Literature and Science* 23 (Jun. 1879): 673. Throughout the 1870s and into the 1890s, articles on the ruins of Paris – and the Tuileries ruins in particular – were featured in US mass and middlebrow periodicals,

prominent literary and political journals, humor magazines, and even children's periodicals, among them *Frank Leslie's Sunday Magazine*, *Harper's Weekly*, *The Independent*, *Appleton's Journal*, *Lippincott's Magazine of Popular Literature and Science*, *The Century*, *Puck*, and *The Youth's Companion*. See, for example, John Burroughs, "A Glimpse of France." *Appleton's Journal* Jan. 18, 1873: 107, and J. A. Priest, D.D., "Paris and France." *New York Evangelist* Jan. 6, 1881: 1.

30. James, *The Tragic Muse*, 181.
31. Priest, "Paris and France," 1; emphasis mine.
32. Wister, "Why Do We Like Paris?", 673.
33. "The Ruins of Paris." *New York Times* Jun. 16, 1871: 2.
34. "The Last of the Tuileries." *The Youth's Companion* Feb. 15, 1883: 60.
35. *Puck* Mar. 29, 1882: 55.
36. "The Tuileries Doomed." *The Washington Post* Aug. 27, 1879: 2. It bears remarking the incredible incongruity of Paris's venerable "demolition artist," Baron Haussmann, championing the cause of leaving the Tuileries ruins intact.
37. Holmes, *Our Hundred Days in Europe*, 177.
38. Bicknell, "The Tuileries Under the Second Empire." *The Century* 47.5 (Mar. 1894): 651.
39. Marx, *The Civil War in France*, 113.
40. James, *Transatlantic Sketches*, 100.
41. See Walker, "Henry James, Cultural Critic," 249–60. To further illustrate this point, at the time of this writing a Modern Language Association (MLA) database search yields 113 hits for the it-text of the 1990s, *The American Scene*, while *Parisian Sketches* and *Transatlantic Sketches* each garner a modest 2 hits.
42. Buzard, "A Continent of Pictures," 35.
43. Ibid., 36.
44. Edel, *Henry James: The Conquest of London, 1870–1881*, 63. Although Fussell suggests that James accesses the ruined Tuileries by way of Zola's 1892 novel, *Le Débâcle*, Edel notes that James specifically toured the ruins of Paris in 1872, and as James's later biographer, Fisher, points out, James and his sister Alice toured the Louvre and Tuileries area extensively. See Fussell, *The French Side of Henry James*, 187; and Fisher, *House of Wits*, 289.
45. Lee, "Rimbaud's Ruin of French Verse," 73. Lee writes suggestively of the "open ruins" of the Commune: "If the ruin is an architectural object that *disrupts* the confines of architecture per se, if it undermines architecture's attempt to divide and give measure to space, then the open ruin is one of its most synthetic models" (69; emphasis mine).
46. James, *Transatlantic Sketches*, 100.
47. William James's description of "afterimages" seems particularly intriguing in relation to Henry's historic "sense":

> As a rule sensations outlast for some little time the objective stimulus which occasioned them. This phenomenon is

the ground of those "afterimages" which are familiar in the physiology of the sense-organs. If we open our eyes instantaneously upon a scene, and then shroud them in complete darkness, it will be as if we saw the scene in ghostly light through the dark screen. We can read off details in it which were unnoticed whilst the eyes were open.

See *The Principles of Psychology*, 645.

48. Ann Stoler's recent work to theorize ruination as residual traces of violence on ostensibly post-colonial landscapes and temporalities is similarly concerned with apprehending ruins by other sensory means. See her introduction to *Imperial Debris*.

49. Henry James, Letter to Henry James, Sr. and Mary Walsh James, Jun. 28, 1872. I am extremely grateful to Dr. Zacharias at the Center for Henry James Studies for providing me with the transcriptions and facsimiles of this and the other letters from James's 1872 travels, and also for his thorough and helpful suggestions on the 1872 trip and James's early Parisian writings as I worked on early drafts of this chapter.

50. What interests me most about James's choice of the term "impressions" is the fact that it implies both a surface on which an imprint can be made (a writing surface, a spatial terrain, and skin/flesh/affect in the case of James) and the remainders inhabiting the palimpsestic space.

51. James, *Henry James: Letters*, 300; original emphasis.

52. Ibid., 300.

53. Raskin, "Henry James and the French Revolution," 724.

54. Ibid., 724. Raskin emphasizes that "James's entire generation focused on 1789, for the Victorians were terrified by the thought of social revolution" (725). While I do not doubt this, I do find it curious that Raskin overlooks the way Europe's most recent (and more radical) social revolution – namely, the Paris Commune – amplified those fears.

55. In "The Politics of Innocence: Henry James's *The American*," Rowe suggestively argues that "the political and historical aspects of the international theme were of considerable importance to Henry James as he began work on *The American*," and contrasts Newman's problematic ignorance of the political situation in France with James's own avid reading of French newspapers and reports in the *Tribune*. Rowe, "The Politics of Innocence," 179.

56. Argues Rowe, "The rapid change in the political revenge drama acted out in France after the Franco-Prussian War has certain similarities with the cycles of revenge that organize the plot of *The American*." Rowe, "The Politics of Innocence," 190. See also his intriguing reading of Christopher Newman and *The American*'s collapse of the "distinction between Europe and America," in *The Other Henry James*, 56–74.

57. It seems worth mentioning that while partisans of the Commune referred to *themselves* as Communards, their critics – both in the UK and the US – quickly labeled them "Communists." James's choice of nomenclature is therefore surprisingly sympathetic. Of course, the

novel never tires of ironizing Poupin, of pointing to the ways in which there is something a little hollow – or rather, a little performative – to his politics and "the bitterness" of his exiled state.

58. Clymer similarly suggests that

> James's terrorist fiction is particularly fascinating because it enacts a remarkable series of displacements. Despite the fact that working-class deprivation and anger loom everywhere in the shadows of the plotline, James's model of terrorist violence and revolution is against aristocratic rather than capitalist foes. Moreover, his terrorists are Russian, German, and French rather than the Irish and Irish Americans who were performing terrorist acts throughout London in the 1880s. And most notoriously, he arms his ill-fated terrorist, Hyacinth, with a small pistol rather than with dynamite, the bête noire of the 1880s.

See *America's Culture of Terrorism*, 72.

59. James, *The Princess Casamassima*, 114.
60. Ibid., 379.
61. Ibid., 380; emphasis mine.
62. Ibid., 382.
63. Ibid., 380. Meissner argues that the "splendid Paris" that Hyacinth finds is largely one of his own design, mediated by his ideas about and early reading of the city. See Meissner, "The Princess Casamassima," 66.
64. Seltzer, "*The Princess Casamassima*," 508.
65. James, *The Princess Casamassima*, 381. Graham reads the intriguing presence of Hyacinth's grandfather as part of the larger subterranean queer politics of the novel:

> Hyacinth's imaginary encounter with his maternal grandfather, the French revolutionary "who had known the ecstasy of the barricade and had paid for it with his life," exemplifies the novel's parallel discourse, in which the political forces proscribing nonreproductive sexuality and the psychic forces repressing homogenic desire mirror each other.

Graham, "Henry James's Subterranean Blues," 181.

66. James, *Princess Casamassima*, 380–1.
67. Ibid., 381.
68. Freud famously likens the unconscious and the subterranean strata of Rome's history to one another, but ultimately suggests that

> it is clearly pointless to spin out this fantasy any further: the result would be unimaginable, indeed absurd. If we wish to represent a historical sequence in spatial terms, we can do so only by juxtaposition in space, *for the same space cannot accommodate two different things.*

See *Civilization and Its Discontents*, 9; emphasis mine.

69. Shaer, Review of *Foreign Bodies* by Cynthia Ozick.
70. Fussell, *The French Side of Henry James*, 185.
71. Ibid., 183.
72. James, *The Ambassadors*, 125.
73. *Paris in a Week*, 5.
74. Edel, *Henry James: A Life*, 25. James himself discusses the recollection in *A Small Boy and Others*.
75. Ross, *The Emergence of Social Space*, 8.
76. James, *The Ambassadors*, 111.
77. Ibid.
78. Ibid.
79. Ibid.
80. Pana-Oltean, "'The Extravagant Curve of the Globe.'"
81. James, *The Ambassadors*, 111. Griffin persuasively points out that Strether's mode of visual perception is always akin to a metonymic slide, "saturated with associations, associations that are themselves not only visual but also verbal, aural and the like." See *The Historical Eye*, 39.
82. For a rich analysis of the Tuileries Palace as ruin and circulating fragment in James, see McCracken, "The Author as Arsonist."
83. Hutchison, *Seeing and Believing*, 105.
84. James, *The Ambassadors*, 425.
85. Pana-Oltean, "'The Extravagant Curve of the Globe,'" 192.
86. James, *The Ambassadors*, 111.
87. Ibid., 123.
88. Ibid., 146 and 130.
89. Ibid., 286.
90. Ibid., 426.
91. Ibid., 400; emphasis mine.
92. Ibid., 390.
93. Nesher-Wirth, "If This Is Liberty, It Must Be Paris," 248.
94. James, *The Ambassadors*, 235, 363; 475.
95. Ibid., 475.
96. Ibid.
97. Ibid.
98. Fussell, *The French Side of Henry James*, 194.
99. Forster, *Aspects of the Novel*, 155.

Chapter 5

1. See "Communists Crowd Madison Square Garden." *Boston Globe* Mar. 16, 1925: 15 and "7,000 Reds Cheer For Commune." *New York Times* Mar. 16, 1925: 1.
2. "Communists Crowd Madison Square Garden," 15.
3. "Dancing Followed." *New York Times* Mar. 17, 1925: 20.

4. "Paris Commune Pageant To Be Greatest Ever: New York Workers to See Mass Action." *Daily Worker* Mar. 6, 1925: 4.
5. "7,000 Reds Cheer For Commune," 1–2.
6. Commune celebrations and retrospectives garnered considerable annual coverage in periodicals sponsored by the Worker's Party of America and later the CPUSA throughout the 1920s and 1930s. See, for example, "Paris Commune – The First Proletarian Dictatorship." *Young Worker* Mar. 1932: 5; The Jack London Drama Group, "Paris Commune Mass Recitation." *Workers Theatre* Mar. 1933: 9; "Lenin on the Commune." *The Communist* Mar. 1931: 263; and "Paris Commune Meets To Be Held Throughout U.S." *Daily Worker* Mar. 13, 1928: 2.
7. Conn, *The American 1930s*, 222.
8. Castronovo, *Beautiful Democracy*, 74.
9. Siegel's work appeared regularly in *The New Masses* and his illustrations graced a range of radical texts in the 1930s, many of them aimed at children, including "American History Retold in Pictures" (1931). On Siegel's career and illustrations for children, see Mickenberg and Nel, *Tales for Little Rebels*, 173.
10. Trachtenberg, "Introduction," in Siegel, *The Paris Commune: A Story in Pictures*, 3.
11. Rideout, *The Radical Novel in the United States, 1900–1954*, 211.
12. Olgin, "Introduction," in Spiro, *Paris on the Barricades*, 4.
13. Ibid., 6; emphasis mine.
14. Spiro, *Paris on the Barricades*, 43. Spiro writes, for example, of the new Paris unfolding, "There were no strangers in those blissful days in Paris! All were brothers, all were citizens of the first Universal Republic. French as well as foreigners, even the Prussians with whom we had just been at war. A new spirit pervaded the air." See *Paris on the Barricades*, 19.
15. Ibid., 60.
16. Ibid., 36–7.
17. Ibid., 39.
18. Ibid., 43.
19. Ibid., 40.
20. Denning, *The Cultural Front*, xvii.
21. This appropriation of mass-cultural forms is, of course, not new. For a discussion of the ways in which postbellum radicals repurposed media spectacles and sentimental culture, see Chapter 3. On the ways in which radicals such as Lucy Parsons disrupted nineteenth-century "practices of looking," see Streeby, *Radical Sensations*.
22. Siegel, *The Paris Commune*, 25; 22.
23. Olgin, "Introduction," in Spiro, *Paris on the Barricades*, 5.
24. Siegel, *The Paris Commune*, 31.
25. Spiro, *Paris on the Barricades*, 64.
26. Quoted in Starr, *Commemorating Trauma*, 169.

27. Starr, *Commemorating Trauma*, 169.

28. Siegel, *The Paris Commune*, 25.

29. Spiro, *Paris on the Barricades*, 64.

30. Crary, "Spectacle, Attention, Counter-Memory," 107.

31. Trachtenberg, "Introduction," *The Paris Commune*, 3.

32. Ibid., 3.

33. Siegel, *The Paris Commune*, 30.

34. Trachtenberg, "Introduction," in Siegel, *The Paris Commune*, 4.

35. Ibid., 5; original emphasis. Marian Sawyer noted in the aftermath of the Commune's centennial in 1971 that

> while the Paris Commune has become part of the living memory of the workers' state, it has undergone a strange metamorphosis. Elsewhere a symbol of heroic protest against a treacherous government of privilege or privilege of government, in the Soviet Union the Paris Commune has become part of the legitimating apparatus of a bureaucratic state.

See "The Soviet Image of the Commune," 245.

36. Eagleton, "Foreword," in Ross, *The Emergence of Social Space*, xiv.

37. Olgin, "Introduction," in Spiro, *Paris on the Barricades*, 3.

38. Ibid., 3.

39. Conn, *The American 1930s*, 58.

40. Ibid., 102. In the mid-1920s, Gorman penned a popular exegesis of *Ulysses* and, in turn, garnered the distinction of being Joyce's authorized biographer. He also published a number of other biographies, historical romances, and works of criticism over the course of his extremely prolific career. For a further discussion of Gorman's work, see Horace Reynold's review, "The Man Who Wrote Ulysses." *New York Times* Feb. 18, 1940, and Conn, *The American 1930s*, 12.

41. Jane Spence Southron, "A Novel of Strength and Stature." Review of *Jonathan Bishop*. *The New York Times* Nov. 26, 1933: BR6. Clipping of Farrar & Rinehart's advertisement for *Jonathan Bishop*, Herbert S. Gorman Papers, "Promotional Material," Box 7 Folder 8, Rare Books and Special Collections, Princeton University.

42. Walter Snow, "Gorman's Picturesque Puppets." Review of *Jonathan Bishop*. *Partisan Review* (Apr.–May 1934): 56–8.

43. "Yankee Spectator." Review of *Jonathan Bishop*. *Time* Dec. 4, 1933; Gorman, *Jonathan Bishop*, 226.

44. Gorman, *Jonathan Bishop*, 227.

45. Rideout, *The Radical Novel in the United States, 1900–1954*, 181.

46. This vision of revolution continues to exert traction in the American imaginary, resurfacing in, for example, the echo of Occupy Wall Street in Christopher Nolan's 2012 film, *The Dark Knight Rises*, and the figure of Bane "pulling the strings" of the seemingly populist anti-capitalist movement.

47. Gorman, *Jonathan Bishop*, 21.
48. Ibid., 372. It seems worth noting that the novel's account is lifted almost word for word from British foreign correspondent Ernest Alfred Vizetelly's description of the felling:

> Loud were the shouts of "Vive La Commune." Right quickly did one of the Guard's bands strike up the "Marseillaise" but amidst and above it I suddenly heard strains of "Hail, Columbia" played violently on a piano by some Yankee girl belonging to a party of Americans who had installed themselves on the first floor of the Hotel Mirabeau. They came out onto the balcony and were loud in their plaudits.

See *My Adventures in the Commune, Paris, 1871*, 281.
49. Gorman, *Jonathan Bishop*, 372.
50. Ibid., 8.
51. Ibid., 402.
52. Oliver, "Writing From the Right During the 'Red Decade,'" 134. Oliver points out that the racial component of radical politics in the 1930s was met with a fierce counter-reaction in a variety of literary texts; the issue, he explains, became most pressing in the aftermath of the 1931 resolution by "the Communist International . . . stating that 'the Negro Problem' must be part and parcel of every campaign conducted by the Party" (134).
53. Gorman, *Jonathan Bishop*, 282; 275.
54. Ibid., 284.
55. Ibid., 365.
56. Ibid., 380; 407.
57. Ibid., 408.
58. Conn, *The American 1930s*, 103.
59. Gorman, *Jonathan Bishop*, 431–2.
60. Ibid., 433.
61. Wald, *Exiles from a Future Time*, 3.
62. Ibid., 2.
63. Foley, *Radical Representations*.
64. Several otherwise excellent re-evaluations of horror fiction have largely overlooked werewolves. See, for example, Halberstam, *Skin Shows*; and Newitz, *Pretend We're Dead*. The most exhaustive text on the subject might be Brian J. Frost's *The Essential Guide to Werewolf Literature* (2003), aimed at scholars and fans of the genre.
65. See Ball, "Guy Endore's *The Werewolf of Paris*: The Definitive Werewolf Novel?" *Studies in Weird Fiction* 17.2 (1995): 4.
66. William C. Weber, Review of *The Werewolf of Paris*. *Saturday Review*, Apr. 22, 1933. Clipping from Guy Endore's Scrapbook, S. Guy Endore Papers, Collection 279, Box 69, UCLA's Special Collections.

67. Fluet, "Hit-Man Modernism," in Mao and Walkowitz, *Bad Modernisms*, 269.
68. Sorensen, "A Weird Modernist Archive," 501.
69. On the ways in which modernist writers such as William Carlos Williams, Tillie Olsen, Richard Wright, and Pietro di Donato drew on "the aesthetics of astonishment" to inspire outrage at social and racial injustices, see Entin, *Sensational Modernism*. In my reading, we might include both Endore's bestselling werewolf novel and the agitprop pamphlets that most seem to energize it as examples of what Entin has termed "sensational modernism."
70. Halberstam, *Skin Shows*, 1.
71. Ibid., 21.
72. Endore, *The Werewolf of Paris*, 3. On the ennui and unavoidable interconnectedness of the expatriate community that Endore here archives, see also Cowley, *Exile's Return: A Literary Odyssey of the 1930s*.
73. Ibid., 13.
74. Ibid., 3.
75. Ibid., 295.
76. Ibid., 3.
77. Woloch, *The One vs. the Many*, 2.
78. Robbins, Bruce. "The Moment of Deep Time." Transforming Henry James Conference. John Cabot University, Rome, Italy, Jul. 9, 2011. Keynote address.
79. Endore, *The Werewolf of Paris*, 17.
80. Ibid., 323.
81. Ibid., 145.
82. Ibid., 184.
83. Ibid., 225.
84. Woolcott, "Circulating Library," review of *The Werewolf of Paris* by Guy Endore. *New Yorker* Mar. 25, 1933.
85. Endore, *The Werewolf of Paris*, 243.
86. Quoted in Baring-Gould, *The Book of Were-wolves*, 255.
87. Endore, *The Werewolf of Paris*, 211.
88. Ibid., 285.
89. Ibid., 289.
90. Ibid., 288.
91. Ibid., 291; 290.
92. Ibid., 290.
93. Ibid., 294; 295.
94. Ibid., 262.
95. Quoted in "The Paris Commune: The Truth Told About That Terrible Struggle By the Late Mr. Pixley." *The Labor World* (Duluth, MN) Apr. 15, 1899: 2.
96. Marcus, *Lipstick Traces*, 127.
97. Endore, *The Werewolf of Paris*, 214.

Epilogue

1. Robin D. G. Kelley, interview by Benjamin Holtzman, *In the Middle of a Whirlwind: 2008 Convention Protests, Movement and Movements*, Apr. 21, 2008, <https://inthemiddleofthewhirlwind.wordpress.com/an-interview-with-robin-dg-kelley/> (last accessed Oct. 31, 2015).
2. "*Los Angeles Times* interview with President Clark Kerr (January 6, 1965)," clipping in Hal Draper, *The FSM Papers: Unpublished Documents and Ephemera Relating to the Free Speech Movement at UC Berkeley in 1964–1965*, on microfilm. Berkeley: Independent Socialist Press, 1969.
3. Ibid.
4. Ibid.
5. Marvin Garson, "Berkeley, A Follow-Up," *Solidarity* Pamphlet 3.7 (1965): 3.
6. Savio, "Questioning the Vietnam War." Speech in *Freedom's Orator*, 333–4.
7. Kunen, *The Strawberry Statement*, 30.
8. Draper, *Karl Marx and Friedrich Engels*, 7.
9. Mark Rudd, email to author, Apr. 29, 2015.
10. Spiro, *Paris on the Barricades*, 64.
11. Rudd, *Underground*, 78.
12. Hayden, *Reunion*, 275–6.
13. For more on the timeline and actions of this student movement, see, for example, "Campus Politics: A Cheat Sheet," *The Atlantic Monthly* Dec. 2, 2015, <http://www.theatlantic.com/education/archive/2015/12/campus-protest-roundup/417570/> (last accessed Dec. 2, 2015).
14. Dr. Everett Piper, "This is Not a Day Care," <http://www.okwu.edu/blog/2015/11/this-is-not-a-day-care-its-a-university/> (last accessed Dec. 2, 2015).
15. "Columbia at Bay: When Students Revolt the Target can be Cafeteria Food – or Society Itself." *Newsweek* May 6, 1968: 40–53.
16. Tav Nyong'o. "The Student Demand" Nov. 17, 2015, <https://bullybloggers.wordpress.com/2015/11/17/the-student-demand/> (last accessed Nov. 26, 2015).
17. I am riffing here on the question that German sociologist Werner Sombart famously posed in 1906: "Why is there no socialism in America?" For further discussion of Sombart's question, see Foner, "Why Is There No Socialism in the United States?" and Denning, "'The Special American Conditions.'"
18. Fiedler, "The Two Memories," 3–25.
19. Rancière, *The Politics of Aesthetics*.

Bibliography

Manuscripts and Archival Collections

Billy Rose Theater Collection, New York Public Library
Programs Collection

Charles E. Young Research Library Department of Special Collections, UCLA
S. Guy Endore Papers
Socialist and Labor Movements Pamphlets Collection

Harry Ransom Center, University of Texas at Austin
Photography Collection

Library Company of Philadelphia
Centennial Collection

Musée d'art et d'histoire, St. Denis (France)
Paris Commune Collection

Rare Books and Special Collections, Library of Congress
Paul Avrich Collection

Rare Books and Special Collections, Princeton University
Centennial Exhibition Collection
Herbert S. Gorman Papers
Miriam Y. Holden Collection

Tamiment Library, New York University
Radical Pamphlet Literature Collection
Reference Center for Marxist Studies Collection

Newspapers and Magazines

Albion: A Journal Of News, Politics and Literature (New York)
The American Monthly Review of Reviews (New York)
Anthony's Photographic Bulletin (New York)
Appleton's Journal (New York)
Atchison Champion (Atchison, KS)
Atlanta Daily Sun
Atlantic Monthly (Boston)
Belford's Monthly and Democratic Review (Chicago)
Bismarck Weekly Tribune (Bismarck, ND)
The Blast (San Francisco)
The Bookman (New York)
Boston Globe
Boston Tribune
Bronson Pilot (Bronson, KS)
Brooklyn Daily Eagle
Buchanan's Journal of Man (Cincinnati)
Century Illustrated Magazine (New York)
Chicago Daily Tribune
Cincinnati Enquirer
The Communist (New York)
Current Literature: A Magazine of Contemporary Record (New York)
Daily Cleveland Herald
Daily Worker (New York)
Decatur Weekly Republican (Decatur, IL)
The Dial (Boston)
Evening World (New York)
Every Saturday (Boston)
Frank Leslie's Illustrated Newspaper (New York)
Galveston Daily News (Galveston)
Garnett Journal (Garnett, KS)
Georgia Weekly Telegraph (Macon)
Harper's Weekly (New York)
The Independent (New York)
Indianapolis Journal
Junction City Weekly Union (Junction City, KS)
Labor World (Duluth, MN)
Lawrence Daily Journal (Lawrence, KS)
Lawrence Gazette (Lawrence, KS)
Lippincott's Magazine of Popular Literature and Science (Philadelphia)
Literary World (New York)
Los Angeles Times
McCook Tribune (McCook, NE)
Milwaukee Sentinel
Milwaukee Weekly Sentinel

Morning Oregonian (Portland)
Morning Republican (Little Rock)
Mother Earth (New York)
Nation (New York)
New York Evangelist
New York-Staats Zeitung
New York Sun
New York Times
New York Tribune
New Yorker
News and Observer (Raleigh)
The North American (Philadelphia)
Ohio Democrat (New Philadelphia, OH)
Osage County Chronicle (Burlingame, KS)
Partisan Review (New York)
Peterson's Magazine (Philadelphia)
Philadelphia North American and United States Gazette
Pittsburgh Daily Post
Pittsburgh Dispatch
Poughkeepsie Daily Eagle (Poughkeepsie, NY)
Puck (St. Louis)
Rocky Mountain News (Denver)
St. Louis Globe-Democrat
San Francisco Chronicle
Saturday Review (New York)
Scranton Republican (Scranton)
Scribner's Monthly (New York)
Topeka Daily Capital (Topeka, KS)
Vermont Chronicle (Bellows Falls, VT)
Washington Post
Winnipeg Tribune (Winnipeg, Canada)
Woman's Journal (Boston)
Woodhull and Claflin's Weekly (New York)
Worker's Monthly (New York)
Workers' Theater (New York)
Young Worker (New York)
Youth's Companion (Boston)

Primary and Secondary Sources

Abel, Elizabeth. *Signs of the Times: The Visual Politics of Jim Crow*. Berkeley: University of California Press, 2010.

Allen, Brooke. "G. A. Henty and the Vision of Empire" *New Criterion* Apr. 2002: 20–4.

Anker, Elisabeth. *Orgies of Feeling: Melodrama and the Politics of Freedom*. Durham, NC: Duke University Press, 2014.

Ashbaugh, Carolyn. *Lucy Parsons: American Revolutionary*. Chicago: Charles H. Kerr, 1976.

Avrich, Paul. *An American Anarchist: The Life of Voltairine de Cleyre*. Princeton: Princeton University Press, 1978.

—. *The Haymarket Tragedy*. Centennial edition. Princeton: Princeton University Press, 1986.

Baedeker, Karl. *Paris and Northern France: A Handbook for Travellers*. Coblenz: Karl Baedeker, 1872.

—. *Paris et ses environs*. Paris: Paul Ollendorf, 1889.

Baldwin, Kate A. *Beyond the Color Line and the Iron Curtain: Reading Encounters Between Black and Red, 1922–1963*. Durham, NC: Duke University Press, 2002.

Ball, Jerry. "Guy Endore's *The Werewolf of Paris*: The Definitive Werewolf Novel?" *Studies in Weird Fiction* 17.2 (1995): 2–12.

Balliet, Barbara J. "Let Them Study as Men and Work as Women: Georgina Davis, New Women and Illustrated Papers." *Revolution in Print: Graphics in Nineteenth-Century America*. Special issue of *Common-place: The Interactive Journal of Early American Life* 7.3 (Apr. 2007), <http://www.common-place.org/vol-07/no-03/balliet/> (last accessed Nov. 6, 2009).

Baring-Gould, Sabine. *The Book of Were-Wolves: Being an Account of a Terrible Superstition*. London: Smith, Elder, & Co., 1865.

Barnes, Elizabeth. *States of Sympathy: Seduction and Democracy in the American Novel*. New York: Columbia University Press, 1997.

Beaumont, Matthew. *Utopia Ltd.: Ideologies of Social Dreaming in England, 1870–1900*. Leiden and Boston: Brill, 2005.

Bederman, Gail. *Manliness and Civilization: A Cultural History of Gender and Race in the United States 1880–1917*. Chicago: University of Chicago Press, 1995.

Bellesiles, Michael A. *1877: America's Year of Living Violently*. Reprint edition. New York: New Press, 2012.

Bencivenni, Marcella. *Italian Immigrant Radical Culture: The Idealism of the Sovversivi in the United States, 1890–1940*. New York: NYU Press, 2011.

Benjamin, Walter. "Paris: Capital of the Nineteenth Century (Exposé of 1939)." *The Arcades Project*. Ed. Rolf Tiedemann. Trans. Howard Eiland and Kevin McLaughlin. Cambridge, MA: Harvard University Press, 1999.

Bennett, Paula. *Nineteenth Century American Women Poets*. Oxford: Blackwell, 1998.

—. *Poets in the Public Sphere: The Emancipatory Project of American Women's Poetry*. Princeton: Princeton University Press, 2003.

—, ed. *Palace-Burner: The Selected Poetry of Sarah Piatt*. Champaign: University of Illinois Press, [2001] 2005.

Berkman, Alexander, ed. *Selected Works of Voltairine de Cleyre*. New York: Mother Earth Publishing Association, 1914.

Berlant, Lauren. *The Female Complaint: The Unfinished Business of Sentimentality in American Culture*. Durham, NC: Duke University Press, 2008.

Bernstein, Samuel. "The Impact of the Paris Commune in the United States." *Revolution and Reaction: The Paris Commune 1871*. Ed. John Hicks and Robert Tucker. Boston: University of Massachusetts Press, 1973.

Blanton, De Anne, and Lauren M. Cook. *They Fought Like Demons: Women Soldiers in the Civil War*. New York: Vintage, 2003.

Blight, David W. *Race and Reunion: The Civil War in American Memory*. Cambridge, MA: Harvard University Press, 2001.

Blix, Göran Magnus. *From Paris to Pompeii: French Romanticism and the Cultural Politics of Archaeology*. Philadelphia: University of Pennsylvania Press, 2009.

Bodnar, John. *The "Good War" in American Memory*. Baltimore: Johns Hopkins University Press, 2010.

Boime, Albert. *Art and the French Commune: Imagining Paris after War and Revolution*. Princeton: Princeton University Press, 1995.

Bolter, Jay David, and Richard Grusin. *Remediation: Understanding New Media*. Cambridge, MA: MIT Press, 2000.

"The Boston Cyclorama." *Adventures in Cybersound*. Australian Center for the Moving Image. Nov. 1999, <http://www.acmi.net.au/AIC/CYCLORAMA_BOSTON.html> (last accessed May 10, 2011).

Boudreau, Kristin. "Elegies for the Haymarket Anarchists," *American Literature* 77.2 (2005): 319–47.

Brickhouse, Anna. *Transamerican Literary Relations and the Nineteenth-Century Public Sphere*. Cambridge: Cambridge University Press, 2009.

Bristow, Joseph. *Empire Boys: Adventures in a Man's World*. London: HarperCollins Academic, 1991.

Brooks, Daphne. *Bodies in Dissent: Spectacular Performances of Race and Freedom, 1850–1910*. Durham, NC: Duke University Press, 2006.

Brooks, Peter. *Henry James Goes to Paris*. Princeton: Princeton University Press, 2007.

Brown, Bill. *A Sense of Things: The Object Matter of American Literature*. Chicago: Chicago University Press, 2003.

Brown, Joshua. *Beyond the Lines: Pictorial Reporting, Everyday Life, and the Crisis of Gilded Age America*. Berkeley: University of California Press: 2002.

Brown, Wendy. "Resisting Left Melancholy." *boundary 2* 26.3 (1999): 26.

Buhle, Paul. *Marxism in the United States: Remapping the History of the American Left*. 2nd edition. London: Verso Books, 2013.

Burwood, Stephen. "Debsian Socialism Through a Transnational Lens." *The Journal of the Gilded Age and Progressive Era* 2.3 (2003): 253–82.

Butts, Dennis. "Exploiting a Formula: The Adventure Stories of G. A. Henty." *Popular Children's Literature in Britain*. Ed. Julia Briggs, Dennis Butts, and M. O. Grenby. London: Ashgate, 2008.

Buzard, James. "A Continent of Pictures: Reflections on the 'Europe' of Nineteenth-Century Tourists." *PMLA* 108 (1993): 30–44.

Castillo, Greg. *Cold War on the Home Front: The Soft Power of Midcentury Design*. Minneapolis: University of Minnesota Press, 2010.

Castronovo, Russ. *Beautiful Democracy: Aesthetics and Anarchy in a Global Era*. Chicago: University of Chicago Press, 2007.

Chambers, Robert W. *The Red Republic: A Romance of the Commune*. New York: G. P. Putnam's Sons, 1895.

Clark, Gail S. "Imperial Stereotypes: G. A. Henty and the Boys' Own Empire." *Journal of Popular Culture* 18 (1985): 43–51.

Clavin, Matthew J. *Toussaint Louverture and the American Civil War: The Promise and Peril of a Second Haitian Revolution*. Philadelphia: University of Pennsylvania Press, 2009.

Clayson, Hollis. *Paris in Despair: Art and Everyday Life under Siege (1870–71)*. Chicago: University of Chicago Press, 2002.

Cloyd, Benjamin G. *Haunted by Atrocity: Civil War Prisons in American Memory*. Baton Rouge: Louisiana State University Press, 2010.

Clymer, Jeffory A. *America's Culture of Terrorism: Violence, Capitalism, and the Written Word*. Chapel Hill: University of North Carolina Press, 2003.

Cohen, Lara Langer. *The Fabrication of American Literature: Fraudulence and Antebellum Print Culture*. Philadelphia: University of Pennsylvania Press, 2011.

Cohoon, Lorinda B. *Serialized Citizenships: Periodicals, Books, and American Boys, 1840–1911*. Lanham, MD: Scarecrow Press, 2006.

Colomina, Beatriz, Anne Marie Brennan, and Jeannie Kim, eds. *Cold War Hothouses: Inventing Postwar Culture, from Cockpit to Playboy*. New York: Princeton Architectural Press, 2009.

Colosseum Hand Book: Descriptive of the Cyclorama of Paris by Night. Philadelphia: Allen, Lane & Scott's Printing House, 1876.

Conn, Peter. *The American 1930s: A Literary History*. Cambridge: Cambridge University Press, 2009.

Connolly, Brian. *Domestic Intimacies: Incest and the Liberal Subject in Nineteenth-Century America*. Philadelphia: University of Pennsylvania Press, 2014.

Constantine, James Robert, ed. *Letters of Eugene V. Debs*. Vol. 1. Chicago: University of Illinois Press, 1990.

Cordell, Ryan. "Reprinting, Circulation, and the Network Author in Antebellum Newspapers." *American Literary History* 27.3 (2015): 417–45.

Cowley, Malcolm. *Exile's Return: A Literary Odyssey of the 1930s*. New York: Norton, [1951] 1994.

Crary, Jonathan. "Spectacle, Attention, Counter-Memory." *October* 50 (1989): 97–107.

Cvetkovich, Ann. *Mixed Feelings: Feminism, Mass Culture and Victorian Sensationalism*. New Brunswick, NJ: Rutgers University Press, 1992.

Davis, Angela Y. *Women, Race, and Class*. New York: Vintage, 1983.

DeLamotte, Eugenia C. *Gates of Freedom: Voltairine de Cleyre and the Revolution of the Mind*. Ann Arbor: University of Michigan Press, 2004.

—. "Refashioning the Mind: The Revolutionary Rhetoric of Voltairine de Cleyre." *Legacy* 20.1 (2003): 153–74.

Denning, Michael. *The Cultural Front: The Laboring of American Culture in the Twentieth Century*. London: Verso, 1997.

—. "'The Special American Conditions': Marxism and American Studies." *American Quarterly* 38 (1986): 356–80.

Derrida, Jacques. *Specters of Marx: The State of the Debt, the Work of Mourning, and the New International*. New York and London: Routledge, 1994.

Dillon, Elizabeth Maddock, and Michael Drexler, eds. *The Haitian Revolution and the Early United States: Histories, Textualities, Geographies*. Philadelphia: University of Pennsylvania Press, 2016.

Donner, Frank. *Protectors of Privilege: Red Squads and Police Repression in Urban America*. Berkeley: University of California Press, 1990.

Doss, Erica. *Memorial Mania: Public Feeling in America*. Chicago: University of Chicago Press, 2010.

Draper, Hal. *Karl Marx and Friedrich Engels: Writings on the Paris Commune*. New York and London: Monthly Review Press, 1971.

Dumas, Alexandre, fils. *Une Lettre sur les choses du jour*. Paris: Michel Lévy Frères, 1871.

Eagleton, Terry. "Foreword," in Kristin Ross. *The Emergence of Social Space: Rimbaud and the Paris Commune*. Minneapolis: University of Minnesota Press, 1998.

Edel, Leon. *Henry James: A Life*. New York: Harper & Row, 1985.

—. *Henry James: The Conquest of London, 1870–1881*. Philadelphia: Lippincott, 1962.

—. "Introduction." *The American Scene*. Bloomington: Indiana University Press, 1968.

Edwards, Brent Hayes. *The Practice of Diaspora: Literature, Translation, and the Rise of Black Internationalism*. Cambridge, MA: Harvard University Press, 2003.

Edwards, Stewart. *The Paris Commune of 1871*. London: Eyre & Spottiswoode, 1971.

Eichner, Carolyn J. *Surmounting the Barricades: Women in the Paris Commune*. Bloomington: Indiana University Press, 2004.

Ellis, Havelock. *Man and Woman: A Study of Human Secondary Sexual Characters*. New York: Scribner's Sons, 1894.

Endore, Guy. *The Werewolf of Paris*. New York: Farrar & Rinehart, 1933.

Engels, Friedrich. "Preface." Karl Marx. *The Civil War in France*. Chicago: Charles H. Kerr & Co., [1891] 1934.

Entin, Joseph P. *Sensational Modernism: Experimental Fiction and Photography in Thirties America*. Chapel Hill: University of North Carolina Press, 2007.

Fah, Alice. *The Imagined Civil War: Popular Literature of North and South, 1861–1865*. Chapel Hill: University of North Carolina Press, 2003.

Falk, Candice, Barry Pateman, and Jessica M. Moran, eds. *Emma Goldman: Making Speech Free, 1902–1909*. Berkeley: University of California Press, 2004.

Fiedler, Leslie. "The Two Memories: Reflections on Writers and Writing in the 1930s." *Proletarian Writers of the Thirties*. Ed. David Madden. London: Southern Illinois Press, 1968.

Field, Douglas. *All Those Strangers: The Art and Lives of James Baldwin*. Oxford: Oxford University Press, 2015.

Finseth, Ian. "The Civil War Dead: Realism and the Problem of Anonymity." *American Literary History* 25.3 (2013): 535–62.

Fisher, Paul. *House of Wits: An Intimate Portrait of the James Family*. New York: Henry Holt & Company, 2009.

Flores, Richard. *Remembering the Alamo: Memory, Modernity and the Master Symbol*. Austin: University of Texas Press, 2002.

Foley, Barbara. *Radical Representations: Politics and Form in U.S. Proletarian Fiction, 1929–1941*. Durham, NC: Duke University Press, 1993.

Foner, Philip S. "French Trade Union Delegation to the Philadelphia Centennial Exposition, 1876." *Science and Society* 40.3 (1976): 257–87.

—. "Why Is There No Socialism in the United States?" *History Workshop Journal* 17.1 (1984): 57–80, <hwj.oxfordjournals.org> (last accessed Oct. 31, 2015).

Forster, E. M. *Aspects of the Novel*. New York: Harcourt, [1927] 1985.

Fournier, Éric. "Les Photographies des ruines de Paris en 1871 ou les faux-semblants de l'image." *Revue d'histoire du XIXe siècle. Société d'histoire de la révolution de 1848 et des révolutions du XIXe siècle* 32 (2006): 137–51.

—. *Paris en ruines: Du Paris haussmannien au Paris communard*. Paris: Imago, 2008.

Freeman, Elizabeth. *Time Binds: Queer Temporalities, Queer Histories*. Durham, NC: Duke University Press, 2010.

Freud, Sigmund. *Civilization and Its Discontents*. Harmondsworth: Penguin, 2002.

Friedman, Gerald. *State-Making and Social Movements: France and the United States, 1876–1914*. Ithaca, NY: Cornell University Press, 1988: 87–8.

Frost, Brian J. *The Essential Guide to Werewolf Literature*. Madison: University of Wisconsin Press, 2003.

Funchion, John. *Novel Nostalgias: The Aesthetics of Antagonism in Nineteenth Century U.S. Literature.* Columbus: Ohio State University Press, 2015.

Fussell, Edwin Sill. *The French Side of Henry James.* New York: Columbia University Press, 1990.

Gabriel, Mary. *Notorious Victoria: The Life of Victoria Woodhull, Uncensored.* New York: Algonquin Books, 1998.

Garvey, Ellen Gruber. "Nineteenth-Century Abolitionists and the Databases They Created." *Legacy: A Journal of American Women Writers* 27.2 (2010): 357–66.

—. *Writing with Scissors: American Scrapbooks from the Civil War to the Harlem Renaissance.* Oxford: Oxford University Press, 2012.

Giles, Paul. *The Global Remapping of American Literature.* Princeton: Princeton University Press, 2011.

Ginsberg, Elaine K, ed. *Passing and the Fictions of Identity.* Durham, NC: Duke University Press, 1996.

Giordano, Matthew. "'A lesson from' the Magazines: Sarah Piatt and the Post-bellum Periodical Poet." *American Periodicals* 16.1 (2006): 23–51.

Glassgold, Peter, ed. *Anarchy!: An Anthology of Emma Goldman's Mother Earth.* Berkeley, CA: Counterpoint Press, 2012.

Goldberg, Shari. *Quiet Testimony: A Theory of Witnessing from Nineteenth-Century American Literature.* New York: Fordham University Press, 2013.

Gomez, Manuel, ed. *Poems for Workers: An Anthology.* Chicago: Daily Workers Publishing Co., 1925.

Gorman, Herbert. *Jonathan Bishop.* New York: Farrar & Rinehart, 1933.

Gornick, Vivian. *Emma Goldman: Revolution as a Way of Life.* Reprint edition. New Haven, CT: Yale University Press, 2013.

Goyens, Tom. *Beer and Revolution: The German Anarchist Movement in New York City, 1880–1914.* Urbana: University of Illinois Press, 2007.

Graham, Wendy. "Henry James's Subterranean Blues." *Modern Fiction Studies* 40.1 (Spring 1994): 51–84.

—. "Notes of a Native Son: Henry James's New York." *American Literary History* 21.2 (2009): 239–67.

Gray, Janet Sinclair. *Race and Time: American Women's Poetics from Antislavery to Racial Modernity.* Iowa City: University of Iowa Press, 2004.

Green, James. *Death in the Haymarket: A Story of Chicago, the First Labor Movement and the Bombing That Divided Gilded Age America.* Reprint edition. New York: Anchor Books, 2007.

Greeson, Jennifer Rae. "Expropriating *The Great South* and Exporting 'Local Color': Global and Hemispheric Imaginaries of the First Reconstruction." *American Literary History* 18.3 (2006): 496–520.

Gribble, Francis. *The Red Spell.* Westminster: A. Constable, 1895.

Griffin, Susan M. *The Historical Eye: The Texture of the Visual in Late James.* Boston: Northeastern University Press, 1991.

Griffiths, Alison. *Shivers Down Your Spine: Cinema, Museums, and the Immersive View*. New York: Columbia University Press, 2008.

Grim, Ryan, and Mike Sacks. "Corporate Citizenship: How Public Dissent in Part Sparked Creation of the Corporate Person." *Huffington Post Politics* Oct. 12, 2011.

Grob, Gerald N. *The Impact of the Paris Commune upon the American Imagination*. M.A. Thesis, Columbia University, 1952.

Gullickson, Gay L. "La Pétroleuse: Representing Revolution." *Feminist Studies* 17.2 (Summer 1991): 248.

—. *Unruly Women of Paris: Images of the Commune*. Ithaca, NY: Cornell University Press, 1996.

Gutman, Herbert George and Donald H. Bell. *The New England Working Class and the New Labor History*. Chicago: University of Illinois Press, 1987.

Halberstam, Judith. *Skin Shows: Gothic Horror and the Technology of Monsters*. Durham, NC: Duke University Press, 1995.

—. *The Queer Art of Failure*. Durham, NC: Duke University Press, 2011.

Harvey, David. *Paris, Capital of Modernity*. New York: Routledge, 2003.

—. *Rebel Cities: From the Right to the City to the Urban Revolution*. London: Verso, 2012.

Hay, John. *Pike County Ballads and Other Pieces*. Boston: James R. Osgood & Company, [1871] 1873.

Hayden, Tom. *Reunion: A Memoir*. New York: Random House, 1988.

Hendler, Glenn. *Public Sentiments: Structures of Feeling in Nineteenth-Century American Literature*. Chapel Hill: University of North Carolina Press, 2001.

Henty, G. A. *A Woman of the Commune: A Tale of Two Sieges of Paris*. Cave Junction, OR: Robinson Books, [1895] 2002.

Herron, George. *From Revolution to Revolution: An Address in Memory of the Paris Commune of 1871*. Chicago: Charles H. Kerr, 1903: 13.

Hollander, John and Eric Harlson. *Encyclopedia of American Poetry: The Nineteenth Century*. Chicago: Fitzroy Dearborn, 1998.

Holmes, Oliver Wendell. *The Autocrat of the Breakfast Table: The Works of Oliver Wendell Holmes*. Vol. 1. Boston: Houghton, Mifflin and Company, 1892.

—. *Our Hundred Days in Europe*. Cambridge, MA: Riverside Press, 1887.

Howells, William Dean. "Mr. John Hay's Volume of Poetry." *Editor's Study. The Atlantic Monthly* Sep. 1890: 638.

Hugo, Victor. *L'Année terrible*. Paris: Michel Lévy Frères, 1872.

Hunt, Peter. "G. A. Henty." *Children's Literature*. London: Wiley–Blackwell, 2001.

Hutchison, Hazel. *Seeing and Believing: Henry James and the Spiritual World*. New York: Palgrave, 2006.

Huyssen, Andreas. *Present Pasts: Urban Palimpsests and the Politics of Memory*. Palo Alto: Stanford University Press, 2003.

Hyde, Ralph. *Panoramania: The Art and Entertainment of the "All-Embracing" View*. London: Trefoil Publications, 1988.

Immerso, Michael. *Coney Island: The People's Playground*. Piscataway, NJ: Rutgers University Press, 2002.

Jacobson, Marcia. *Being a Boy Again: Autobiography and the American Boy Book*. Tuscaloosa: University of Alabama Press, 1994.

James, Henry. *The Ambassadors*. New York: Penguin, [1903] 2003.

—. *The American Scene*. Ed. Leon Edel. Bloomington: Indiana University Press, [1907] 1968.

—. *The Bostonians*. New York: Penguin, [1886] 2000.

—. The Complete Letters of Henry James, 1855–1872. Vol. 1. Ed. Pierre A. Walker and Greg W. Zacharias. Lincoln: University of Nebraska Press, 2009.

—. *Henry James: Letters*. Vol. 1: 1843–1875. Ed. Leon Edel. Cambridge, MA: Harvard University Press, 1974.

—. *The Princess Casamassima*. Ed. Derek Brewer. London: Penguin, [1886] 1987.

—. *The Tragic Muse*. Boston: Houghton Mifflin Company, 1890.

—. *Transatlantic Sketches*. Boston: Osgood and Company, 1875.

James, William. *The Principles of Psychology*. Vol. I. London: Macmillan, 1891.

Kammen, Michael. *The Mystic Chords of Memory: The Transformation of Tradition in American Culture*. New York: Vintage Books, 1993.

Kaplan, Alice. *Dreaming in French: The Paris Years of Jacqueline Bouvier Kennedy, Susan Sontag, and Angela Davis*. Chicago: University of Chicago Press, 2012.

Kaplan, Amy. *The Anarchy of Empire in the Making of U.S. Culture*. Cambridge, MA: Harvard University Press, 2002.

—. "Nation, Region, Empire." *The Columbia History of the American Novel*. Ed. Emory Elliot. New York: Columbia University Press, 1991.

—. "Romancing the Empire: The Embodiment of American Masculinity in the Popular Historical Novel of the 1890s." *American Literary History* 4 (1990): 659–90.

Katz, Philip M. *From Appomattox to Montmartre: Americans and the Paris Commune*. Cambridge, MA: Harvard University Press, 1998.

Keil, Hartmut, John B. Jentz, and Chicago Project (Universität München). *German Workers in Chicago: A Documentary History of Working-Class Culture from 1850 to World War I*. Chicago: University of Illinois Press, 1988.

Kelley, Robin D. G. *Freedom Dreams: The Black Radical Imagination*. Boston: Beacon Press, 2003.

Kennedy, J. Gerald. *Imagining Paris: Exile, Writing, and American Identity*. New Haven, CT: Yale University Press, 1994.

Kidd, Kenneth. *Making American Boys: Boyology and the Feral Tale*. Minneapolis: University of Minnesota Press, 2004.

King, Edward. *Europe in Storm and Calm*. Springfield, MA: C. A. Nichols and Company, 1885.

—. *Under the Red Flag: Or, the Adventures of Two American Boys During the Paris Commune*. Philadelphia: Philip Coates & Co., 1895.

—. "A Woman's Execution (Paris, 1871)." *Scribner's Monthly* 2 (Sep. 1871): 500.

Kirkpatrick, D. L., ed. *Reference Guide to American Literature*. Chicago: St. James Press, 1987.

Klein, Stacy Jean. *Margaret Junkin Preston, Poet of the Confederacy: A Literary Life*. Columbia, SC: University of South Carolina Press, 2006.

Kristeva, Julia. *Powers of Horror: An Essay on Abjection*. New York: Columbia University Press, 1982.

Kropp, Phoebe. *California Vieja: Culture and Memory in a Modern American Place*. Berkeley: University of California Press, 2006.

Kunen, James Simon. *The Strawberry Statement: Notes of a College Revolutionary*. New York: Random House, 1969.

Landsberg, Alison. *Prosthetic Memory: The Transformation of American Remembrance in the Age of Mass Culture*. New York: Columbia University Press, 2004.

Lee, Anthony, and Elizabeth Young. *On Alexander Gardner's Photographic Sketch Book of the Civil War*. Berkeley: University of California Press, 2007.

Lee, Daryl. "Rimbaud's Ruin of French Verse: Verse Spatiality and the Paris Commune Ruins." *Nineteenth-Century French Studies* 32.1–2 (Fall–Winter 2003–4): 69–82.

Lefebvre, Henri. "La Commune: dernière fête populaire." *Images de la Commune/Images of the Commune*. Ed. James A. Leith. Montreal: McGill–Queen's University Press, 1978.

Lerer, Seth. *Children's Literature: A Reader's History from Aesop to Harry Potter*. Chicago: University of Chicago Press, 2009.

Levenstein, Harvey A. *Seductive Journey: American Tourists in France from Jefferson to the Jazz Age*. Chicago: University of Chicago Press, 1998.

Litwicki, Ellen M. *America's Public Holidays, 1865–1920*. Washington, DC: Smithsonian Books, 2003.

Lowry, Bullitt, and Elizabeth Gunter, eds. *The Red Virgin: Memoirs of Louise Michel*. 2nd edition. Tuscaloosa: University of Alabama Press, 2003.

Luciano, Dana, and Ivy Wilson, eds. *Unsettled States: Nineteenth-Century American Literary Studies*. New York: NYU Press, 2014.

Luxenberg, Alisa. "Creating *Désastres*: Andrieu's Photographs of Urban Ruins in the Paris of 1871." *The Art Bulletin* 80.1 (1998): 113–38.

Macaulay, Rose. *The Pleasure of Ruins*. London: Weidenfeld & Nicolson, 1953.

Mailloux, Steven. *Rhetorical Power*. Ithaca, NY: Cornell University Press, 1989.

Makalani, Minkah. *In the Cause of Freedom: Radical Black Internationalism from Harlem to London, 1917–1939.* Chapel Hill: University of North Carolina Press, 2014.

Mao, Douglas, and Rebecca L. Walkowitz, eds. *Bad Modernisms.* Durham, NC: Duke University Press, 2006.

Marcus, Greil. *Lipstick Traces: A Secret History of the Twentieth Century.* Cambridge, MA: Harvard University Press, 1989.

Marx, Karl. *The Civil War in France.* Chicago: Charles H. Kerr & Co., 1934.

Maxwell, William J. *F. B. Eyes: How J. Edgar Hoover's Ghostreaders Framed African American Literature.* Princeton: Princeton University Press, 2015.

McCracken, Scott. "The Author as Arsonist: Henry James and the Paris Commune." *Modernism/Modernity* 21.1 (2014): 71–87.

McCullough, David. *The Greater Journey: Americans in Paris.* New York: Simon & Schuster, 2013.

McGill, Meredith. *American Literature and the Culture of Reprinting, 1834–1853.* University of Philadelphia: Pennsylvania Press, 2003.

Meissner, Collin. "The Princess Casamassima: 'A Dirty Intellectual Fog.'" *The Henry James Review* 19.1 (Winter 1998): 53–71.

Méral, Jean. *Paris in American Literature.* Chapel Hill: University of North Carolina Press Enduring Editions, 2009.

Merrifield, Andrew. *Metromarxism: A Marxist Tale of the City.* New York: Routledge, 2002.

Merriman, John. *Massacre: The Life and Death of the Paris Commune.* New Haven, CT: Yale University Press, 2014.

Messer-Kruse, Timothy. *The Yankee International: Marxism and the American Reform Tradition.* Chapel Hill: University of North Carolina Press, 1988.

Michels, Tony. *A Fire In Their Hearts: Yiddish Socialists in New York.* Cambridge, MA: Harvard University Press, 2005.

Mickenberg, Julia L., and Philip Nel, eds. *Tales for Little Rebels: A Collection of Radical Children's Literature.* New York: NYU Press, 2008.

Miller, Angela. "The Panorama, the Cinema, and the Emergence of the Spectacular." *Wide Angle* 18.2 (1996) 34–69.

Moten, Fred. "Black Op," *PMLA* 123.5 (2008): 1743–7.

Muñoz, José Esteban. *Cruising Utopia: The Then and There of Queer Futurity.* New York: NYU Press, 2009.

Nelson, Megan Kate. *Ruin Nation: Destruction and the American Civil War.* Athens: University of Georgia Press, 2012.

Nesher-Wirth, Hana. "If This Is Liberty, It Must Be Paris: Landmarks and Home in *The Ambassadors*." *Homes and Homelessness in the Victorian Imagination.* Ed. Murray Baumgarten and H. M. Daleski. New York: AMS Press, 1998.

Newitz, Annalee. *Pretend We're Dead: Capitalist Monsters in American Popular Culture.* Durham, NC: Duke University Press, 2006.

Nora, Pierre. "Between Memory and History: Les Lieux de mémoire." *Representations* 26 (Spring 1989): 7–24.

—. *Les Lieux de mémoire*. Paris: Gallimard, 1984–92.

Oettermann, Stephan. *The Panorama*. Trans. Deborah Lucas Schneider. New York: Zone Books, 1997.

Oldenziel, Ruth, and Karin Zachmann. *Cold War Kitchen: Americanization, Technology, and European Users*. Cambridge, MA: MIT Press, 2011.

Oliver, Lawrence J. "Writing from the Right During the 'Red Decade': Thomas Dixon's Attack on W. E. B. DuBois and James Weldon Johnson in The Flaming Sword." *American Literature* 70.1 (1998): 131–52.

Oppenheimer, Mark. "What They're Reading at the Kitchen Table: Home-schoolers of All Stripes Find Common Ground in Some Good, Old Fashioned Books." *The Wall Street Journal* Sep. 2, 2005, <http://online.wsj.com/article/SB112563097775330026.html> (last accessed Apr. 3, 2009).

Painter, Nell Irvin. *Standing at Armageddon: The United States, 1877–1919*. New York: Norton, 1989.

Pana-Oltean, Roxana. "'The Extravagant Curve of the Globe': Refractions of Europe in Henry James's 'An International Episode' and *The Ambassadors*." *The Henry James Review* 22 (2001): 180–99.

Panero, James. "Commune Plus One: On Occupy Wall Street and the Legacy of the Paris Commune." *The New Criterion* Dec. 2011, <http://www.newcriterion.com/articles.cfm/Commune-plus-one-7227> (last accessed Nov. 1, 2015).

Paris in a Week. London: Hachette & Co., 1910.

Parsons, Lucy, ed. *Life of Albert R. Parsons*. Chicago: L. E. Parsons, 1889.

Peterson, Merrill D. *Lincoln in American Memory*. New York: Oxford University Press, 1994.

Piatt, Sarah M. B. "The Palace-Burner: A Picture in a Newspaper." *The Independent* Nov. 1872.

Pizer, Donald. *American Expatriate Writing and the Paris Moment: Modernism and Place*. Baton Rouge: Louisiana State University Press, 1997.

Pratt, Lloyd. *Archives of American Time: Literature and Modernity in the Nineteenth Century*. Philadelphia: University of Pennsylvania Press, 2009.

Presley, Sharon, and Crispin Sartwell, eds. *Exquisite Rebel: The Essays of Voltairine de Cleyre –Anarchist, Feminist, Genius*. Albany, NY: State University of New York Press, 2005.

Preston, Margaret Junkin. *Cartoons*. Boston: Roberts Brothers, 1875.

—. "The Hero of the Commune." *Scribner's Monthly* Apr. 1872: 660–1.

Przyblyski, Jeannene. "Moving Pictures: Photography, Narrative, and the Paris Commune of 1871." *Cinema and the Invention of Modern Life*. Ed. Leo Charney and Vanessa R. Schwartz. Berkeley and Los Angeles: University of California Press, 1993: 253–78.

Rancière, Jacques. *The Politics of Aesthetics*. Trans. Gabriel Rockhill. London: Continuum, 2006.

Raskin, Jonah. "Henry James and the French Revolution." *American Quarterly* 17 (1965): 724–33.

Rees, Laura L. *We Four, Where We Went and What We Saw in Europe*. Philadelphia: J. B. Lippincott & Co., 1880.

Renan, Ernest. "What is a Nation?" Trans. Martin Thorn. *Nation and Narration*. Ed. Homi Bhabha. New York: Routledge, 1990.

Reynolds, Larry J. *European Revolutions and the American Literary Renaissance*. New Haven, CT: Yale University Press, 1988.

Richardson, Heather Cox. *The Death of Reconstruction: Race, Labor, and Politics in the Post-Civil War North, 1865–1901*. Cambridge, MA: Harvard University Press, 2001.

Rideout, Walter Bates. *The Radical Novel in the United States, 1900–1954: Some Interrelations of Literature and Society*. New York: Columbia University Press, 1992.

Rigney, Ann. *The Afterlives of Walter Scott: Memory on the Move*. Oxford and New York: Oxford University Press, 2012.

—. *Imperfect Histories: The Elusive Past and the Legacy of Romantic Historicism*. Ithaca: Cornell University Press, 2001.

Robbins, Bruce. *Feeling Global: Internationalism in Distress*. New York: NYU Press, 1999.

"Robert W. Chambers." *The New American Supplement to the Encyclopedia Britannica*. Ed. Day Otis Kellogg, D.D. New York: Werner, 1897.

Roberts, Timothy Mason. *Distant Revolutions: 1848 and the Challenge to America Exceptionalism*. Charlottesville: University of Virginia Press, 2009.

Robinson, Cedric J. *Black Marxism: The Making of the Black Radical Tradition*. Chapel Hill: University of North Carolina Press, 2000.

Roediger, David, and Franklin Rosemont, eds. *Haymarket Scrapbook*. Chicago: Charles Kerr, 1986.

Rogin, Michael Paul. *Subversive Genealogy: The Politics and Art of Herman Melville*. Berkeley: University of California Press, 1992.

Romano, Renee Christine, and Leigh Raiford. *The Civil Rights Movement in American Memory*. Athens: University of Georgia Press, 2006.

Rosier, Paul C. "'They Are Ancestral Homelands': Race, Place, and Politics in Cold War Native America, 1945–1961." *The Journal of American History* 92.4 (2006): 1300–26.

Ross, Kristin. *Communal Luxury: The Political Imaginary of the Paris Commune*. London: Verso, 2015.

—. *The Emergence of Social Space: Rimbaud and the Paris Commune*. Minneapolis: University of Minnesota Press, 1988.

—. *May 68 and Its Afterlives*. Chicago: University of Chicago Press, 2002.

Rowe, John Carlos. *The Other Henry James*. Durham, NC: Duke University Press, 1998.

—. "The Politics of Innocence: Henry James's *The American*." *At Emerson's Tomb: The Politics of Classic American Literature*. New York: Columbia University Press, 1997.

Rudd, Mark. *Underground: My Life with SDS and the Weathermen*. New York: HarperCollins, 2009.

Rumble, Walker. *The Swifts: Printers in the Age of Typesetting Races*. Charlottesville: University of Virginia Press, 2003.

Rusert, Britt. "The Science of Freedom: Counterarchives of Racial Science on the Antebellum Stage." *African American Review* 45.3 (2012): 291.

Rydell, Robert W. *All the World's a Fair: Visions of Empire at American International Exhibitions, 1876–1916*. Chicago: University of Chicago Press, 1984.

Savidge, Eugene Coleman. *The American in Paris: A Biographical Novel of the Franco-Prussian War, the Siege and Commune of Paris from an American Stand-point*. New York: Lippincott, 1896.

Savio, Mario. "Questioning the Vietnam War." *Freedoms Orator: Mario Savio and the Radical Legacy of the 1960s*. Ed. Robert Cohen. Oxford: Oxford University Press, 2009.

Sawyer, Marian. "The Soviet Image of the Commune: Lenin and Beyond." *Images of the Commune*. Ed. James A. Leith. Montreal: McGill–Queen's University Press, 1978.

Schechter, Patricia A. *Ida B. Wells-Barnett and American Reform, 1880–1930*. Chapel Hill: University of North Carolina Press, 2001.

Schneirov, Matthew. *The Dream of a New Social Order: Popular Magazines in America 1893–1914*. New York: Columbia University Press, 1994.

Schneirov, Richard. *Labor and Urban Politics: Class Conflict and the Origins of Modern Liberalism in Chicago, 1864–97*. Chicago: University of Illinois Press, 1998.

Scriabine, Christine Brendel, Edmund B. Sullivan, and Paul Buhle. *Voices of the Left, 1870–1960: Exhibit, December 6, 1990 through June 2, 1991*. Museum of American Political Life. Hartford, CT: University of Hartford Press, 1990.

Seawell, Molly Elliot. *The Commune of Paris: In Three Parts*. *Munsey's Magazine* Aug.–Oct. 1897.

Sedgwick, Eve Kosofsky. *Touching Feeling: Affect, Pedagogy, Performativity*. Durham, NC: Duke University Press, 2003.

Seltzer, Mark. "*The Princess Casamassima*: Realism and the Fantasy of Surveillance." *Nineteenth-Century Fiction* 35 (1981): 506–34.

Shackel, Paul A. *Memory in Black and White: Race, Commemoration, and the Post-Bellum Landscape*. Walnut Creek, CA: Altamira Press, 2003.

Shaer, Matthew. Review of *Foreign Bodies*, by Cynthia Ozick. *Book Forum* Oct. 28, 2010, <http://www.bookforum.com/review/6591> (last accessed Sep. 1, 2014).

Siegel, William. *The Paris Commune: A Story in Pictures*. New York: International Pamphlets (No. 12.), 1932.

Smith, Carl. *Urban Disorder and the Shape of Belief: The Great Chicago Fire, the Haymarket Bomb, and the Model Town of Pullman*. Chicago: University of Chicago Press, 2008.

Sorensen, Leif. "A Weird Modernist Archive: Pulp Fiction, Pseudobiblia, H. P. Lovecraft." *Modernism/modernity* 17.3 (2010): 501–22.

Spark, Sidney I. *The Stranger's Vade Mecum, or, Paris Guide: Compendium of Reliable Information, for the Use of American and English Visitors*. London: Wertheimer, Lea & Co., 1879.

Spiro, George. *Paris on the Barricades*. New York: Workers Library Publishers, 1929.

Stansell, Christine. *American Moderns: Bohemian New York and the Creation of a New Century*. New York: Henry Holt & Co., 2000.

Starr, Peter. *Commemorating Trauma: The Paris Commune and Its Cultural Aftermath*. New York: Fordham University Press, 2006.

Stein, Jordan. "American Literary History and Queer Temporalities." *American Literary History* 25.4 (2013): 855–69, <alh.oxfordjournals.org> (last accessed Aug. 14, 2015).

Stoler, Ann Laura, ed. *Imperial Debris: On Ruins and Ruination*. Durham, NC: Duke University Press, 2013.

Streeby, Shelley S. "Doing Justice to the Archive Beyond Literature." *Unsettled States: Nineteenth-Century American Literary Studies*. Ed. Dana Luciano and Ivy Wilson. New York: NYU Press, 2014.

—. "Labor, Memory, and the Boundaries of Print Culture: From Haymarket to the Mexican Revolution." *ALH* 19.2 (2007): 406–33.

—. *Radical Sensations: World Movements, Violence, and Visual Culture*. Durham, NC: Duke University Press, 2013.

Sturken, Marita. *Tangled Memories: The Vietnam War, the AIDS Epidemic, and the Politics of Remembering*. Berkeley: University of California Press, 1997.

—. *Tourists of History: Memory, Kitsch, and Consumerism from Oklahoma to Ground Zero*. Durham, NC: Duke University Press, 2007.

Sweet, Timothy. *Traces of War: Poetry, Photography and the Crisis of the Union*. Baltimore: Johns Hopkins University Press, 1990.

Talbot, Margaret. "A Mighty Fortress." *New York Times Magazine* Feb. 27, 2000: 34–41.

Tamarkin, Elisa. *Anglophilia: Deference, Devotion, and Antebellum America*. Chicago: University of Chicago Press, 2008.

Tax, Meredith. *The Rising of the Women: Feminist Solidarity and Class Conflict, 1880–1917*. Chicago: University of Illinois Press, 2001.

Thayer, William Roscoe. *The Life and Letters of John Hay*. New York: Houghton Mifflin, 1915.

Tillier, Bertrand. *La Commune de Paris, révolution sans images?: Politique et représentations dans la France républicaine (1871–1914)*. Paris: Editions Champ Vallon, 2004.

Trachtenberg, Alan. *Reading American Photographs: Images as History from Matthew Brady to Walker Evans.* New York: Farrar, Straus, & Giroux, 1989.

Trouillot, Michel-Rolph. *Silencing the Past: Power and the Production of History.* Boston: Beacon Press, 1995.

VanDette, Emily E. *Sibling Romance in American Fiction, 1835–1900.* London: Palgrave Macmillan, 2013.

Vizetelly, Ernest Alfred. *My Adventures in the Commune, Paris, 1871.* New York: Duffield & Company, 1914.

Wahrman, Dror. *The Making of the Modern Self: Identity and Culture in Eighteenth-Century England.* New edition. New Haven, CT, and London: Yale University Press, 2007.

Wald, Alan M. *Exiles from a Future Time: The Forging of the Mid-Twentieth-Century Literary Left.* Chapel Hill: University of North Carolina Press, 2002.

Walker, Pierre A. "Henry James, Cultural Critic." *A Companion to Henry James.* Ed. Greg W. Zacharias. Oxford: Blackwell/Wiley, 2008.

Wearn, Mary. "'She has been burning palaces': The Maternal Poetics of Sarah Piatt." *Negotiating Motherhood in Nineteenth-Century Literature.* New York: Routledge, 2008.

—. "Subjection and Subversion in Sarah Piatt's Maternal Poetics." *Legacy* 23.2 (2006): 168.

White, Ashli. *Encountering Revolution: Haiti and the Making of the Early Republic.* Baltimore and London: Johns Hopkins University Press, 2012.

Wilderson, Frank B. *Red, White and Black: Cinema and the Structure of U.S. Antagonisms.* Durham, NC: Duke University Press, 2010.

Wilson, Colette. "Memory and the Politics of Forgetting: Paris, the Commune, and the 1878 Exposition Universelle." *Journal of European Studies* 35.1 (2005): 47–63.

—. *Paris and the Commune, 1871–78.* Manchester: Manchester University Press, 2007.

Woloch, Alex. *The One vs. the Many: Minor Characters and the Space of the Protagonist in the Novel.* Princeton: Princeton University Press, 2009.

Yablon, Nick. "'A Picture Painted in Fire': Pain's Reenactments of the *Last Days of Pompeii*, 1879–1914." *Antiquity Recovered: The Legacy of Pompeii and Herculaneum.* Ed. Victoria C. Gardner Coates and Jon L. Seydl. Los Angeles: Getty Publications, 2007.

—. *Untimely Ruins: An Archaeology of American Urban Modernity, 1819–1919.* Chicago: University of Chicago Press, 2009.

Young, Elizabeth. *Disarming the Nation: Women's Writing and the American Civil War.* Chicago: University of Chicago Press, 1999.

Zimmerman, David A. *Panic! Markets, Crises, and Crowds in American Fiction.* Chapel Hill: University of North Carolina Press, 2006.

Index

Page numbers for illustrations are in *italics*.

EU representative:
Easy Access System Europe
Mustamäe tee 50, 10621 Tallinn, Estonia
Gpsr.requests@easproject.com

www.ingramcontent.com/pod-product-compliance
Lightning Source LLC
Chambersburg PA
CBHW070405270326
41926CB00014B/2706